DAUGHTERS OF AATAENTSIC

McGILL-QUEEN'S INDIGENOUS AND NORTHERN STUDIES

(In memory of Bruce G. Trigger)

John Borrows, Sarah Carter, and Arthur J. Ray, Editors

The McGill-Queen's Indigenous and Northern Studies series publishes books about Indigenous peoples in all parts of the northern world. It includes original scholarship on their histories, archaeology, laws, cultures, governance, and traditions. Works in the series also explore the history and geography of the North, where travel, the natural environment, and the relationship to land continue to shape life in particular and important ways. Its mandate is to advance understanding of the political, legal, and social relations between Indigenous and non-Indigenous peoples, of the contemporary issues that Indigenous peoples face as a result of environmental and economic change, and of social justice, including the work of reconciliation in Canada. To provide a global perspective, the series welcomes books on regions and communities from across the Arctic and Subarctic circumpolar zones.

1 When the Whalers Were Up North
Inuit Memories from the Eastern Arctic
Dorothy Harley Eber

2 The Challenge of Arctic Shipping
Science, Environmental Assessment, and Human Values
Edited by David L. VanderZwaag and Cynthia Lamson

3 Lost Harvests
Prairie Indian Reserve Farmers and Government Policy
Sarah Carter

4 Native Liberty, Crown Sovereignty
The Existing Aboriginal Right of Self-Government in Canada
Bruce Clark

5 Unravelling the Franklin Mystery
Inuit Testimony
David C. Woodman

6 Otter Skins, Boston Ships, and China Goods
The Maritime Fur Trade of the Northwest Coast, 1785–1841
James R. Gibson

7 From Wooden Ploughs to Welfare
The Story of the Western Reserves
Helen Buckley

8 In Business for Ourselves
Northern Entrepreneurs
Wanda A. Wuttunee

9 For an Amerindian Autohistory
An Essay on the Foundations of a Social Ethic
Georges E. Sioui

10 Strangers Among Us
David Woodman

11 When the North Was Red
Aboriginal Education in Soviet Siberia
Dennis A. Bartels and Alice L. Bartels

12 From Talking Chiefs to a Native Corporate Elite
The Birth of Class and Nationalism among Canadian Inuit
Marybelle Mitchell

13 Cold Comfort
My Love Affair with the Arctic
Graham W. Rowley

14 The True Spirit and Original Intent of Treaty 7
Treaty 7 Elders and Tribal Council with Walter Hildebrandt, Dorothy First Rider, and Sarah Carter

15 This Distant and Unsurveyed Country
A Woman's Winter at Baffin Island, 1857–1858
W. Gillies Ross

16 Images of Justice
Dorothy Harley Eber

17 Capturing Women
The Manipulation of Cultural Imagery in Canada's Prairie West
Sarah Carter

18 Social and Environmental Impacts of the James Bay Hydroelectric Project
Edited by James F. Hornig

19 Saqiyuq
Stories from the Lives of Three Inuit Women
Nancy Wachowich in collaboration with Apphia Agalakti Awa, Rhoda Kaukjak Katsak, and Sandra Pikujak Katsak

20 Justice in Paradise
Bruce Clark

21 Aboriginal Rights and Self-Government
The Canadian and Mexican Experience in North American Perspective
Edited by Curtis Cook and Juan D. Lindau

22 Harvest of Souls
The Jesuit Missions and Colonialism in North America, 1632–1650
Carole Blackburn

23 Bounty and Benevolence
A History of Saskatchewan Treaties
Arthur J. Ray, Jim Miller, and Frank Tough

24 The People of Denendeh
Ethnohistory of the Indians of Canada's Northwest Territories
June Helm

25 The *Marshall* Decision and Native Rights
Ken Coates

26 The Flying Tiger
Women Shamans and Storytellers of the Amur
Kira Van Deusen

27 Alone in Silence
European Women in the Canadian North before 1940
Barbara E. Kelcey

28 The Arctic Voyages of Martin Frobisher
An Elizabethan Adventure
Robert McGhee

29 Northern Experience and the Myths of Canadian Culture
Renée Hulan

30 The White Man's Gonna Getcha
The Colonial Challenge to the Crees in Quebec
Toby Morantz

31 The Heavens Are Changing
Nineteenth-Century Protestant Missions and Tsimshian Christianity
Susan Neylan

32 Arctic Migrants/Arctic Villagers
The Transformation of Inuit Settlement in the Central Arctic
David Damas

33 Arctic Justice
On Trial for Murder – Pond Inlet, 1923
Shelagh D. Grant

34 The American Empire and the Fourth World
Anthony J. Hall

35 Eighteenth-Century Naturalists of Hudson Bay
Stuart Houston, Tim Ball, and Mary Houston

36 Uqalurait
An Oral History of Nunavut
Compiled and edited by John Bennett and Susan Rowley

37 Living Rhythms
Lessons in Aboriginal Economic Resilience and Vision
Wanda Wuttunee

38 The Making of an Explorer
George Hubert Wilkins and the Canadian Arctic Expedition, 1913–1916
Stuart E. Jenness

39 Chee Chee
A Study of Aboriginal Suicide
Alvin Evans

40 Strange Things Done
Murder in Yukon History
Ken S. Coates and William R. Morrison

41 Healing through Art
Ritualized Space and Cree Identity
Nadia Ferrara

42 Coyote and Raven Go Canoeing
Coming Home to the Village
Peter Cole

43 Something New in the Air
The Story of First Peoples Television Broadcasting in Canada
Lorna Roth

44 Listening to Old Woman Speak
Natives and Alternatives in Canadian Literature
Laura Smyth Groening

45 Robert and Francis Flaherty
A Documentary Life, 1883–1922
Robert J. Christopher

46 Talking in Context
Language and Identity in Kwakwaka'wakw Society
Anne Marie Goodfellow

47 Tecumseh's Bones
Guy St-Denis

48 Constructing Colonial Discourse
Captain Cook at Nootka Sound
Noel Elizabeth Currie

49 The Hollow Tree
Fighting Addiction with Traditional Healing
Herb Nabigon

50 The Return of Caribou to Ungava
A.T. Bergerud, Stuart Luttich, and Lodewijk Camps

51 Firekeepers of the Twenty-First Century
First Nations Women Chiefs
Cora J. Voyageur

52 Isuma
Inuit Video Art
Michael Robert Evans

53 Outside Looking In
Viewing First Nations Peoples in Canadian Dramatic Television Series
Mary Jane Miller

54 Kiviuq
An Inuit Hero and His Siberian Cousins
Kira Van Deusen

55 Native Peoples and Water Rights
Irrigation, Dams, and the Law in Western Canada
Kenichi Matsui

56 The Rediscovered Self
Indigenous Identity and Cultural Justice
Ronald Niezen

57 As affecting the fate of my absent husband
Selected Letters of Lady Franklin Concerning the Search for the Lost Franklin Expedition, 1848–1860
Edited by Erika Behrisch Elce

58 The Language of the Inuit
Syntax, Semantics, and Society in the Arctic
Louis-Jacques Dorais

59 Inuit Shamanism and Christianity
Transitions and Transformations in the Twentieth Century
Frédéric B. Laugrand and Jarich G. Oosten

60 No Place for Fairness
Indigenous Land Rights and Policy in the Bear Island Case and Beyond
David T. McNab

61 Aleut Identities
Tradition and Modernity in an Indigenous Fishery
Katherine L. Reedy-Maschner

62 Earth into Property
Aboriginal History and the Making of Global Capitalism
Anthony J. Hall

63 Collections and Objections
Aboriginal Material Culture in Southern Ontario, 1791–1914
Michelle A. Hamilton

64 These Mysterious People
Shaping History and Archaeology in a Northwest Coast Community, Second Edition
Susan Roy

65 Telling It to the Judge
Taking Native History to Court
Arthur J. Ray

66 Aboriginal Music in Contemporary Canada
Echoes and Exchanges
Edited by Anna Hoefnagels and Beverley Diamond

67 In Twilight and in Dawn
A Biography of Diamond Jenness
Barnett Richling

68 Women's Work, Women's Art
Nineteenth-Century Northern Athapaskan Clothing
Judy Thompson

69 Warriors of the Plains
The Arts of Plains Indian Warfare
Max Carocci

70 Reclaiming Indigenous Planning
Edited by Ryan Walker, Ted Jojola, and David Natcher

71 Setting All the Captives Free
Capture, Adjustment, and Recollection in Allegheny Country
Ian K. Steele

72 Before Ontario
The Archaeology of a Province
Edited by Marit K. Munson and Susan M. Jamieson

73 Becoming Inummarik
Men's Lives in an Inuit Community
Peter Collings

74 Ancient Pathways, Ancestral Knowledge
Ethnobotany and Ecological Wisdom of Indigenous Peoples of Northwestern North America
Nancy J. Turner

75 Our Ice Is Vanishing/Sikuvut Nunguliqtuq
A History of Inuit, Newcomers, and Climate Change
Shelley Wright

76 Maps and Memes
Redrawing Culture, Place, and Identity in Indigenous Communities
Gwilym Lucas Eades

77 Encounters
An Anthropological History of Southeastern Labrador
John C. Kennedy

78 Keeping Promises
The Royal Proclamation of 1763, Aboriginal Rights, and Treaties in Canada
Edited by Terry Fenge and Jim Aldridge

79 Together We Survive
Ethnographic Intuitions, Friendships, and Conversations
Edited by John S. Long and Jennifer S.H. Brown

80 Canada's Residential Schools: The History, Part 1, Origins to 1939
The Final Report of the Truth and Reconciliation Commission of Canada, Volume 1

81 Canada's Residential Schools: The History, Part 2, 1939 to 2000
The Final Report of the Truth and Reconciliation Commission of Canada, Volume 1

82 Canada's Residential Schools: The Inuit and Northern Experience
The Final Report of the Truth and Reconciliation Commission of Canada, Volume 2

83 Canada's Residential Schools: The Métis Experience
The Final Report of the Truth and Reconciliation Commission of Canada, Volume 3

84 Canada's Residential Schools: Missing Children and Unmarked Burials
The Final Report of the Truth and Reconciliation Commission of Canada, Volume 4

85 Canada's Residential Schools:
The Legacy
The Final Report of the Truth and Reconciliation Commission of Canada, Volume 5

86 Canada's Residential Schools:
Reconciliation
The Final Report of the Truth and Reconciliation Commission of Canada, Volume 6

87 Aboriginal Rights Claims and the Making and Remaking of History
Arthur J. Ray

88 Abenaki Daring
The Life and Writings of Noel Annance, 1792–1869
Jean Barman

89 Trickster Chases the Tale of Education
Sylvia Moore

90 Secwépemc People, Land, and Laws
Yerí7 re Stsq̓ey̓s-kucw
Marianne Ignace and Ronald E. Ignace

91 Travellers through Empire
Indigenous Voyages from Early Canada
Cecilia Morgan

92 Studying Arctic Fields
Cultures, Practices, and Environmental Sciences
Richard C. Powell

93 Iroquois in the West
Jean Barman

94 Leading from Between
Indigenous Participation and Leadership in the Public Service
Catherine Althaus and Ciaran O'Faircheallaigh

95 Against the Current and Into the Light
Performing History and Land in Coast Salish Territories and Vancouver's Stanley Park
Selena Couture

96 Plants, People, and Places
The Roles of Ethnobotany and Ethnoecology in Indigenous Peoples' Land Rights in Canada and Beyond
Edited by Nancy J. Turner

97 Fighting for a Hand to Hold
Confronting Medical Colonialism against Indigenous Children in Canada
Samir Shaheen-Hussain

98 Forty Narratives in the Wyandot Language
John L. Steckley

99 Uumajursiutik unaatuinnamut / Hunter with Harpoon / Chasseur au harpon
Markoosie Patsauq
Edited and translated by Valerie Henitiuk and Marc-Antoine Mahieu

100 Language, Citizenship, and Sámi Education in the Nordic North, 1900–1940
Otso Kortekangas

101 Daughters of Aataentsic
Life Stories from Seven Generations
Kathryn Magee Labelle in collaboration with the We^{n}dat/Wa^{n}dat Women's Advisory Council

DAUGHTERS OF AATAENTSIC

Life Stories from Seven Generations

KATHRYN MAGEE LABELLE

In collaboration with the members of the We^{n}dat/Wa^{n}dat Women's Advisory Council: Sallie Cotter Andrews, Janith English, Judith Pidgeon-Kukowski, Judith Manthe, Beverlee Pettit, Linda Sioui, Manon Sioui, and Catherine Tàmmaro

McGill-Queen's University Press
Montreal & Kingston | London | Chicago

ISBN 978-0-2280-0529-2 (cloth)
ISBN 978-0-2280-0688-6 (ePDF)

Legal deposit first quarter 2021
Bibliothèque nationale du Québec

Printed in Canada on acid-free paper that is 100% ancient forest free (100% post-consumer recycled), processed chlorine free

This book has been published with the help of a grant from the Canadian Federation for the Humanities and Social Sciences, through the Awards to Scholarly Publications Program, using funds provided by the Social Sciences and Humanities Research Council of Canada.

Funded by the Government of Canada | Financé par le gouvernement du Canada | Canada | Canada Council for the Arts | Conseil des arts du Canada

We acknowledge the support of the Canada Council for the Arts.

Nous remercions le Conseil des arts du Canada de son soutien.

LIBRARY AND ARCHIVES CANADA CATALOGUING IN PUBLICATION

Title: Daughters of Aataentsic : life stories from seven generations / Kathryn Magee Labelle ; in collaboration with the members of the We[n]dat/Wa[n]dat Women's Advisory Council : Sallie Cotter Andrews, Janith English, Judith Pidgeon Kukowski, Judith Manthe, Beverlee Pettit, Linda Sioui, Manon Sioui, and Catherine Tàmmaro.
Names: Labelle, Kathryn Magee, 1983– author.
Description: Series statement: McGill-Queen's Indigenous and northern studies ; 101 | Includes bibliographical references and index.
Identifiers: Canadiana (print) 20200363077 | Canadiana (ebook) 20200363166 | ISBN 9780228005292 (hardcover) | ISBN 9780228006886 (PDF)
Subjects: LCSH: Indigenous women—Ontario—History. | LCSH: Indigenous women—Québec (Province)—History. | LCSH: Indigenous women—Middle West—History. | LCSH: Indigenous women—Ontario—Biography. | LCSH: Indigenous women—Québec (Province)—Biography. | LCSH: Indigenous women—Middle West—Biography. | LCSH: Indigenous women—Ontario—Social life and customs. | LCSH: Indigenous women—Québec (Province)—Social life and customs. | LCSH: Indigenous women—Middle West—Social life and customs.
Classification: LCC E99.H9 L33 2021 | DDC 305.48/897555—dc23

Set in 10.5/14 Gentium Plus with Minion Pro and Brandon Grotesque
Book design & typesetting by Garet Markvoort, zijn digital

etsikweža:raha? aweti? nǫme?šǫ?ǫh
again we remember all women

nęhša? nǫnęh ^{n}deyǫmahšuta?ayęhę?
and also the grandmothers of the past

^{n}daižuh a?ǫkinǫht ^{n}dikyǫte ^{n}dinyǫma?
because they gave to us our own life.

CONTENTS

ACKNOWLEDGMENTS

This book is a gift that comes from many people and places. The project began with a gathering in Saskatoon, Saskatchewan, on Treaty 6 Territory and the Homeland of the Métis. I am so grateful to have the privilege to live and learn on these ancient lands.

The We^{n}dat/Wa^{n}dat Women's Advisory Council, who provided countless hours of guidance and support, were critical throughout the entire process. They are powerful leaders and I am so humbled to know each and every one of them. The Council includes: Chief Janith English (Wyandot Nation of Kansas), Judith Manthe (Wyandot Nation of Kansas), Catherine Tàmmaro (Wyandot of Anderdon Nation), Judith Pidgeon-Kukowski (Wyandot of Anderdon Nation), Sallie Cotter Andrews (Wyandotte Nation), Beverlee Pettit (Wyandotte Nation), Linda Sioui (la Nation huronne-wendat), and Manon Sioui (la Nation huronne-wendat).

Other We^{n}dat/Wa^{n}dat members have made significant contributions to the project through conversations and teachings. Tizameh/Thank you: Richard Zane Smith, D'Arcy Tammaro, Chief Ted Roll, Steve Gronda, Clyde Pigeon, Dorothy Tammaro, Michael Odette, Louisa Libby, Anna Libby, Faith Gronda. Tiawenhk/Merci: George Sioui, Arakwa Sioui, Stephan Picard, Louis Lesage, Jean-Francois Richard, Jonathan Lainey, Sabrina Godbout.

The academic community has also lifted this project up with constructive feedback from: Jim Miller, Carolyn Podruchny, Thomas Peace, Cheryl Troupe, Ashleigh Androsoff, Ben Hoy, Lesley Biggs, Alessio Ponzio, Zach Yuzwa, Erika Dyck, Robert Englebert, Andrew Sturtevant, Stacy Nation-Knapper, Andrew Watson, Erika Dyck, Keith Carlson, Heidi Bohaker, Mari Cowan, Victoria Jackson, Boyd Cothran, Joseph Genetin-Pilawa, Lucy Murphy, Brittany Luby, Elizabeth Mancke, Sarah Nickle, Karen Merraro, Charles Garrad, John Steckley, John Nichols, Barry Shingoose, Jaime Meyer, Anyssa Plan, Krystl Raven, Daniel Palmer, Tarisa Little, Mckelvey Kelly, Erin Isaac, Ronda Lyn, Elizabeth Berton

Riley, Matraeca Munro, Scott Barthelette, Erin Grant, Hannah Cooley, and Fallon Burner. Editorial and administrative support have also been invaluable. Thank you so much: Mark Abley, Rilla Friesen, Sarah Taggart, Jane Westhouse, and Rachel Taylor.

Important conversations took place in specialized forums that brought clarity to many aspects of this story. The research was presented at the History Seminar (University of Saskatchewan) and at several conferences, including those of the History of Indigenous Peoples Network (York University), the American Society for Ethnohistory, the Canadian Historical Association, the Berkshire Conference of Women Historians, the Ontario Archeology Society, the International Studies Association, and the Native American and Indigenous Studies Association.

This project benefited from the financial support of several institutions as well. These funds went beyond facilitating customary research practices, and were used to coordinate We^{n}dat/Wa^{n}dat Women's Advisory Council meetings in the homeland, fund We^{n}dat/Wa^{n}dat student research awards, provide honorariums for community members, support community-run digital history projects, and support an art exhibit at Crawford Lake, Ontario, inspired by the *Daughters of Aataentsic* Project. I am forever grateful for the opportunities supported by: the Newberry Library Short-Term Fellowship, the Association of American University Women, the Interdisciplinary Centre for Culture and Creativity (University of Saskatchewan), the President's SSHRC Research Grant (University of Saskatchewan), and the Insight Grant (Social Science and Humanities Research Council of Canada).

Last but not least, my family have been unrelenting in their support for this work. To my extended family – thank you: Diane Magee, Steve Magee, Sean Magee, Lauren King, Isla King, Kim Magee, Chris Tait, Franklyn Tait, Henry Tait, and Gabriel Tait. Merci: Sylvie Vaillancourt, Julie Lalonde, Sabrina Lalonde-Vaillancourt, Fannie Lalonde-Vaillancourt, Rachelle Labelle, Marty March, Chloée Vernier, and Mathieu Vernier. And to my forever family whose love makes everything possible: I love you forever/Je t'aime toujours Moe, Zeke, Enaïs, and baby Beau.

We^{n}dat/Wa^{n}dat Women's Advisory Council, 2013. *Back row, left to right*: Beverlee Pettit, Judith Manthe, Linda Sioui, Catherine Tàmmaro, Kathryn Labelle. *Front row, left to right*: Sallie Cotter Andrews, Judith Kukowski, Chief Janith English. *Not pictured*: Manon Sioui. *Photo courtesy of Maurice Labelle, used by permission of the 2013 We^{n}dat/Wa^{n}dat Women's Advisory Council.*

We^{n}dat/Wa^{n}dat Women's Advisory Council, 2015. *Back row, left to right*: Sallie Cotter Andrews, Judith Manthe, Kathryn Labelle, Thomas Peace, Chief Janith English. *Front row, left to right*: Linda Sioui, Manon Sioui, Catherine Tàmmaro. *Not pictured*: Beverlee Pettit and Judith Kukowski. *Photo courtesy of Brenna Bartley and the author, used by permission of the 2015 We^{n}dat/Wa^{n}dat Women's Advisory Council.*

(*opposite, top*) Gravestone of Eliza Burton Conley, Kansas City, Kansas. *Kansas Room Special Collections, Kansas City, Kansas Public Library, with thanks to Anne Lacey.*

(*opposite, bottom*) Fort Conley, Kansas. *Kansas Room Special Collections, Kansas City, Kansas Public Library, with thanks to Anne Lacey.*

ELIZA BURTON CONLEY
DEPARTED THIS LIFE MAY 28, 1946
ATTORNEY AT LAW.
ONLY WOMAN EVER ADMITTED TO
THE UNITED STATES SUPREME COURT

WENDAT
GEORGES-A. SIOUI
1918 — 1984
ÉPOUX DE
ELEONORE SIOUI
1920 — 2006
YOSKAHA, GRAND ESPRIT
EMBAUME NOTRE REPOS DE ROSES TENDRES

(*opposite, top*) Gravestone of Éléonore Sioui, Wendake, Quebec. *Photo by the author.*

(*opposite, bottom left*) Ashley Simmons (Wyandotte Nation) in Jane Zane Gordon's dress, holding a picture of Gordon wearing the dress and standing next to President Harding. *Photo courtesy of Wyandotte Nation, with thanks to Sherri Clemons and Ashley Simmons.*

(*opposite, bottom right*) Jane Zane Gordon meeting with President Harding. *Photo courtesy of Wyandotte Nation, with thanks to Sherri Clemons.*

(*right*) Mary McKee, Essex, Ontario, photographed by Marius Barbeau, 1912. *Canadian Museum of History, image no. 19931.*

(*below*) Gravestone of Mary McKee, Wyandotte, Oklahoma. *Photo courtesy of Sallie Cotter Andrews.*

Eliza B. Conley, 1902. *WikiCommons. Public domain.*

(*opposite, top*) Alexander Zane's farm, Wyandotte reservation, Oklahoma. *Photo courtesy of Sallie Cotter Andrews.*

(*opposite, bottom left*) Mary McKee with a mortar, pestle, and baskets, Essex, Ontario, photographed by Marius Barbeau, 1912. *Canadian Museum of History, image no. 19945.*

(*opposite, bottom right*) Eliza B. Conley. *Thanks to archivists and librarians at University of Missouri–Kansas City Special Collections, the Kansas City, Kansas Public Library, and the Kansas City Public Library. Photo courtesy of Chief Janith English. Public domain.*

John Grey Eyes. *Kansas Room Special Collections, Kansas City, Kansas Public Library, with thanks to Anne Lacey.*

Nancy Quindaro. *Kansas Room Special Collections, Kansas City, Kansas Public Library, with thanks to Anne Lacey.*

Silas Armstrong. *Kansas Room Special Collections, Kansas City, Kansas Public Library, with thanks to Anne Lacey.*

Lucinda Young-Pidgeon. *Photo courtesy of Judith Kukowski.*

Archie Pidgeon. *Photo courtesy of Judith Kukowski.*

Stella Chene. *Photo courtesy of Judith Kukowski.*

Joseph Warrow and his family. *Kansas Room Special Collections, Kansas City, Kansas Public Library, with thanks to Anne Lacey.*

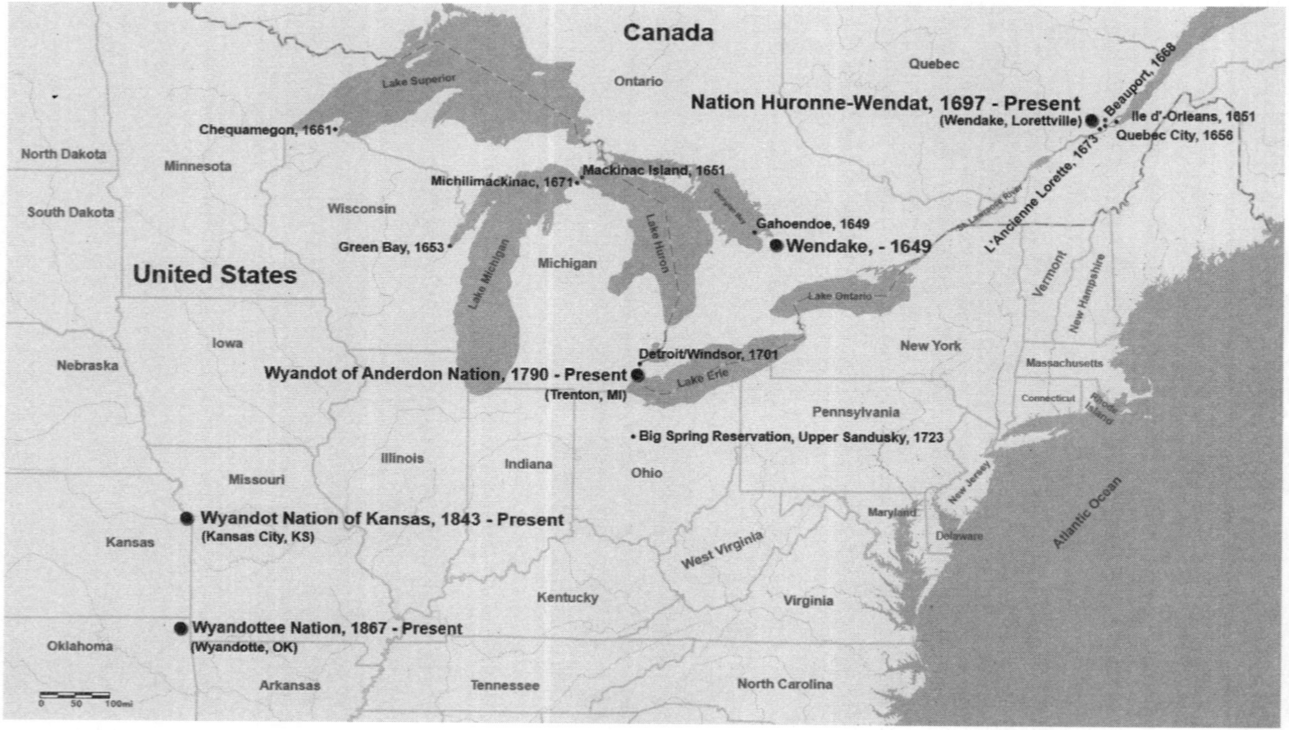

Migrations and communities of the We^{n}dat/Wa^{n}dat from 1600 to the present

DAUGHTERS OF AATAENTSIC

INTRODUCTION

Aataentsic, also known as Sky Woman, holds a special place in the history of the Iroquois and is the central figure in their origin story.[1] She is not only responsible for the creation of Turtle Island – the North American continent – she is also the grandmother of the People. Among her descendants are her We^{n}dat/Wa^{n}dat children, a People who have also been known variously as the Huron, the Wendat, the Wyandot, and the Wyandotte.[2] For over 350 years, the We^{n}dat/Wa^{n}dat People (originally consisting of a confederacy of five First Nations: Bear, Cord, Rock, Deer, and Swamp) have travelled the vast territory of the North American continent. Forced from their seventeenth-century villages – known collectively as Wendake and located along the shores of Georgian Bay, Ontario – We^{n}dat/Wa^{n}dat descendants found refuge both within the borders of their vast territory to the east leading to Quebec, and in new homelands throughout the modern province of Ontario and the states of Michigan, Ohio, Kansas, and Oklahoma. Despite disease, warfare, and colonial regimes, these resilient First Nations remain. Today, their communities consist of the Wyandot of Anderdon Nation (Ontario/Michigan), la Nation huronne-wendat (Quebec), the Wyandot Nation of Kansas (Kansas), and the Wyandotte Nation (Oklahoma).

On 27 August 1999 these First Nations reunited in Wendake Ehen (Old Wendake) to confirm their enduring bond. Chief Janith English (Wyandot Nation of Kansas), Chief Wellie Picard (la Nation huronne-wendat), Second Chief Jim Bland for Chief Leaford Bearskin (Wyandotte Nation), and spokesperson Steven Gronda (Wyandot of Anderdon Nation) signed the Wendat Confederacy, a document that officially reinstated the ancient coalition. Chief English created the document with the consent of the other Chiefs. It concludes, "We vow to attempt to work together in a way that the embers of long ago council fires may be fanned into a flame of kinship, culture, and love that will warm countless generations of Wendat people."[3]

The story of Aataentsic is also the story of her People. Originally recorded by skilled knowledge keepers and passed on through sacred oral history, her status and role within We^{n}dat/Wa^{n}dat society were transformed by European contact and the imposition of settler colonialism. The earliest written accounts come from seventeenth-century French missionaries who believed the We^{n}dat/Wa^{n}dat "recognize as the head of their Nation a certain woman whom they call *Ataentsic*."[4] Two hundred years later, ethnographers translated We^{n}dat/Wa^{n}dat descriptions of "Yaa'tayehtsih" (phonetically Aataentsic) as "witch."[5] This recasting of Sky Woman, from the head of a nation to a witch, demonstrates a departure from the value of We^{n}dat/Wa^{n}dat women within a customarily matricentric society.[6] No longer the ultimate matriarch of humankind and homeland, Aataentsic was stripped of her feminine power by Eurocentric influences to fit Western models of patriarchal dominance and Indigenous subordination. Similarly, these same influences subjugated her We^{n}dat/Wa^{n}dat children and, more specifically, vilified her *daughters* to fit these foreign frameworks. Inextricably connected to the history of her People, Aataentsic's story serves as a cultural indicator of the lived experiences of her We^{n}dat/Wa^{n}dat daughters within the North American colonial world.

Much has been written on the disruptive effects of patriarchal policies on North American Indigenous societies and the decline in women's status, power, and authority.[7] Clan Mothers stood at odds with the male-dominated European systems of hierarchy, so dismantling female power became critical in colonial conquest. Violence, chaos, and conflict typified the lives of Indigenous women. In many cases, the story remains one of victimhood and cultural corrosion, with an emphasis on the constant struggles to protect both their Indigeneity and their womanhood. While acknowledging the validity of this declension model, *Daughters of Aataentsic* offers an alternative narrative by considering the ways in which individual We^{n}dat/Wa^{n}dat women resisted colonialism, preserved their culture, and maintained their status as matriarchs. More specifically, it looks at how We^{n}dat/Wa^{n}dat women have engaged with colonial institutions in ways steeped in We^{n}dat/Wa^{n}dat feminine traditions.

Within We^{n}dat/Wa^{n}dat studies there is very little published about We^{n}dat/Wa^{n}dat women's history. In 1976, Bruce Trigger published his foundational work *The Children of Aataentsic*, about the We^{n}dat/Wa^{n}dat

Confederacy up until 1650. His meticulous study was, and continues to be, a standard reference for those interested in Native-Newcomer relations, colonialism, and Indigenous cultures, politics, and economies around the Great Lakes of North America. Despite its utility over the last forty years, Trigger's research lacked gender analysis, provoking sociologist Karen Anderson to look more closely at the experience of Native women in seventeenth-century New France. Inspired by the rise of social history and cultural studies, Anderson argued in her book *Chain Her by One Foot* that the relationship between French missionaries and We^{n}dat/Wa^{n}dat had devastating effects on We^{n}dat/Wa^{n}dat women, resulting in a total loss of social, political, and economic power.[8]

While not rejecting Anderson's conclusions (missionaries most certainly transformed We^{n}dat/Wa^{n}dat women's roles), my first book complicated our understanding of seventeenth-century We^{n}dat/Wa^{n}dat women and Anderson's declension thesis. In *Dispersed but Not Destroyed,* I dedicated a chapter to exploring how women's power was maintained at least until the eighteenth century in the wake of several We^{n}dat/Wa^{n}dat migrations and episodes of warfare.[9] There, I argued that rather than losing authority, women exerted power as keepers of the land and people. This kind of collective power fostered unity and strength among We^{n}dat/Wa^{n}dat women, creating opportunities to further their communities' goals and secure a future beyond their former homeland in present-day Ontario.

Daughters of Aataentsic fits into a growing body of literature that redresses the historical conversation from a discourse of destruction to discussions of cultural healing, resistance, and resilience.[10] While not ignoring the significant changes experienced by Indigenous North Americans and the overt attacks Indigenous societies have suffered throughout colonial history, these works describe the strength of Indigenous women throughout this history and the many ways that they have protected, and continue to protect, their communities from colonial harm. Anishinaabeg women, for instance, may have converted to Christianity, but they did not necessarily assimilate into mainstream society. Similarly, Métis daughters may have married French men, but they did not give up their Indigenous traditions. Together, this scholarship recognizes the critical and persistent actions of Indigenous women in the history of cultural survival.

Daughters of Aataentsic extends this conversation by focusing exclusively on We^{n}dat/Wa^{n}dat women. The research summarized in these pages explores how We^{n}dat/Wa^{n}dat women have consistently turned to traditions of "motherwork" – work that is geared towards bettering their family and community's circumstances rather than those of a single person. Lisa Udel has demonstrated specific ways that Indigenous women have found motherwork to be a useful model. Her research indicates that Indigenous women tend to see "individual survival, empowerment, and identity" as reliant on "group survival, empowerment, and identity." Further, she contends that motherwork extends beyond the realm of giving birth – it is not necessarily the physical act itself but rather the responsibilities associated with nurturing, teaching, and protecting Indigenous cultures for future generations.[11] For many Indigenous women, part of this work aims to reinstate a pre-colonial "mother-centred" value system – one that re-establishes the authority of women. Put another way, Indigenous women do not seek to establish new positions of special or equal status within society, but rather they strive to regain or maintain a status that was historically already present.[12]

While motherwork provides the conceptual framework for this book, it is the We^{n}dat/Wa^{n}dat themselves who have provided the project design. In November 2013, after consultation with We^{n}dat/Wa^{n}dat Chiefs and leaders, a We^{n}dat/Wa^{n}dat Women's Advisory Council was established to guide my work. Eight We^{n}dat/Wa^{n}dat women agreed to serve on this council, with representation from all four modern We^{n}dat/Wa^{n}dat nations. The members are: Chief Janith English (Wyandot Nation of Kansas), Judith Manthe (Wyandot Nation of Kansas), Catherine Tàmmaro (Wyandot of Anderdon Nation), Judith Pidgeon-Kukowski (Wyandot of Anderdon Nation), Beverlee Pettit (Wyandotte Nation), Sallie Cotter Andrews (Wyandotte Nation), Linda Sioui (la Nation huronne-wendat of Quebec), and Manon Sioui (la Nation huronne-wendat of Quebec).[13]

What followed, and what continues beyond this book project, are the results of a collaborative process based on ethnohistorical methodologies, community engagement, and consensus decision-making. Community-based participatory research requires ongoing and genuine relationship-building and support with a commitment to action and social change.[14] Consequently, as a settler scholar, my connections with the Wendat Confederacy and the advisory council go beyond scholarship. In 2014 I became an adopted member of the Wyandot Nation of Kansas and was given the Wyandot name Ontidesonk (the Eagle That Soars High and Sees Far). Three years later, the Wyandot of Anderdon Nation gave me the honour name Yari:memaʔ (She Carries the Story Along) at their annual Green Corn Ceremony. As a result, these women and their communities have become my aunties and cousins – my family.

With family comes responsibilities. Reciprocity and process over progress are crucial elements of my work. The manner in which decisions were made for the project design of this book reflects this methodology. Shortly after the creation of the advisory council, I organized a gathering to facilitate conversation and consultation. Council members travelled from across North America – from Alaska, Texas, Kansas, Michigan, Ontario, and Quebec – in order to meet in person at the University of Saskatchewan. Some of the women had met before; for others, it was the first time. I myself had only met a fraction of the council before the Saskatoon gathering. We began the meeting with a question: "How can my work as a historian best serve the communities?" The answer was unequivocal: a compilation of published biographies of notable We^{n}dat/Wa^{n}dat women – the council members' cultural, and in some cases literal, grandmothers. The idea was to provide published accounts that would act as a written reference for future generations. Remarkably, oral histories have maintained much of the information preserved among We^{n}dat/Wa^{n}dat families, but 450 years of colonialism have made the dissemination of that information difficult.

A focus on life stories provides what scholar Nick Salvatore describes as a "light far beyond the individual" and is, as historian Jean Barman explains, a means to make connections to broader historical change.[15] Further, (her)stories – that is, histories about individual women – deliver a "wealth of specific information about the life course of differently positioned women, whose lives can be viewed collectively and separately" to make informed revisions of male-dominated interpretations.[16] Indigenous feminist scholars see the publication of Indigenous women's biographies in particular as an important component of the decolonizing process and critical to developing cultural pride and leadership.[17] Renya Ramirez, an Indigenous studies scholar and the granddaughter of acclaimed Native American intellectual Henry Roe Cloud, argues that the publication of Indigenous biographies is an act of countering colonialism and can "help us reconstruct a Native-centric history as well as empower us as a people."[18] Each case study in this book, therefore, contributes to this trend and provides chapters that highlight the lives of important We^{n}dat/Wa^{n}dat women, while situating them within the larger context of North American settler colonialism.

Over four days, advisory council members discussed possible candidates for the book's biographies. Names and rationales were submitted, revised, and voted on. The council justified their final selections through recognition of significant family connections, community importance, evidence of motherwork, and cultural legacies. The chapters in this book reflect the advisory council's desire to capture a related set of critiques of colonialism and patriarchy through historical examples of We^{n}dat/Wa^{n}dat motherwork. Combined, the case studies document how We^{n}dat/Wa^{n}dat women have consistently drawn upon their knowledge of matricentric traditions to inspire successful initiatives that nurture, teach, and protect Indigenous culture.

Critics might be quick to dismiss this work as hagiographic, but such dismissal implies a lack of understanding and consideration of the historical and persistent colonial tradition of discrimination and dehumanization of Indigenous women. For too long, Indigenous women have been the target of Christian, governmental, and patriarchal regimes deeming them unfit mothers, wives, and citizens. We are still witnessing and experiencing the systemic results of these tactics today. As a result, this work does not provide a deep critique of these women; to do so would counter the goals of the project. We^{n}dat/Wa^{n}dat women have been blamed for centuries as the instigators of community struggles. It is, therefore, neither helpful nor insightful to contribute more to this kind of analysis. We are not there yet; before we can engage with complicating the accomplishments of these women, we must first acknowledge their successes.

Chapter 1 introduces Cécile Gannendâris (?–1669), a woman threatened by Iroquois attacks, forced relocations, and a new colonial patriarchy. Gannendâris led strategic initiatives that delivered critical support for her family and community during this time of crisis. Christian conversion, maternal diplomacy, and membership in the Catholic women's organization the Holy Family Society remained at the heart of her successful motherwork. While on the surface this may seem like a case of assimilation, Gannendâris drew upon We^{n}dat/Wa^{n}dat traditions of women's circles and matriarchy as means to maintain Indigenous cultural practices for future generations.

Chapter 2 focuses on Marie Catherine Jean dit Vien (1676–1767), who was born in Quebec but lived most of her life among the Detroit River We^{n}dat/Wa^{n}dat. Although there have been persistent colonial efforts to erase her We^{n}dat/Wa^{n}dat identity, this chapter draws attention to testimony from her family and the legacy of her motherwork as evidence to highlight her status as a significant and influential member of eighteenth-century We^{n}dat/Wa^{n}dat society. Her descendants, including Chiefs Isadore Chesne, Adam Brown, Billy Friend, and Clyde Pidgeon, follow a long line of leadership grounded in customary female mentorship and support.

The public motherwork of Margaret "Mother" Grey Eyes Solomon (1816–1890) is the subject of Chapter 3. This chapter explores Solomon's position as a Chief's daughter during the forced removal of the We^{n}dat/Wa^{n}dat from Ohio to Kansas in 1843. In addition, her efforts to protect and promote We^{n}dat/Wa^{n}dat culture through the Wyandot Mission Church in Upper Sandusky, Ohio present a clear example of successful motherwork in the nineteenth century.

Chapter 4 discusses the life of Mary McKee (1838–1922), who lived in We^{n}dat/Wa^{n}dat communities in Detroit, Kansas, and Oklahoma. McKee became famous when her words and knowledge about the We^{n}dat/Wa^{n}dat were recorded by the well published ethnographer Marius Barbeau, resulting in one of the few sources about We^{n}dat/Wa^{n}dat culture recorded before the language was lost. This, however, has overshadowed other motherwork, as she also fought and won the right to maintain property, despite government threats to ignore We^{n}dat/Wa^{n}dat territorial rights and the traditional connection of matriarchal authority over land.

Chapter 5 highlights the accomplishments of Eliza Burton Conley Jr (1869–1946), who was the first woman admitted to the Kansas bar. Conley addressed colonial policies concerning We^{n}dat/Wa^{n}dat sacred spaces and ancestral protection through protests, petitions, and legal action over the Wyandot National Burial Ground in Kansas City. This activism led her to become the first Indigenous woman to argue a case before the Supreme Court of the United States.

Another trailblazer, and the subject of Chapter 6, is Jane Zane Gordon (1871–1963) of the Wyandotte Nation (Oklahoma). Gordon was an author, playwright, and activist at the turn of the twentieth century. She dedicated her life to supporting Indigenous artists and preserving their practice with national organizations. Her motherwork was so influential that she was granted an audience with US president Warren Harding, bringing national awareness to Indigenous rights.

Finally, Chapter 7 concludes the book with a chapter on Dr Éléonore Sioui (1924–2006). An avid proponent of education, Dr Sioui used the written word to counter colonial policies and promote Indigenous teachings at home as well as abroad. As a result, this We^{n}dat/Wa^{n}dat intellectual's transnational motherwork, which sought to provide support for Indigenous Peoples throughout the world, was recognized in 2001 with the Order of Canada.

Each chapter is organized into four sections: Family, Community, Motherwork, and Legacy. One of the first teachings I received from my We^{n}dat/Wa^{n}dat mentors was the importance of *family*. Family situates who you are and where you come from. For the We^{n}dat/Wa^{n}dat, family is more than bloodlines; it is the tracing of historical relationships that evolved into kinship connections. Family explains identity and the motivations behind certain events. It is a means by which the We^{n}dat/Wa^{n}dat find inspiration and guidance. Family ties are the foundation upon which communities are built. *Community* explains not just the people, but the place in which the people live. Each time I visit one of the modern We^{n}dat/Wa^{n}dat communities or their ancestral homelands, I am asked to engage with the landscape – the rivers, creeks, prairie grass, caves, and mountains. Many We^{n}dat/Wa^{n}dat have experienced multiple homelands and each relocation resulted in new sources of knowledge and identity, derived from the land. Providing a description of these places is therefore an essential component to later analysis of We^{n}dat/Wa^{n}dat culture and world views. Family and community serve as the inspiration for the next section, *motherwork*. Here the focus is exclusively on each woman's unique activism. Although this work is seemingly different in many respects, each chapter finds common threads that distinguish a consistent goal of creating opportunities for cultural survival and resilience. Finally, each chapter concludes by outlining the significant and long-term effects of motherwork. The *legacy* of these women is evident in not only the way their descendants have commemorated them over time but the many ways in which the modern We^{n}dat/Wa^{n}dat have benefited from their motherwork.

Although the writing and analysis for this book is my own, it is the result of invaluable insight and oversight by the We^{n}dat/Wa^{n}dat Women's Advisory Council. Drafts of the manuscript were presented to the council at various stages of the project. This practice of conversation and consultation allowed for the application of community-based perspectives and family histories to the narrative. Put another way, this research is intimately related to the advisory members. The case studies are not abstract historical figures; rather, they are their We^{n}dat/Wa^{n}dat relations. Discrepancies were inevitable as we attempted to align various national, religious, familial, and linguistic differences. This was not an easy process and required extra time, care, and respect. Each opinion needed equal attention, a balancing act that led to deeper questions and multi-perspective analyses. What follows in these pages is my sincere attempt to reflect the desires of the council, while maintaining a commitment to historical practice and integrity.

This process also provided unique opportunities to access rare and often overlooked sources. Alongside settler archival documents and published primary sources, this research benefits from the collections of the We^{n}dat/Wa^{n}dat themselves. The community archives of both the Wyandot Nation of Kansas and la Nation huronne-wendat of Quebec provided generous documentation about their histories. I also had the opportunity to use several private collections. These collections included the genealogical records of Judith Pidgeon-Kukowski, which served as a wealth of knowledge concerning the generational links between the case studies. Sallie Cotter Andrews provided her personal records pertaining to Jane Zane Gordon, shared with her by Wyandotte elder Mary Jane Gallaspy. Chief Janith English contributed unpublished written reflections on her family history and several guided visits to the Wyandot National Burial Ground. Similarly, Judith Manthe gave me permission to view her family's collection of legal documents concerning Eliza Conley. Finally, Dr Éléonore Sioui's eldest son, Dr Georges Sioui, donated her personal papers for exclusive use for this project. Combined, these gifts are reflections of the We^{n}dat/Wa^{n}dat people who created and preserved them. They have allowed for deeper understandings of the case studies in this book, as well as the world in which they lived.

The story of Aataentsic is an important one. It is a story that has guided the We^{n}dat/Wa^{n}dat people since time immemorial.[19] It describes the creation of the world and the value systems that give that world shape. Despite the ways in which colonial influences have transformed her narrative, Aataentsic's legacy remains to this day, continuing to inform her descendants. Her daughters – generations of We^{n}dat/Wa^{n}dat women, including the case studies in this book, as well as the members of the advisory council – are a testament to this fact.

Seven case studies for seven generations – and beyond.

CHAPTER 1

Cécile Gannendâris (?–1669)

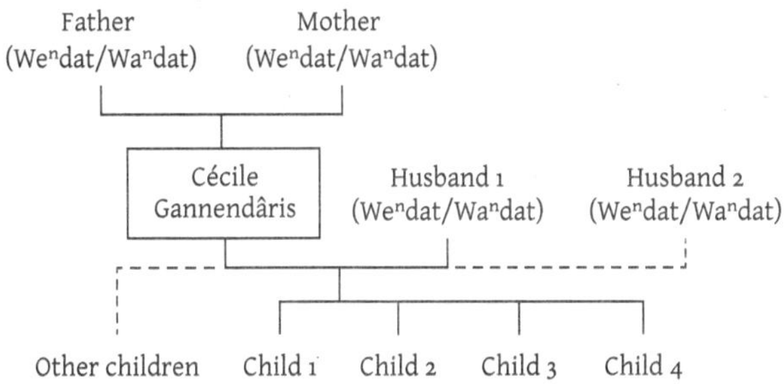

INTRODUCTION

Heads hung low as church bells rang through the frosty February air and the procession completed its journey through the centre of town. Despite the cold, a mixed crowd of First Nations people and French Canadians pushed one another to get a glimpse of the well-known and recently deceased We^{n}dat/Wa^{n}dat woman Cécile Gannendâris. Born sometime between 1620 and 1630, Gannendâris joined hundreds of We^{n}dat/Wa^{n}dat refugees who decided in 1650 to evacuate their villages near Georgian Bay on Lake Huron due to Iroquois military strikes. With sadness in their hearts, she and her family re-settled farther east: first at the French colonial village of Sillery and later near Quebec City. After the relocation, Gannendâris made motherwork her foremost priority, taking advantage of every opportunity to ensure her position as an influential matriarch and better the lives of We^{n}dat/Wa^{n}dat women. This was not an easy task, as European patriarchal world views had begun to reshape We^{n}dat/Wa^{n}dat society. Matrilineal and matrifocal traditions gave way to French customs that introduced male heads of households and privileged We^{n}dat/Wa^{n}dat headmen over Clan Mothers. Still, at the time of her death in 1669 Gannendâris remained a powerful force within her community; so much so that upon her passing, French bishop François Laval ordered a formal public funeral held in her honour at Notre-Dame de Québec.[1] Similar arrangements were made by the We^{n}dat/Wa^{n}dat headman Ignace Saouhenhohi, who hosted a public feast in Gannendâris's honour.[2] At the We^{n}dat/Wa^{n}dat memorial, Saouhenhohi encouraged those who had gathered to "not forget Gannendâris."[3] Yet, despite this request, little record of her existence has survived.

Contemporaries who attended the funeral services took note of her influence, documenting these events and her death in 1669. French Jesuit missionaries dedicated an entire entry in their annual reports, or *Relations*, describing who she was and the relationships she had forged with the Christian community. Naturally, their focus was on Christian conversion and she was highlighted as an exemplary case of a faithful We^{n}dat/Wa^{n}dat ally and a critical component to the success of the missions in New France.[4] Similar remarks were made by the Mother Superior at the Québec Seminary, Marie de l'Incarnation, as well as her fellow Ursuline Mother, Marie Forestier de Saint Bonaventure.[5] These religious women reiterate the same information as is relayed in the *Jesuit Relations* and call attention to Gannendâris's "vertueuse" nature.

Her story remained within these seventeenth-century accounts until 1918 when Narcisse-Eutrope Dionne published a collection of forty biographies of Christian "servants" in Canada. Within these pages, Dionne highlights again Gannendâris's Christian virtues – her chastity, her piety, and her "zeal" for the Catholic church.[6] One hundred years later I incorporated Gannendâris's story into a study of the seventeenth-century We^{n}dat/Wa^{n}dat diaspora. I highlighted Gannendâris's story to illustrate how We^{n}dat/Wa^{n}dat women in the post-dispersal period negotiated their relocation near Quebec City and used Christianity as a means to create support networks in a colonial society.[7] This brief analysis, however, does little to tease out the full significance of this remarkable woman. It alludes to, but does not investigate fully, Gannendâris's actions in relation to motherwork.

Scholars have demonstrated various ways that Indigenous women have infiltrated colonial regimes by using the very institutions that are the source of their subjugation and discrimination. These examples call attention specifically to how conversion to Christianity led to a religious culture that gave Indigenous women a voice in settler society. This "oratorical voice" attracted young women, like Gannendâris, to convert because they could transport the We^{n}dat/Wa^{n}dat Longhouse practices to Christian "women's teachings."[8] This strategy is reflected in the case study of Cécile Gannendâris. The dispersal marked a new era for the We^{n}dat/Wa^{n}dat. Options were limited for women of the diaspora, while the number of threats continued to grow. Warfare and drought threatened lives, as did the European onslaught of disease, trade of alcohol, and a rising number of single, lonely men who saw Indigenous women as part of the colonial conquest. Ultimately, this chapter highlights one strategy to preserve and protect We^{n}dat/Wa^{n}dat women and the community. Where We^{n}dat/Wa^{n}dat men converts had the benefit of trade and firearms, women converts used their feminine status to join Christian networks, gaining access to not only extended support but also clothes, shelter, and food for their family. Women like Gannendâris had to create alliances with non-Indigenous actors, such as French nuns, bishops, and high-society women, to achieve these goals.

FAMILY

The woman who came to be known as Cécile Gannendâris was most likely not born with that name. Born during the first few decades of French missionary work in Wendake, it is likely that she gained the name Cécile not from her We^{n}dat/Wa^{n}dat family, but from her Christian European neighbours. There are mentions of other "Ceciles," for instance, baptized by Jesuit priests during the same period.[9] Sainte Cécile de Rome was the patron of music and musicians and it is perhaps this model of a woman that the Indigenous women were named after. Gannendâris's Christian naming took place during a key moment in We^{n}dat/Wa^{n}dat history. Epidemics of smallpox, measles, and scarlet fever swept We^{n}dat/Wa^{n}dat communities in the 1630s, pushing many to accept Christian beliefs with the hope that their lives might be saved. The Jesuits had an aggressive campaign to "cure" the We^{n}dat/Wa^{n}dat.[10]

Initially women were hesitant to accept the new faith, but extreme circumstances gave way to new traditions. One mother expressed her conversion as a means to manage her sense of loss as death rates increased and disease engulfed communities. The mother explained: "I used to be inconsolable, in the past, when any of my near relatives died; but, since I have become [the Holy Virgin's] daughter, and know that, to please [her], one must wish what is God's will, I am content to see my dear child die."[11] It is not clear why Gannendâris received baptism, whether it was the decision of her mother, father, or a last attempt to save the soul of an orphaned child. What is likely, however, is that her baptism was not an isolated event and that she joined a growing number of We^{n}dat/Wa^{n}dat Christian kin.

The surname "Gannendâris" gives further clues to the origins of this remarkable woman. The name is likely of We^{n}dat/Wa^{n}dat origin. According to Wyandot linguist John Steckley, there are many We^{n}dat/Wa^{n}dat names that have the noun root "-nnenh-," meaning "corn," in them, and there is no noun root "-nnend-." This makes it possible that, with the verb root "-ri-," meaning "to spread," we actually have the name *Gannenharis* – meaning "she (habitually) spreads out the corn."[12] The seventeenth-century We^{n}dat/Wa^{n}dat were farmers and built traditions and cultural practices around the "Three Sisters": corn, beans, and squash. The We^{n}dat/Wa^{n}dat had a special relationship with corn and many of their names reflect this important food source.[13]

As with so much history of the early contact period, there is no definitive proof in regard to the origin of this person's name, but through a linguistic, historical, and cultural analysis we can come to understand that the woman recorded in New France letters, reports, and books as "Cécile Gannendâris" was identified by her contemporaries with both European and We^{n}dat/Wa^{n}dat names. "Cécile" is evidence of European encounters, as well as confirmation of her Christian baptism. Similarly, "Gannendâris" alludes to her identity as a We^{n}dat/Wa^{n}dat woman (with a We^{n}dat/Wa^{n}dat name), connecting her to We^{n}dat/Wa^{n}dat heritage and culture.

The identity of Cécile Gannendâris can be further defined through her family and her responsibilities as a We^{n}dat/Wa^{n}dat woman. Pre-dispersal seventeenth-century We^{n}dat/Wa^{n}dat families were both matrilineal and matrifocal. In a world created by Aataentsic, it is no surprise that the main social structures relied heavily on the responsibilities of We^{n}dat/Wa^{n}dat women. Women were not only the heads of their immediate families, but also their extended families and Clans. These Clan Mothers held significant authority within We^{n}dat/Wa^{n}dat society, designating both civil and war leaders, making decisions to enter into battle, and deciding the fate of prisoners. Women also controlled the food supplies and it was the women who kept the land.[14] Gannendâris was born into this pre-dispersal mother-centred society and witnessed its transition to a European patriarchy as she relocated farther east towards Quebec after 1650. Still, while intermarriage and colonial pressure changed certain aspects of former We^{n}dat/Wa^{n}dat customs, many remained intact throughout Gannendâris's life.

As a wife, Gannendâris exercised her influence on her partners by convincing them to adopt her values, including conversion to Christianity. According to Jesuit accounts, she was happily married twice – both times to We^{n}dat/Wa^{n}dat Traditionalists. The first marriage lasted several years and was cut short with the untimely death of her husband due to an unknown disease.[15] Although originally unbaptized, this man agreed to Gannendâris's request to accept the Christian faith. The missionaries took note of how easily he transitioned and they believed that this was due in large part to his wife's explanation of the Christian traditions as well as his long-time exposure to the customs of the French.[16] Not long after her first husband passed away, Gannendâris married again. This husband was equally devoted to her and demonstrated his commitment through Christian conversion. This, however, was not an easy task. Unlike her first husband, this We^{n}dat/Wa^{n}dat man struggled with the differences between We^{n}dat/Wa^{n}dat codes of conduct and those of the Catholic faith. His road to "salvation" took much more time, but, eventually, he was baptized. Despite this strained negotiation, the eager husband fulfilled his wife's desires and became "one of the best Christians in the Colony."[17] We^{n}dat/Wa^{n}dat marriages in the post-dispersal period took many forms. It was not uncommon for We^{n}dat/Wa^{n}dat women to marry French men, for instance. Consequently, marriage culture transformed We^{n}dat/Wa^{n}dat society as We^{n}dat/Wa^{n}dat women began to adhere to European traditions of patrifocal and patriarchal customs. This was not the case with Gannendâris. Because she chose to marry We^{n}dat/Wa^{n}dat men, it is likely that she maintained matrifocal customs. Her noted ability to persuade her spouses into conversion further demonstrates this point.

In addition to two loving marriages, Gannendâris's immediate family included several children. She had at least four children with her first husband, all of whom passed away before her death in 1669. We also know that she was survived by a number of other children, although we do not know how many there were, or which father they belonged to.[18] Motherwork describes work designed to better the lives of Indigenous women and communities and Cécile Gannendâris took special attention to support her daughters. This was made clear when the girls became deathly ill. Although the girls were already devoted little Christians, according to the Jesuits their mother went to great lengths to ensure their salvation in case they did not survive. Gannendâris's twelve-year-old daughter, for instance, no longer able to walk due to a debilitating disease, was wrapped in a moose-skin robe and carried with the help of another We^{n}dat/Wa^{n}dat woman to the Church during Easter to receive communion.[19] Her other daughter, age seven, was instructed by her mother to continue to say her rosary throughout an illness that would eventually take her life. The child took this to such an extreme that she insisted on adhering to her mother's instructions even when she had lost the ability to speak.[20] The Christian devotion expressed by Gannendâris's daughters was the result of their mother's own loyalty to the religion. Gannendâris's children's spiritual beliefs were, like those of her husbands, shaped almost exclusively by her.

Gannendâris's kinship relationships demonstrate healthy and customary ties built on We^{n}dat/Wa^{n}dat traditions of women's roles and responsibilities. As a wife to We^{n}dat/Wa^{n}dat men, she held her position as the foremost guide to her family's values and spiritual practices. As a mother, she paid close attention to the well-being of her daughters, girls who could potentially continue the traditions of We^{n}dat/Wa^{n}dat Longhouse women in the post-dispersal period. Contemporaries made note of this familial devotion, a passion that would eventually go beyond her immediate and biological family and extend to the larger local We^{n}dat/Wa^{n}dat community as well as neighbouring Indigenous societies.

COMMUNITY

Cécile Gannendâris belonged to multiple communities within her lifetime. It is likely that Gannendâris was born in historic Wendake shortly before the We^{n}dat/Wa^{n}dat dispersal. This would have been a time of great unrest for the people residing around present-day Georgian Bay, Ontario. The We^{n}dat/Wa^{n}dat were at war with the Iroquois and villages were constantly under attack. Further, by 1650 the We^{n}dat/Wa^{n}dat Confederacy had been in contact with French missionaries for almost thirty years and, in return, European diseases had ravaged the population with an estimated loss of at least 60 per cent.[21] This placed immense pressure on their society, as many leaders were lost during a short amount of time. The epidemics had left communities without Civil Chiefs, replacing them with War Chiefs who had little experience with diplomatic matters. Further, We^{n}dat/Wa^{n}dat Healers lost influence as their traditional remedies had little effect on European diseases.[22] The circumstances were so destructive that the Confederacy, after much deliberation, decided to divide into several groups and evacuate Wendake. One group travelled to the west towards Michilimackinac and their Anishinaabeg allies, others joined Iroquois villages, and a third group of roughly 300 survivors travelled east towards the French settlements of Montreal and Quebec City.[23]

As a child, Gannendâris had few options. By the time of the dispersal she would have survived disease and starvation and most likely witnessed the deaths of numerous family members. Yet she still found the strength (with little choice) to join the eastern We^{n}dat/Wa^{n}dat and leave the land of her birth. The exact location of her birth is speculative. We know that she was eventually baptized, and so it may be that she was born into a We^{n}dat/Wa^{n}dat village where Jesuit priests also lived. Perhaps the most famous of these is the great village of the Bear Nation, Ossossané. If this was the case, it may have been that she lived in one of twelve smaller villages or "hamlets" that surrounded Ossossané, in particular, the village of Ste Cécile.[24] It was common practice in seventeenth-century Wendake to allocate the French names of villages to We^{n}dat/Wa^{n}dat Christian converts.

Beyond Wendake and along the shores of the St Lawrence, the eastern We^{n}dat/Wa^{n}dat (along with Gannendâris) found refuge at the village of Sillery, close to Quebec City. This town was established in 1638 and by the time Gannendâris arrived with the We^{n}dat/Wa^{n}dat refugees, it was a multicultural hub for trade and political activity. The population included Anishinabeg people as well as a minority of We^{n}dat/Wa^{n}dat who had relocated before the mass migration. In addition, French settlers and priests also called Sillery their home. This community was both Christian and Traditionalist.[25]

Father Jean de Quen was the resident missionary and enforced strict Christian protocols for the converted. While missionaries had been present in historic Wendake, at Sillery the mixed demographic provided leverage for the priests and allowed them to exert more influence on the community. It is here that we can begin to see the way Christianity and its patriarchal practices transformed We^{n}dat/Wa^{n}dat society. Gannendâris would have been born into a system where marriages were seen as partnerships and premarital relations were encouraged. Moreover, women had the right to leave the marriage at any time.[26] In stark contrast, Christian marriages were patriarchal and hierarchical, and women could not divorce their husbands.

Marie de l'Incarnation, the famous Ursuline Mother Superior at Québec, made note of an incident illustrating the severity of this system reported to her by Father de Quen in 1642. An unconverted Indigenous woman had become involved with a married Christian Indigenous man. The Christian community was outraged at the transgression and demanded she be punished. The woman begged De Quen to baptize her and forgive her mistake, but he refused. He then watched as a crowd formed and forced the young woman into the centre of town where she was publicly whipped three times.[27] On another occasion, Father de Quen was made aware of an Indigenous woman who had tried to divorce her husband "without just cause."[28] De Quen responded by jailing the woman. The prison sentence took place during the middle of January and the woman received no fire or source of insulation throughout her stay. When she entered the cell, one of the most prominent Christian headmen at Sillery exclaimed, "My niece, pray earnestly to God all night, – thou wilt have leisure; ask him that thou mayst become sensible, and that thou mayst no longer be self-willed. Endure this prison for thy sins. Take courage; if thou wilt be obedient, thou wilt not stay there long."[29] The woman was released later the next day and she promised to return to her husband. The punishment was viewed as such a success that, Father de Quen noted, several other women were also subject to imprisonment.[30] This was the community where Gannendâris would raise her children and live most of her adult life. Indigenous women were subject to French laws and customs that countered previous traditions of matricentric power. These laws systematically attacked women, which not only allowed for further misogyny but fostered and encouraged the oppression of women.

Gannendâris herself was threatened at one point. A young French man had made inappropriate advances towards her and she consistently refused him. He ignored her rejections and persisted in "tempting her to sin."[31] The situation developed into such extreme circumstances that Gannendâris grabbed a firebrand and ran after the perpetrator to the edge of town. She made sure to articulate clearly her devotion to her husband and her disgust at the young man's advances.[32] A crowd gathered to observe the confrontation.

Threats such as these would not have been tolerated in historic Wendake, yet they were common to everyday life in the patriarchal society of Sillery. Marie de l'Incarnation wrote to her son on 9 August 1668, describing the circumstances and the incessant threats to Indigenous girls. She had decided to take in as many girls as possible at the seminary in order to protect them from the abuses of village men. The nuns created a unique opportunity within New France society, where girls entered into a gendered space that was meant for pious women and that generally received respect from settler society.[33]

In addition to the constant threat of sexual assault, the threat of Iroquois military attacks remained a constant worry for the We^{n}dat/Wa^{n}dat. Ursuline nuns made particular observations about the insecurity felt by Indigenous women. According to their accounts, the Iroquois continued to kill hundreds of We^{n}dat/Wa^{n}dat. This created another reason for the Ursulines to seek out, and take in, We^{n}dat/Wa^{n}dat girls.[34] In 1651, around the time of Gannendâris's arrival at Sillery, the We^{n}dat/Wa^{n}dat headman Louys Taiaeronk recognized the critical nature of the We^{n}dat/Wa^{n}dat situation. Their strategy to avoid conflict by moving east had failed. They needed help to support their struggling population. With this in mind, Taiaeronk approached the French nuns for assistance; specifically, he asked them to help protect the We^{n}dat/Wa^{n}dat women and girls. His address was desperate:

> Holy virgins, you see before you miserable carcasses, the remnant of a country that once was flourishing and that is no more, the

> country of the Hurons. We have been devoured and gnawed to the very bones, by war and famine. These carcasses are able to stand only because you support them. You have learned from letters, and now you see with your own eyes, to what extreme misery we are reduced. Look at us on all sides, and consider whether there is anything in us that does not compel us to weep for ourselves, and to shed unceasing torrents of tears.[35]

The headman then presented the nuns with two wampum[36] belts, asking them, firstly, to remain in North America and not return to France and, secondly, to build a school so We^{n}dat/Wa^{n}dat girls could be educated in French ways and remain under the protection of the French. He explained the wampum by saying,

> To strengthen you in these resolutions, here is a present of twelve hundred porcelain beads which will root your feet so deeply in the soil of this country that no love for your kindred or for your own country can withdraw them from it. The second present, which we beg you to accept, is a similar collar of twelve hundred porcelain beads, to lay the foundation of an entirely new building wherein shall be the house of JESUS, the house of prayer; wherein your classes will be held, in which you may teach our little Huron girls. Such are our desires; they are likewise yours, for doubtless you could not die happy if, when dying, this reproach could be cast at you that, through too tender a love for your relatives, you had not contributed to the salvation of so many souls which you have loved for the sake of God, and which will be your crown in Heaven.[37]

The nuns accepted the gifts and continued to support the We^{n}dat/Wa^{n}dat in their quest for refuge.[38]

Physical escape accompanied cultural preservation at the seminary. Despite the fact that it was a settler institution, it did not require complete assimilation into settler society. The Ursuline nuns negotiated the degree to which they implemented the French colonial policy of "francisation,"[39] opting more readily for a strategy of hybridity and acculturation. While students learned French religion and culture, they were not required to replace their Indigenous customs entirely.[40] The Jesuits made note of a We^{n}dat/Wa^{n}dat student who could read and write in Latin, French, and We^{n}dat. Rather than reprimand the student for maintaining her Indigenous language, the Ursulines celebrated her achievements, presenting her to colonial officials who sent an example of her writing in both We^{n}dat/Wa^{n}dat and French to France.[41] The seminary, therefore, maintained a safe space and supportive practice of conserving We^{n}dat/Wa^{n}dat culture for future generations.

The protection provided by the nuns at the seminary was limited to girls and beyond the reach of their mothers – including young women like Gannendâris. Thus, the questions remained: what strategies were available to a We^{n}dat/Wa^{n}dat woman? How could she conduct motherwork in a time of community crisis and in a world dominated by discriminatory patriarchal policies?

MOTHERWORK

The answer to Cécile Gannendâris's predicament was to engage in colonial institutions. Most notably, she became a member of the Holy Family Society. Officially established at the Quebec City parish of Notre-Dame de Québec on 14 March 1664, this Catholic organization was originally intended for female participation exclusively.[42] Although similar societies existed elsewhere, the Quebec City version was initially the idea of Barbe de Boullongne, the wife of Louis d'Ailleboust, the third governor of New France. Support quickly grew from other colonial aristocrats, including Jesuit Father Pierre-Joseph-Marie Chaumonot, Gabriel Souart, Marguerite Bourgeois, Jeanne Mance, Judith Moreau de Brésoles, and, most importantly, the first bishop of Canada, François de Laval.[43] The idea was that the society would be a model for family virtues. It would conduct work that expressed French Catholic concepts of traditional households and values. Members were to reflect the Christian holy family: fathers aspiring to imitate Joseph, mothers to imitate Mary, and children the baby Jesus.

Most women joined around the age of forty. Contemporaries took note of the immediate success of the society. In particular, Marie de l'Incarnation made sure to document the progress of the Holy Family at Quebec and the inclusion of military families in the society.[44] Membership was technically open to all Catholics, but the majority came from the highest ranks of French-Canadian society. Notable female members included Mme Vaudreuil, the wife of the last Governor of New France; Mme de Champigny, the wife of the New France intendant; and Mme d'Youville, the founder of the Grey Nuns.[45] The membership also included approximately 1,010 settler women, 148 nuns, and 64 "Indiennes" – one of whom was Cécile Gannendâris.[46] Combined, they were known collectively as the "Women of the Holy Family."

The numbers only increased over the years, especially after 1668 when the official policy of New France was to "frenchify" the Indigenous allies.[47] We^{n}dat/Wa^{n}dat Christians in particular had a reputation of being more French than the French during this period, making it easier for them to gain membership than for other Indigenous Traditionalists. Indeed, the Jesuits recorded how one We^{n}dat/Wa^{n}dat woman inspired "virtuous and devout" French ladies to be better Christians.[48] Gannendâris had a similar reputation. The French missionaries continuously took note of her successful efforts to teach her We^{n}dat/Wa^{n}dat family and community about Christian values. As mentioned earlier, she converted her husbands and children through Catholic baptisms. Additionally, she was often asked to instruct foreign Indigenous people on the ways of the Church.[49]

Actions such as these were celebrated (and mandatory) for women of the Holy Family. In 1675, Bishop Laval published a manual outlining the principles that were to guide the conduct of these women. Produced roughly a decade after the organization began, the document made official the past practices of the Holy Family. In addition to imitating the Virgin Mary, there were seven rules the Women of the Holy Family were to follow. In brief, they were obliged to submit and conform to the service of the saints; love their husbands cordially and sincerely; raise their children in the ways of God; make sure their servants refrained from sin; conduct themselves in a charitable fashion, with humility, peace, and kindness towards their servants; be vigilant in their chores; temper their drinking and eating; and be modest in their comments.[50] In addition, the manual included a list of qualities deemed essential for the Women of the Holy Family. These qualities were subject to judgment by the other members and required proof delivered in the women's devout actions. There were four qualities in this category: a devotion and tenderness to members of the Holy Family Society; the avoidance of scandal, and if scandal occurred, an effort made to change their lifestyle to avoid scandal in the future; a concerted effort to correct weaknesses; and willingness to assist with the society and instruction.[51] The justification for these qualities was that "the Holy Family is for those who seek perfection, not those who are perfect."[52]

Before Gannendâris could become a member, she would have had to go through a series of tests. The first test took place over four months. During this period, she would have been educated by other women of the Holy Family about their rules and regulations. They would have pointed out any faults she might have, and given her ways to correct them before her inauguration. Once she had passed this first evaluation, the society would have given her fifteen days to prepare for the official receiving. On the day of reception, Gannendâris would have taken communion, recited the "oraison" from memory, taken a lit candle and consecrated herself, her family, Jesus, Mary, Joseph, and Sainte Agnes, and, finally, concluded by reciting the "Gloria Patri" nine times.[53]

Membership could last a lifetime, but it was not a permanent position. The society had a long list of offences that could disqualify membership. Some of these included: trading alcohol with Natives, drinking too much, inappropriate public behaviour, vanity, educating your children poorly, and divorcing your husband. The process for dismissal was not meant to be quick, however, and members were given several warnings so that they might correct their behaviour.[54]

Gannendâris refrained from all of these offences and made a concerted effort to challenge others within her community to do the same. Gannendâris took special care to make sure her family followed the rules of the Holy Family, and she incorporated French traditions in order to appease the society. Perhaps one of the clearest examples of this was her adoption of corporal punishment. To the dismay of her children and others within the We^{n}dat/Wa^{n}dat community, Gannendâris justified her actions by pointing to the necessity of performing public displays of her devotion. She further argued her approach by explaining to her children, "Ah, my child, how wouldst thou bear the strange tortures of the demons, if thou canst not bear so light a punishment? Take good care not to fall again into this fault for which I have just chastised thee, for fear lest thou be condemned to sufferings that never end."[55] This strategic display of conformity and acculturation may have seemed extreme, but it was a means to an end. The family and We^{n}dat/Wa^{n}dat community members that Gannendâris had as followers could potentially also gain from her association with the Holy Family and the support networks that resulted from her position within the society.

The role and structure of the Holy Family Society was not completely foreign to Gannendâris. Similar organizations were integral to We^{n}dat/Wa^{n}dat customs in historic Wendake. Ritual societies, for instance, existed among many seventeenth-century First Nations. Women gained status through their membership and role within them.[56] Curing societies were also prevalent among the We^{n}dat/Wa^{n}dat. These were community-based organizations that specialized in healing various illnesses. In some cases, each illness would have its own specific membership, that is, people who were trained to treat the illness through dances, prayers, and songs.[57] The Bear Dance, for instance, involved a group of selected intergenerational women, including at least four or five Elders. This group focused their efforts on sick women. If a woman was sick, the association was called upon to dance and sing in ceremony. At first, the patient sat and watched the society members perform several songs and dances. The healers were nude except for their heads, which were covered in bearskins. Once the first round of songs finished, the sick woman was lifted up and included in the next series of dances and songs.[58]

The work of the Women of the Holy Family achieved many of the same goals as these ancient We^{n}dat/Wa^{n}dat societies. It was a vehicle to access protection, food, and spiritual salvation through a network of powerful women. By becoming a member, Gannendâris gained support, as well as a platform to better the situation of her family and her community as a whole. Above and beyond teaching her husbands and children European values, social conduct, and Christian theology, Gannendâris became a notable teacher to Indigenous women within the community and throughout the region. Women often sought out her guidance to learn Christian morals and conduct. This became such common practice that the Jesuits believed she could prepare someone for baptism within three days.[59]

Her reputation was known within French Canadian society as well. The Jesuits themselves went to Gannendâris for teaching. She taught the missionaries the We^{n}dat/Wa^{n}dat language.[60] It is likely that this kind of reputation, along with her connections to high society women in the Holy Family, led to special attention from Bishop François Laval. Perhaps one of the most important figures in French-Canadian society at the time, Laval made a concerted effort to get to know Gannendâris. The bishop often visited her in her home and brought her gifts.[61]

This seemingly personal relationship was possibly an indication of a larger strategy by Laval to support Indigenous communities. Although Laval had officially allocated "Indian Affairs" to the Jesuits, he had maintained an agenda that suggests a genuine interest in the Indigenous people living in New France. He had direct contact with his Indigenous neighbours, as he performed the sacrament of confirmation for hundreds of Indigenous converts. During those occasions he might have noticed the threatening behaviour of settler men towards Indigenous women. He might have also come to understand the concerning issues around the sale of alcohol and alcohol abuse within these communities. As we saw in his manual for the Holy Family Society, according to him, drinking was a clear transgression of Christian values. The bishop took his concerns to the King of France, Louis XIV, in 1662. He received a warm reception and the King agreed to ban the liquor trade in light of Laval's observations.[62] This victory had direct implications for We^{n}dat/Wa^{n}dat women like Cécile Gannendâris. Indigenous women were often the victims of violence exacerbated by intoxication. Perhaps it was even Gannendâris herself who shared these circumstances with Laval, an additional testament to his growing list of grievances stemming from the sale of spirits in North America.

The optics of these meetings and relationships are worth consideration. Gannendâris had carved out a space for herself among the eastern We^{n}dat/Wa^{n}dat and drew upon French traditions to secure a formidable position within this geopolitical arena. She not only became a member of one of the most elite groups of women, but subsequently had private meetings with powerful leaders such as Bishop Laval. Although her spiritual gains are worth consideration, the secular pragmatic benefits are also significant. We^{n}dat/Wa^{n}dat conversions were often silent forms of diplomacy done for practical reasons, such as to create allies during times of cultural insecurity.[63] This kind of silent diplomacy, or perhaps in this case more appropriately *maternal* diplomacy, was made possible by

Gannendâris's status as a woman and mother. Gender was more important than the racial hierarchy that existed in New France. Gannendâris successfully manoeuvred colonial institutions and engaged with colonial officials to meet the needs of her family and community.

LEGACY

The legacy of Gannendâris's motherwork through the Holy Family Society had immediate results, as well as effects that would be felt for generations. She remained a member of the society up until her early death in 1669. By the summer of 1668, it was clear that she could no longer avoid the diseases that had plagued her first husband and several children.[64] For the next eight months she received constant support from a wide range of people – the results of the relationships and reputation she had forged throughout her life.

Too sick to remain in her home, Gannendâris moved to the newly built Hôtel-Dieu de Québec. There she received special attention from the hospital nuns. They would have paid particular attention to the "virtuous" We^{n}dat/Wa^{n}dat woman who the second superior of the Hôtel-Dieu, Mother Marie Forestier de Saint-Bonaventure, had written about in her letters.[65] The nuns had a long history of helping We^{n}dat/Wa^{n}dat women and providing refuge for the most vulnerable in society, with specific preference given to young girls. Gannendâris's reputation as a Christian convert and leader within the community would have been enough for the nuns to take her in. Likewise, the hospital had a reputation among the We^{n}dat/Wa^{n}dat. Since the dispersal, We^{n}dat/Wa^{n}dat women had not only received medical attention from the hospital nuns, but also had become hospital nuns themselves.[66] We^{n}dat/Wa^{n}dat viewed their relationship to the hospital much like they viewed the seminary and convent, in terms of trust and dependency during a tumultuous time in their history. At one point a priest asked a group of We^{n}dat/Wa^{n}dat women how they felt about taking advantage of the services at the hospital despite the fact that they had never met any of the French benefactors who provided the financial support for the Hôtel-Dieu. The women replied that they viewed the relationship in a similar way to their relationship with God – they could not see their benefactors, but they felt their love.[67]

The Women of the Holy Family would have also provided support for their We^{n}dat/Wa^{n}dat sister. As the requirements stated in Bishop Laval's manual, "When there are members of the society that are sick, the Women of the Holy Family must assist them to the best of their ability and provide charity, and pray for them; who are considered sisters."[68] It is not surprising then that the Jesuits made note of "several persons of quality" who visited Gannendâris, bringing refreshments and "all having tenderness for so virtuous a person."[69] The sisterhood of the Holy Family acted as an extended kinship community that would ensure that its members were never alone. In times of extreme desperation, such as illness or death, this remained a security net for members and their dependents.

Other notable members of French-Canadian society called on Gannendâris. Bishop Laval, for instance, continued to pay visits throughout her sickness, before and after her arrival at the hospital. The Bishop brought Gannendâris food while she was sick at home and they discussed Christian teachings. He continued this tradition at the hospital where he supplied her with food again and they maintained frequent conversations about faith and the afterlife. Gannendâris told her husband how grateful she was for these visits and how she believed that the Bishop's attention was the direct result of her involvement with the Holy Family and her work as a Christian. This only served to reinforce her motherwork strategy as she confided to her husband, "I have seen the charity exercised toward me by a person of that quality and of that rank … who has done me so much good that I cannot thank him."[70]

Records indicate that Gannendâris received visits from We^{n}dat/Wa^{n}dat women while at the hospital. This was both to give the dying woman support and to gain a final audience with the respected leader. On one occasion a woman came to get counselling on how to abstain from a "certain vice to which she was addicted."[71] On other occasions Gannendâris catered to larger groups and used the visits to continue to conduct motherwork and encourage the women of her community to find salvation in Christian teachings and customs. According to Jesuit observers, she explained to her visitors: "My Sisters, I was formerly regarded among you as fairly good-looking, and now I am hideous to look at. I used to love cleanliness, and now my body is a mass of corruption. I was not the poorest person in our Village, and today I get no help from my possessions. That is the condition in which you will find yourselves some day. Do many good deeds during your lives, for from them only will you receive any consolation in the hour of death."[72]

This teaching encapsulates a number of aspects of Gannendâris's motherwork. First, she targeted a female audience, and therefore was able to address the mothers and leaders who would guide her community in the future. Second, she reinforced the precarious circumstances of the We^{n}dat/Wa^{n}dat, reminding the women that they would need to rely on larger support networks to survive. If they did this, she explained, they would be able to die in peace.

Her advice became a reality soon after. Because of her reputation as a devout Catholic, maternal diplomat, and member of the Holy Family Society, Gannendâris received help not only for herself but for her family during and after her illness. Security and survival were her ultimate goals. Her first husband had expressed sincere anxiety over the future care of their children if either parent did not survive the epidemics. With confidence, Gannendâris had responded, "Do not weep, my dear husband; our children will not remain fatherless after your death. The Fathers who instruct them will be fathers to them, so long as our children are good Christians; and I will take all possible care to make them become so."[73] In other words, as long as Gannendâris maintained her reputation and work to further the Christian faith and social moral code among her family, she believed her children would benefit in the same way.

Gannendâris tried to ensure her hard work would not be forgotten by employing the We^{n}dat/Wa^{n}dat custom of wampum. Wampum belts and beads have a long history of being used among the Indigenous Peoples of the Great Lakes. They were a material reminder of important treaties and events and were often used as gifts to acknowledge alliances.[74] Around the time of Gannendâris's illness, the headman Ignace Saouhenhohi began to promote the gifting of wampum to the resident church in order to demonstrate loyalty to the Christian faith. He explained his belief at an Elders' Council, telling them that he would set the example by offering a wampum belt of 4,000 beads as the first gift at the next service.[75] Gannendâris followed this custom and left the Women of the Holy Family a wampum belt of 6,000 black beads upon her death.[76] This belt would have been of high value in terms of wampum. The black beads symbolized not only the death of Gannendâris, but her life as well. It would serve as a material reminder of her dedication to the Holy Family Society and to Christianity. Finally, it called the Women of the Holy Family to honour her lifetime of service by supporting her children and family.

Gannendâris's strategy made sense. At a time when options were limited and the familiar ways of dealing with crises – such as We^{n}dat/Wa^{n}dat ritual and healing societies – could not be relied upon, new paths needed to be broken. The Women of the Holy Family presented a solution that would serve to protect We^{n}dat/Wa^{n}dat women like Gannendâris from sexual assault, exploitation, and starvation. Through her role as a woman and mother, Gannendâris became a maternal diplomat and conducted motherwork that promoted Christian teachings in order to safeguard her family against the colonial transformations of patriarchy, war, and disease.

The gains achieved by women like Gannendâris through membership in the Holy Family Society were not without their price. The Holy Family maintained a strict and rigid assimilationist approach. Demonstrations of French language, religion, and laws were essential to acquiring membership and support from Christian colonists. Their rules reflect a seventeenth-century focus on creating French citizens in New France. It would not suffice to have members of one of the most elite sororities in the colony be anything but "frenchified." As a result, Gannendâris felt compelled to adopt customs that were in stark contrast to We^{n}dat/Wa^{n}dat traditions. Corporal punishment and patricentric value systems had to be enforced. Any transgression risked an eventual expulsion.

The integration of colonial ways did not, however, mean a complete loss of culture. Gannendâris demonstrated her retention of We^{n}dat/Wa^{n}dat practices, for instance, with her gift of wampum to the Women of the Holy Family at the time of her death. Its message went beyond a plea for recognition of her work and a reminder to support her family. The elaborate wampum called attention to her We^{n}dat/Wa^{n}dat heritage and demonstrated a preservation of Indigenous practices. Further, she chose to marry We^{n}dat/Wa^{n}dat men. Despite the advances of French settlers, she selected partners who were deemed "Traditionalists" by Jesuits. During this period, so-called Traditional We^{n}dat/Wa^{n}dat were not only non-Christians but keepers of We^{n}dat/Wa^{n}dat language, culture, and faith. It is likely, even after their conversion to Catholicism, that her husbands maintained this knowledge. Gannendâris had chosen these men to be the fathers and uncles of We^{n}dat/Wa^{n}dat children, ensuring a degree of exposure to We^{n}dat/Wa^{n}dat teachings for her family. Finally, the seminary provided a possible opportunity for cultural preservation for her daughters. Where she had to publicly sacrifice We^{n}dat/Wa^{n}dat beliefs to gain support from the Holy Family Society, her We^{n}dat/Wa^{n}dat children were given a hybrid option through the education of the Ursuline nuns.

Many We^{n}dat/Wa^{n}dat were willing to engage with settler society, and particularly the French, to save their kin. The records are replete with the military and diplomatic strategies of leading men. But what about the We^{n}dat/Wa^{n}dat women? Throughout her lifetime, Cécile Gannendâris would have witnessed the success of Christian converts, such as the We^{n}dat/Wa^{n}dat headman Ignace Saouhenhohi who delivered wampum to the Ursulines and requested protection for We^{n}dat/Wa^{n}dat girls. While these public accounts demonstrate the agency of community leaders, they neglect the leading and critical role of women. Although disadvantaged by the continuing focus on reshaping We^{n}dat/Wa^{n}dat society into a patriarchy, these women held a particular advantage during this period in their ability to join female sororities such as the Women of the Holy Family. As a result, Gannendâris died with the peace of mind that her family would be cared for and that another generation might survive.

CHAPTER 2

Marie Catherine Jean dit Vien (1676–1767)

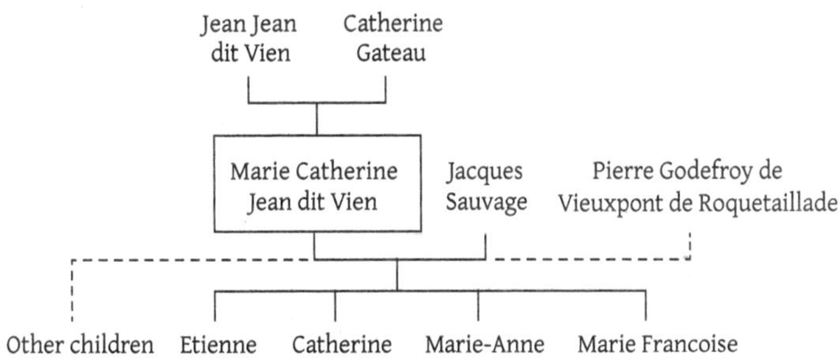

INTRODUCTION

Christianity continued to play an important role within We^{n}dat/Wa^{n}dat communities well past the death of Cécile Gannendâris. Part of a colonial package to "frenchify" the Indigenous populations of North America, French Christian ceremonies and customs were one way that We^{n}dat/Wa^{n}dat women constructed new worlds in the wake of their dispersal in 1649. Still, these changes in cultural practices and belief systems did not erase We^{n}dat/Wa^{n}dat traditions. While We^{n}dat/Wa^{n}dat took French names, baptized their children, and buried their dead according to Christian protocols, they maintained their Indigenous practices and their We^{n}dat/Wa^{n}dat identity.

Scholars have tried to unravel the complicated nature of seventeenth- and eighteenth-century Indigenous identity during the first century of colonization by analyzing degrees of assimilation and racialization within the French colonial context.[1] In the beginning, European administrators tried to create a society that was "ethnically mixed but culturally French as Amerindians were encouraged to assimilate to French religion and civility."[2] Yet the records and research indicate that despite their efforts, there was a clear "French failure." Indigenous women, in particular, refused to unequivocally trade their traditions for French customs. As we saw with Cécile Gannendâris, acceptance of non-Indigenous practices was often a means to an end, reflecting acculturation rather than assimilation. European officials made note of this reality, explaining that "even when [Indigenous women] married Frenchmen, they chose to remain barbarous, indeed even dangerous as they kept their sexual freedom, divorced their husbands when they wanted to, and continued to observe their traditional values."[3] Overall, scholars contend that assimilation policies were unsuccessful during this period. We^{n}dat/Wa^{n}dat women and their Indigenous neighbours refused to reject their ancestral teachings and culture, despite their intimate relationships with the French.[4]

The case of the We^{n}dat/Wa^{n}dat woman Marie Catherine Jean dit Vien supports this research. Although often recorded as a French woman, Catherine Jean is remembered by her family and community as a strong We^{n}dat/Wa^{n}dat woman who engaged wholeheartedly in both French and We^{n}dat/Wa^{n}dat societies. Born during the culmination of Iroquois attacks near Quebec and witness as an adult to Pontiac's War and the Seven Years' War/French and Indian War, Catherine Jean knew very well the casualties of colonial conquest. We^{n}dat/Wa^{n}dat continued to call upon past practices and traditional responses to warfare. While men engaged in military battle and performed diplomatic negotiations, women held the power to decide when to engage in combat, who to select as War Chiefs, and the fate of prisoners.[5] Strong female leadership was crucial to the success of these endeavours. As a We^{n}dat/Wa^{n}dat mother and grandmother, Catherine Jean would have participated in this process. Her motherwork, therefore, focused on the training of future We^{n}dat/Wa^{n}dat leaders who could bridge the colonial divide. As a result, her grandsons played important roles in countering colonial aggressions and preserving We^{n}dat/Wa^{n}dat rights for future generations.

FAMILY

Much of what we know about Catherine Jean rests in the French colonial archives. Through baptismal, immigration, marriage, and death documents, a shadow of an eighteenth-century woman begins to take shape. According to French records, Catherine Jean was born 31 August 1676 in Charlesbourg, New France.[6] Her parents were Jean Jean dit Vien and Catherine Gateau, both considered French citizens.[7] Catherine Jean was baptized 1 September 1676 in Champlain, Quebec.[8] We know little about her childhood other than the fact that her parents raised their family in the Champlain area.[9] In 1690, she reappears in the record at the age of fourteen and marries Jacques Sauvage, a trader based out of the Quebec City region.[10] Together the couple had at least four children: Etienne (1693–?), Catherine (1695–1778), Marie-Anne (1697–?), and Marie Françoise (1700–1792).[11] Jacques died sometime before 1720, and in 1724, Catherine Jean married Pierre Godefroy de Vieuxpont de Roquetaillade, who was listed as a "canadien de Trois Rivière" in Detroit.[12] Catherine Jean died in June 1767 and was buried inside the church of Ste Anne de Détroit.[13]

Through this description it would seem that Catherine Jean was French. Born to Catholic parents, baptized by French Catholic priests, married in the churches of New France, and buried in a French Catholic cemetery, her world seemed to have been culturally and ancestrally French. Yet consider the adamant and necessary strategy of Cécile Gannendâris less than a decade before Catherine's birth. Gannendâris had made it her mission to demonstrate public acts of acculturation to European society in order to survive the devastating circumstances faced by the We^{n}dat/Wa^{n}dat community. With this case alone, we are reminded that many We^{n}dat/Wa^{n}dat women found sanctuary through French Christianity and used their Catholic networks to safeguard their families for future generations.

Further, there has been a significant amount of work that outlines the problematic and often erroneous dependency on written names. The Detroit area, where Catherine Jean spent most of her life, was particularly problematic. Often French names were altered to reflect the community. In addition, familiar French Christian names were given to Indigenous neighbours. This re-naming of individuals convoluted people's identities during their own lifetimes, as well as later within the records.[14] This historical context requires an investigation beyond the limited records of church events pertaining to Catherine Jean, incorporating other evidence and a multi-perspective analysis in order to fully understand the family of Marie Catherine Jean dit Vien.

First, there is a chance that Catherine Jean's parents may not have been French. There is well-supported documentation that Indigenous children were taken from North America and sent to France throughout the seventeenth century.[15] The Jesuit priests made specific references to We^{n}dat/Wa^{n}dat who went to France during this period. There, they received baptism, returning to North America with French-Catholic names and a strong grasp of French customs and culture.[16] Louis Amantacha, a well-known We^{n}dat/Wa^{n}dat leader, for instance, was baptized in France.[17] The Jesuits explained this phenomenon in the following way: "As to the children of the Savages in this country, there will be more trouble in keeping them; I see no other way than that which Your Reverence suggests, of sending a child every year to France. Having been there two years, he will return with a knowledge of the language, and having already become accustomed to our ways, he will not leave us and will retain his little countrymen."[18] Speaking of a particular We^{n}dat/Wa^{n}dat child, Jesuits wrote to their French superiors:

> A little Huron is going to see you; he longs to see France. He is very fond of us and manifests a strong desire to be instructed; nevertheless, his father and the Captain of the nation wishes to see him next year, assuring us that, if he is satisfied, he will give him to us for some years. It is of importance that he should be thoroughly satisfied; for, if this child is once instructed, it will open the way to many tribes where he will be very useful. And the return of the interpreter of that tribe to France is very opportune – the Interpreter whom he loves so much, that he calls him his father.[19]

With this in mind, it is not out of the realm of possibility that one or both of Catherine's so-called French parents were among the cohort of We^{n}dat/Wa^{n}dat children sent to France and returned to their homeland with new French names.

The ambiguity and complexity of We^{n}dat/Wa^{n}dat identity and heritage in the seventeenth century is further illustrated by the comparable case of Catherine Pillard. Although Pillard was defined by historians for centuries as a "French" woman, her We^{n}dat/Wa^{n}dat descendants have proven otherwise.[20] The evidence was published in both French and English in 2009. In short, through a revision of the Registers of

New France and the *Jesuit Relations*, scholars were able to confirm that Catherine Pillard was actually Catherine Plat or le Plat, the daughter of the We^{n}dat/Wa^{n}dat Chief Atsena Le Plat (Bear Nation).[21]

Beyond Catherine Jean's own ancestral bloodlines, her marriage to Jacques Sauvage in 1790 provides additional circumstances to explain her We^{n}dat/Wa^{n}dat identity. Although French records indicate that Sauvage was born in France and that his parents (Jacques Sauvage and Marie Fageau) were of French origin, there is reason to believe that Jacques Sr was We^{n}dat/Wa^{n}dat and sent to France as a child. "Sauvage" was a popular surname given to Indigenous Christians in the seventeenth century.[22] Catherine Jean's We^{n}dat/Wa^{n}dat identity, therefore, would have been strengthened by her marriage to a We^{n}dat/Wa^{n}dat man. Certainly her children and grandchildren saw themselves as We^{n}dat/Wa^{n}dat. Catherine Jean and Jacques's daughter Catherine Sauvage married the French settler Charles Chesne, but their children identified themselves as We^{n}dat/Wa^{n}dat on their *mother's* side.[23] Similarly, another daughter, Marie-Anne Sauvage, is recorded in 1747 as a "Wyandot" godmother of a "Wyandot" child living in the Petit Village settlement of the Hurons, near Detroit.[24]

Generations of descendants have preserved Catherine Jean's We^{n}dat/Wa^{n}dat identity through oral family histories. Her seventh great-granddaughter, Judith Pidgeon-Kukowski, recalls hearing stories from her grandparents Archie Pidgeon and Stella Chesne about Catherine Jean. "Most of what I know [about Catherine]," she explains, "is the oral history passed down by my grandparents." It is through this kind of sharing that We^{n}dat/Wa^{n}dat have come to understand that "Catherine Jean [would] have been one of those who [had] a deep sense of spirituality. It seems that she was a great leader of her people who spent uncounted hours working for their benefit."[25]

At the very least, a careful reading of this evidence in relation to the historical context of seventeenth- and eighteenth-century New France calls into question general assumptions of who was French and who was We^{n}dat/Wa^{n}dat. Pushed further, it asks us to review our sources and preconceived notions of what is deemed "evidence" and highlights a persistence in colonial methods and the maintenance of old-world views. Current scholarship on Catherine Jean privileges the records of European priests and Quebec notaries during a time of colonial conquest – a time when the frenchification of Indigenous people was integral to the success of French imperial control. It does not give equal weight to the accounts archived by the Wyandot communities and the descendants of Catherine Jean.

The situation is, as one scholar points out, that cultural identity is "fragmented, multiply constructed, and intersected in a constantly changing, sometimes conflicting array."[26] There are three facets of identification that help compartmentalize this process: self-identification, community identification, and external identification. External identification, or, in this case, the denial of Indigenous identity by settlers who cling to a French Catherine Jean, is part of a colonizing practice that leads to oppression and the continued marginalization of the We^{n}dat/Wa^{n}dat.[27] This act of nonrecognition is only made possible by silencing an entire community of We^{n}dat/Wa^{n}dat people. It perpetuates the ability of settlers to erase the We^{n}dat/Wa^{n}dat presence in Detroit and elsewhere, refusing to acknowledge treaty rights and land rights, and protection of sacred spaces.

While it is difficult to know for certain how Catherine Jean self-identified (she left no written records of her thoughts on the matter), there is substantial evidence that the We^{n}dat/Wa^{n}dat community and her children, grandchildren, and extended family claimed her as We^{n}dat/Wa^{n}dat kin. Indigenous identity in particular is associated with a common sense of Peoplehood, linked to sacred traditions, homelands, and a shared history.[28] Community recognition is, at the very least, a powerful, if not critical, tool in deciphering Indigenous identity and claims to membership. It is, therefore, of paramount importance that Catherine Jean's We^{n}dat/Wa^{n}dat community, the keepers of We^{n}dat/Wa^{n}dat identity and definitions, who are maintaining that she is family.

COMMUNITY

The communities Catherine called home were not only French colonial settlements, but We^{n}dat/Wa^{n}dat ones as well. The We^{n}dat/Wa^{n}dat had a long history of using her birthplace near Quebec City as a meeting ground, a central point of collaboration.[29] We^{n}dat/Wa^{n}dat like Cécile Gannendâris had re-established key settlements along the St Lawrence River during the post-dispersal migration from Georgian Bay. This made it possible for Catherine Jean to access networks, including French colonists, Catholic missionaries, and New France soldiers. Still, the We^{n}dat/Wa^{n}dat remained autonomous from their French allies. While some We^{n}dat/Wa^{n}dat found refuge in Sillery, many continued on to a series of temporary locations before settling in Jeune Lorette in 1697.[30] Along this path was the village of Charlesbourg, located approximately ten kilometres from Quebec City and the place of Catherine Jean's birth in 1676. This was a period characterized by relocations, insecurity, and disease. We^{n}dat/Wa^{n}dat were still the targets of Iroquois military strikes and epidemics plagued their struggling population. It would not be until 1701 and the diplomatic intervention known as the Great Peace of Montreal that the We^{n}dat/Wa^{n}dat achieved an agreement of allyship and ceasefire. We^{n}dat/Wa^{n}dat Chief Kondiorọnk led this initiative and although he died during the deliberations, this work reaffirmed the French-We^{n}dat/Wa^{n}dat alliance and encouraged future community-building between the two.[31]

Around the same time, Louis XIV and minister of the marine Louis Phélypeaux, comte de Pontchartrain, authorized Antoine de la Mothe Cadillac to establish a post along the waterways joining Lakes Erie and Huron – a vital North American crossroads known simply as "the straits," or *le détroit*.[32] On 24 July 1701, Cadillac founded Fort Pontchartrain du Détroit, near where Lake St Clair drains into the Detroit River. The initial settlement of 100 French soldiers and farmers grew steadily to 270 French men and women by 1707.[33] Although Cadillac saw the establishment of Detroit as a way to further his own career and finances, colonial officials and metropolitan ministers saw advantages in a concentrated French presence at the straits. Such a presence would guard against English and Haudenosaunee westward expansion by controlling access to the lower Great Lakes, as well as act as a veritable nexus of a trading network that stretched from Montreal to the lower Mississippi River.[34] To ensure Detroit's success, Cadillac instigated a colonial policy to invite disparate Great Lakes Indigenous Peoples – Odawas, Ojibwes, Potawatomis, We^{n}dat/Wa^{n}dat, Miamis, Mississaugas, and, for a short time, Mesquakies – to join the French settlers down at their new post, believing that he would easily control the movements of these peoples, convert them to Catholicism, and impress upon them the imperial power of the French colonial government.[35]

Because of Cadillac's plan, Detroit remained a volatile Euro-Indigenous contact zone for much of the eighteenth century.[36] Nevertheless, Detroit served as a valuable fur trade centre and an interior headquarters and transshipment point, giving merchants and traders easier access to Indigenous people living farther west and south.[37] Although French women lived at Detroit, French-Indigenous marriages, or marriages à la façon du pays (after the custom of the country), were also common at Detroit because they solidified political, commercial, and kinship ties between the various communities at the straits.[38]

After the death of her first husband, Catherine Jean joined the We^{n}dat/Wa^{n}dat at Detroit. It is likely that she moved with a number of her children, including her daughters Marie-Anne, Marie Françoise, and Catherine.[39] Once settled, she actively engaged with the community and her new homeland. In 1724, she married the "canadien" Pierre Godefroy de Vieuxpont de Roquetaillade.[40] Over and above companionship, marriage provided strategic opportunities for a We^{n}dat/Wa^{n}dat woman living at Detroit. Scholars like Karen Marrero and Catherine Cangany have articulated the critical role that European, Euro-American, and Indigenous women played in the commercial activities and economic life of Detroit.[41] As a single woman, Catherine Jean was vulnerable to undesired attention from the growing population of French men. Godefroy was a successful merchant, as well as a Catholic. Marriage, therefore, served to protect Catherine Jean financially and guard her personal safety through the sanctity of a Christian marriage: in theory a married woman would no longer be a target for unwanted and potentially violent advances. In addition, the effects of colonial rule and patriarchal cultural shifts made the environment particularly volatile for Indigenous women. Finally, France's frenchification policies were still in effect, and the pressure from administrators for French men to take Indigenous wives might have also brought the couple together. Their marriage lasted twenty years.[42]

Much like the circumstances in Quebec, the We^{n}dat/Wa^{n}dat lived among, but also autonomous from, their European neighbours. Alliances with the Jesuits remained strong and the We^{n}dat/Wa^{n}dat carved out mission settlements within the vicinity. In 1728, they were located at the Mission of the Assumption among the Hurons of Detroit. In 1742, the mission moved to the secluded Bobloo Island (Ile aux Bois Blancs), where it remained for five years.[43] The island was approximately four kilometres long. The mission was divided into two villages, Petit (small) Village and Grand (big) Village. Ironically, the We^{n}dat/Wa^{n}dat population of Petit Village was approximately 309 whereas Grand Village's population was only 232. People lived in traditional rectangular, round-roofed bark longhouses with more than one nuclear family living inside. Typically, the Petit Village houses held from five to forty-nine residents while the Grand Village houses held from five to seventy-four. On average, a We^{n}dat/Wa^{n}dat household would have roughly nineteen members.[44] In 1748, the We^{n}dat/Wa^{n}dat relocated again to Pointe de Montreal on the south bank of the Detroit River. They stayed in that location for the remainder of Catherine Jean's life.

While We^{n}dat/Wa^{n}dat settlements existed, Catherine Jean did not live on mission grounds. It is likely that Catherine Jean lived with her second husband until his death, and then took up residence with her daughter Catherine Sauvage Chesne.[45] This did not preclude Catherine Jean from accessing her We^{n}dat/Wa^{n}dat kin. Eighteenth-century Detroit was a world bound by family ties, ethnic diversity, and cultural difference. As a We^{n}dat/Wa^{n}dat woman living beside and, at times, with We^{n}dat/Wa^{n}dat people, Catherine Jean continued to be a valuable member of We^{n}dat/Wa^{n}dat society.

Despite these intricate connections between Detroit inhabitants, European strategies of conquest continued. We^{n}dat/Wa^{n}dat engaged in both Indigenous and imperial politics to navigate the volatile conflicts over land and sovereignty in North America that culminated in the Seven Years' War and the French and Indian War (1754–63), Pontiac's War (1763–66), the American War of Independence (1775–83), and the War of 1812.[46] Catherine Jean lived through most of these conflicts, witnessing critical moments of military strategy and diplomacy. We^{n}dat/Wa^{n}dat leaders played an important role in these events, calling upon the traditional training and guidance led by We^{n}dat/Wa^{n}dat women.

MOTHERWORK

Despite the seemingly transformative circumstances of We^{n}dat/Wa^{n}dat life at Detroit, with its growing influences of patricentric models of marriage, spirituality, and governance, We^{n}dat/Wa^{n}dat women continued to practice matricentric traditions. We^{n}dat/Wa^{n}dat Clan Mothers and Women's Councils remained intact during this period. Collectively, these women passed on We^{n}dat/Wa^{n}dat values to their children and retained their authority in training and selecting We^{n}dat/Wa^{n}dat headmen.[47] It is in this way that Catherine Jean's motherwork is best displayed. Through her children we can see that she instilled We^{n}dat/Wa^{n}dat teachings and values that would persist despite imperial wars and colonial policies of assimilation. Catherine Jean had five children and over thirty grandchildren.[48] Of particular significance is how her motherwork informed her daughter Catherine Sauvage Chesne,[49] who would parent prominent We^{n}dat/Wa^{n}dat Chiefs and leaders.

It takes a village to raise a family and Catherine Jean was no exception. As a We^{n}dat/Wa^{n}dat woman and Catholic mother, she had the help of Clan Mothers and anciennes (female Elders). There were approximately twenty-nine women who held these positions in 1747. They were usually between the ages of thirty and fifty.[50] Catherine Jean was part of a complex Clan system that included the Deer, Snake, Bear, Large Turtle, Porcupine, Striped Turtle, Prairie Turtle, Wolf, Hawk, Sturgeon, and Fox Clans.[51] Catherine Jean belonged to the Deer Clan. Through this membership she was intimately connected with other Deer kin. Within this group were several other notable "Catherines." Catherine Onnond8annon was an important figure, leading Christian ceremonies and anniversary services. Her role within these activities remained steeped in We^{n}dat/Wa^{n}dat traditions of female faith-keeping, while at the same time influencing others to ask her for further mentorship as she became godmother to nine We^{n}dat/Wa^{n}dat children.[52] Both these positions incorporated parallel responsibilities concerning spiritual leadership and teachings. Another We^{n}dat/Wa^{n}dat woman, Catherine Sk8ateenre (who was named after Caterine Skouatenhré, a seventeenth-century We^{n}dat/Wa^{n}dat woman who lived with the Jesuits), was called "la vieille Catherine" by the missionaries. Much like Onnond8annon, Sk8ateenre became known as a leader within the community and was godmother ten times between the years 1730 and 1740.[53]

These women were part of an ancient We^{n}dat/Wa^{n}dat leadership system, one that had been preserved for centuries. Women were charged with training and selecting future headmen. It was the women who were responsible for choosing Chiefs and making decisions on war.[54] Observing the role of women during this time period, Jesuit historian Pierre François de Charlevoix wrote in 1721 that among the We^{n}dat/Wa^{n}dat, the women "always deliberate first on whatever is proposed in council."[55] Charlevoix further observed that "amongst the Huron, where this dignity is hereditary, the succession is continued through the women, so that at the death of a chief, it is not his own, but his sister's son who succeeds him; or in default of which, his nearest relation in the female line. When the whole branch happens to be extinct, the noblest matron of the tribe or in the nation chuses [*sic*] him chief."[56] Jesuit Joseph Francois Lafitau expanded on this as he observed similar Iroquoian practices among the Mohawk in a 1724 publication. "There is nothing more real, however," he explained, "than the women's superiority."[57]

This history remains among the We^{n}dat/Wa^{n}dat as well. Tribal genealogist and Elder Judith Pidgeon-Kukowski explains:

> Perhaps intentionally omitted by the Jesuits and early historians was the Women's Council. Each clan's longhouse had a female Elder with one woman appointed to be the main Elder of the clan. So you have a female clan Elder in charge of each longhouse that was shared by the clan and an Elder who represented the entire clan and was called the Clan Mother. These women held council to discuss the needs of the people. They decided whether the fields were no longer producing enough and needed to be moved. This could precipitate the removal of the entire village to a new location. When a Civil or Head Chief died or was deemed unsatisfactory, the women discussed his replacement. They then told the Men's Council who they supported and why. After the women returned to their longhouses, the men discussed the pros and cons of the women's choice and came to a decision. Seldom did they disagree. They were collaborative.[58]

With this in mind, Catherine Jean, Catherine Onnond8annon, and Catherine Sk8ateenre would have been responsible for selecting, training, and supporting We^{n}dat/Wa^{n}dat headmen. Matrilineal lines were important. Future and current male leadership rested on the endorsement and guidance of mothers, grandmothers, and aunties. Sk8ateenre, for instance, lived in 1717 with Sastaretsi, the Grand Chief of the We^{n}dat/Wa^{n}dat.[59] His policies and actions throughout his tenure were reflections of the desires of Sk8ateenre and other clan mothers. We^{n}dat/Wa^{n}dat Chiefs were spokesmen rather than dictators, and they had to follow the agendas of the Councils or risk being replaced.

The case of Catherine Jean's daughter Catherine Sauvage Chesne provides evidence of this process. Catherine Sauvage moved to Detroit with her mother around the age of twenty-eight. There she met and married the French-Canadian man Charles Chesne in 1722.[60] The Chesne family was well known at Detroit and Chesne himself was known among the We^{n}dat/Wa^{n}dat community.[61] Sauvage parented four sons with Chesne: Isadore, Charles, Elleopole, and Adam. In addition, she would act as godmother at least twice.[62] These children were raised among both French-Canadian and We^{n}dat/Wa^{n}dat kin. It is also likely that Sauvage's children lived with their grandmother Catherine Jean until her death in 1767.[63] This set the stage for We^{n}dat/Wa^{n}dat leadership training and policy-shaping, as Sauvage's sons and grandsons took on significant roles as diplomats and Chiefs.

Reputations of strong leadership and diplomacy have a long history with the We^{n}dat/Wa^{n}dat. Since the early days of European encounters, the We^{n}dat/Wa^{n}dat had held a special place as diplomats in Great Lakes geopolitics. This role did not diminish with their move to Detroit. General Butterfield reflected in 1782 that "of all the savage allies of Great Britain in the West, the Wyandots were the most powerful. This arose not so much from the number of their warriors, as from their superior intelligence. Their long association with the French at Detroit, and, after that post fell into the possession of Great Britain, with its later occupants, had advanced them in many respects over the surrounding nations."[64] In many ways, Butterfield's observations are the result of the public work done by Catherine Jean's grandchildren and the private work of We^{n}dat/Wa^{n}dat Clan Mothers.

Catherine Jean's grandson Isadore Hayanemade Chesne was born on 6 January 1738. He spent his life in Detroit and married Thérese, a Shawnee woman, in 1758. Hayanemade died on 1 July 1793.[65] His life work was as a spokesperson for the We^{n}dat/Wa^{n}dat people, with many of his most important interventions as a diplomat taking place during the Seven Years' War and Pontiac's War. Having both French and We^{n}dat/Wa^{n}dat community connections, Hayanemade navigated the settler and Indigenous worlds. He had a reputation as an influential negotiator and arbitrator of peace.[66] This reputation continued throughout the American Revolution, where he again acted as an interpreter and a diplomat. Later he became a captain for the British.[67] In recognition of his work he received land along the Detroit River.[68] His actions were not independent of his family and community; rather, they would have been made in consultation with them. In the end, the success of the We^{n}dat/Wa^{n}dat in maintaining their homes and land around Detroit, despite the multiple attempts to remove them by French, British, and American colonists, depended on innovative approaches that maintained a cohesive and aggressive diplomatic strategy.[69]

Isadore's son, Catherine Jean's great-grandson, would follow in his father's path. Isadore Roniatere Chesne Jr was born in 1772 and died on 20 July 1828. At the time of his death, his title was recorded by the French as "Chef Principal de la nation des Hurons": Principal Chief of the Huron Nation.[70] During the War of 1812, Roniatere continued the work of his father, acting as a diplomat and key negotiator between the Americans and the British.[71] On a number of occasions he represented the Detroit River We^{n}dat/Wa^{n}dat at meetings with the Shawnee leader Tecumseh. Tecumseh had successfully gathered support to counter the American threats and was looking to confirm We^{n}dat/Wa^{n}dat allegiance. Roniatere was perhaps able to do this more easily than others as he was fluent in Shawnee, as well as French and We^{n}dat/Wa^{n}dat. He eventually gained the trust of the Shawnee Chief and helped write Tecumseh's speeches. Rather than taking a military role in the conflict, Roniatere chose a supportive, non-violent approach. He was captured during a siege at Detroit, but was returned unharmed to his community. After the war, Roniatere settled permanently on the "Canadian" side of the Detroit River. He was buried alongside other prominent We^{n}dat/Wa^{n}dat Chiefs in Amherstburg, Ontario.[72]

Chief Roniatere's uncle was also a significant leader during the War of 1812. Chief Adam Ta-Haw-Na-Haw-Wie-Te Brown was born in 1740 to a settler family in Virginia.[73] A party of Mingo and Delaware warriors raided a nearby fort and captured Adam and his brother Samuel when Adam was eight years old. Samuel returned to the settler community five years later, but Adam was adopted into the We^{n}dat/Wa^{n}dat community and remained a We^{n}dat/Wa^{n}dat until this death in 1823.[74] His adoptive parents were Catherine and Charles Chesne, making Catherine Jean his maternal grandmother and Hayanemade his brother. He eventually married Teressa, a We^{n}dat/Wa^{n}dat woman, and they raised their family among the Detroit River Wa^{n}dat. Like his brother and nephew, Ta-Haw-Na-Haw-Wie-Te received teachings from his We^{n}dat/Wa^{n}dat kin. He gained a reputation as a notable leader, eventually becoming a Chief. Part of his responsibilities included the care and preservation of tribal archives, consisting of wampum belts and written records pertaining to the $We^{n}dat/Wa^{n}dat$. He kept these items in a trunk among his personal belongings.

During the War of 1812, Ta-Haw-Na-Haw-Wie-Te demonstrated considerable support for the British. Unlike his nephew Chief Roniatere, he accompanied British soldiers during military strikes. Still, he cautioned other $We^{n}dat/Wa^{n}dat$ from engaging further and opposed them serving as British scouts.[75] His allegiance to the British served his family and community well. The British favoured the loyalty of the $We^{n}dat/Wa^{n}dat$ and honoured previous treaties that set aside land for the $We^{n}dat/Wa^{n}dat$ around the Detroit area. Brownstown, Michigan, located at the junction of the Huron and Detroit rivers, was one such spot – named after this $We^{n}dat/Wa^{n}dat$ Chief.[76]

The leadership presented by Isadore Sr and Chiefs Isadore Jr and Adam Brown had significant and immediate effects for the Detroit River $We^{n}dat/Wa^{n}dat$. Eighteenth-century and early nineteenth-century warfare threatened the physical, cultural, and economic security of the $We^{n}dat/Wa^{n}dat$ – to the point of complete collapse. The trauma of this experience remains within the collective memory of the Wyandot of Anderdon Nation. Former Grand Chief Steve Gronda believes that "the War of 1812 holds no honor to what was done to indigenous peoples … It was used to denude native society, steal the land and repress native tradition and culture."[77] Similar observations have been made on the detrimental effects these wars had on $We^{n}dat/Wa^{n}dat$ women. Tribal genealogist and Elder Judith Pidgeon-Kukowski states that "when the War of 1812 broke out between the Americans and the British, it was the final blow to a way of life for Wyandot women … Neither side had the best interest of the Wyandot people at heart … This was a no-win war for us. Families were being torn apart. It was the women who announced the time for every ceremony. But our women leaders were scattered and our culture was in danger of becoming irrevocably lost."[78]

Yet, despite these threats and the lingering generational effects of historic trauma, the $We^{n}dat/Wa^{n}dat$ people, including their women and ceremonies, were not lost. Pidgeon-Kukowski herself has proven this. With meticulous archival research, she found evidence that the most sacred $We^{n}dat/Wa^{n}dat$ ceremony – Komaskwema'a, which takes place at the Green Corn Feast – continued on an annual basis throughout the nineteenth century. According to Pidgeon-Kukowski, "this was a time for renewing friendship and making alliances. Young men and women could meet and perhaps find spouses." Most importantly, this example reveals how, in the face of all these threats, the women were still able to "hold council and discuss strategies for survival and lend each other the support they needed": by keeping ceremonies such as Komaskwema'a alive.[79]

LEGACY

Catherine Jean's motherwork is best illustrated through her descendants. Beyond the battlefields of imperial wars, her legacy lives on into the twenty-first century. Her children and grandchildren have passed on the teachings of their grandmothers and have maintained their motherwork to preserve the We^{n}dat/Wa^{n}dat way of life. Chief Billy Friend of the Wyandotte Nation (Oklahoma) is a descendant of Chief Adam Brown. Under his direction, the Wyandotte Nation supports initiatives like the annual cultural gathering and pow-wow. Friend consistently makes young people a priority. Every year, Wyandotte youth participate in a historical journey to key Wyandotte heritage sites. Speaking of the 2017 journey, Chief Friend said, "We have a great group of young men and women working with us this year and it makes me very confident that someday we will continue to be in great hands."[80] That same year, the Chief provided the opening remarks for the Gathering of Little Turtles. This event drew twenty-eight Wyandotte children together for several days of cultural activities and education. The Chief began the gathering by teaching the children about the importance of smudging in Wyandotte traditions. Other activities included lacrosse, language classes, and dance lessons.[81] The youth hold a special position within the Wyandotte Nation and are responsible for the selection of an ambassador, the "Tribal Princess." In 2017, the princess was Emilee Wills, another descendant of Chief Adam Brown. According to Wills, to be Wyandotte means "being a part of something bigger than yourself. It means family, it means support and it means success."[82] Wills's understanding of Wyandotte culture and community follows the leadership of Chiefs like Adam Brown and Billy Friend. When reflecting on his accomplishments as a Wyandotte leader, Chief Friend stated, "Every

Wyandotte citizen today has many opportunities from which to choose. These opportunities extend from education, jobs, housing, health care and so much more. This year for the first time we are able to offer a healthcare benefit that will be available for every Wyandotte citizen to access regardless of where they may reside. Wyandottes today are benefiting from our commercial success in a multitude of ways. The goal, as always, is to improve the quality of life for every Wyandotte citizen."[83]

Further to these initiatives, the We^{n}dat/Wa^{n}dat have continued to practice the Komaskwema'a ceremony. "We are very proud that every year our people can experience educational, governmental, social and ceremonial time together at Wyandotte, Oklahoma," says We^{n}dat/Wa^{n}dat Faith Keeper Sallie Cotter Andrews. "Since 2009, over 80 We^{n}dat/Wa^{n}dat people have received traditional names at the Komaskwema'a ceremony annually held at Wyandotte, Oklahoma. It is also significant that Wandats from all four of our nations (Oklahoma, Kansas, Anderdon and Wendake) attend Komaskwema'a in Oklahoma each year. These times of gathering together definitely improve our quality of life."[84]

Similar achievements have been made by other relatives of Catherine Jean. Chief Isadore Chesne's seventh great-grandson Clyde Pidgeon became Second Chief of the Wyandot of Anderdon Nation in 2009. While Chief, Pidgeon was an advocate for We^{n}dat/Wa^{n}dat rights and educated the public on We^{n}dat/Wa^{n}dat history. In 2012, Chief Pidgeon attended a public celebration that acknowledged the involvement of We^{n}dat/Wa^{n}dat in the Battle of Monguagon. The event took place near Trenton, Michigan, and involved We^{n}dat/Wa^{n}dat Grand Chief Ted Roll, Mayor Kyle Stack, and at least one hundred spectators. Chief Pidgeon performed a smudging ceremony before the historic marker was revealed.[85] This event provides evidence of the sustained and passionate preservation of Catherine Jean's descendants to not only pass on these teachings to their families and communities, but to the public as well. When interviewed about the event and aspects of Wyandot culture, Chief Pidgeon made sure to acknowledge the traditional role of Wyandot women. He said, "Women would run things … Men served on council for the tribe, but as what we might call figureheads."[86]

Chief Pidgeon's sister Elder Judith Pidgeon-Kukowski demonstrates the way in which this type of leadership structure has continued among the We^{n}dat/Wa^{n}dat. Although she is not Chief, she is most certainly a leader. As the tribal genealogist, she is responsible for reconstructing and reconnecting modern We^{n}dat/Wa^{n}dat with their ancestors. Through meticulous research and detailed analysis, she has dedicated her life to helping We^{n}dat/Wa^{n}dat understand their past and confirm their cultural inheritance. Following in her seventh great-grandmother's footsteps, Pidgeon-Kukowski says, "My call to leadership is from what I have learned of the life of my 7x great-grandmother. Isn't there a saying 'up to the 7th generation?' If I can reinvigorate the culture of my people, I will have done well. Catherine is my role model."[87]

Much like her grandmother, Pidgeon-Kukowski is not alone in this work. We^{n}dat/Wa^{n}dat women continue to guide Chiefs, invoke ceremony, and organize women-specific gatherings. In 2012, for instance, the Wyandot of Anderdon Nation officially revived their Women's Sharing Circle. This circle serves to create a confidential safe space for We^{n}dat/Wa^{n}dat women to discuss issues they face, whether they be political, cultural, or spiritual. Women from all across the We^{n}dat/Wa^{n}dat Nations are welcomed into a space dedicated to teachings and reciprocal exchanges of knowledge. The Circle is inspired by past practices of matricentric traditions and the motherwork of We^{n}dat/Wa^{n}dat grandmothers like Catherine Jean.[88]

Combined, the leadership of Catherine Jean's descendants, such as Chiefs Friend and Pidgeon, and of notable women like her seventh great-granddaughter Elder Judith Pidgeon-Kukowski provides evidence that highlights the long-term implications of Catherine Jean's influence and motherwork. As a result, the dedicated mentorship of We^{n}dat/Wa^{n}dat Clan Mothers like Catherine Jean dit Vien informed generations of We^{n}dat/Wa^{n}dat Chiefs who have continued to protect and strengthen their communities for the future. Significantly, We^{n}dat/Wa^{n}dat women remain central to these initiatives, drawing on their historic roles as leaders, matriarchs, and mothers.

CHAPTER 3

Margaret Grey Eyes Solomon (1816–1890)

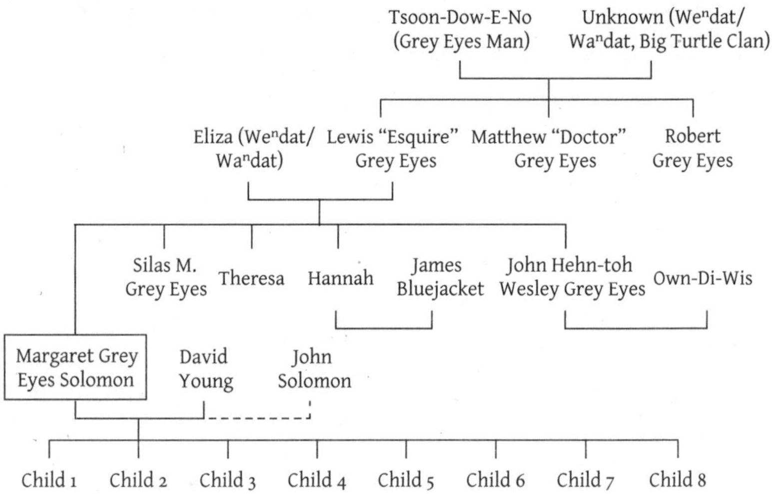

INTRODUCTION

The united and interdependent nature of male and female We^{n}dat/Wa^{n}dat leadership that Catherine Jean witnessed in her Detroit River community was later displayed publicly at the United States Congress in December 1806. The We^{n}dat/Wa^{n}dat had established towns near Upper Sandusky, Ohio at the turn of the eighteenth century.[1] These Ohio We^{n}dat/Wa^{n}dat petitioned the federal government to recognize the importance of place to their collective rights.[2] Representing their community were the "Warriors and Women [who] speak with one voice." Together they begged Congress to respect their attachment to the land, explaining, "It is the place where we were born, where our ancestors were born; and where they, and many of our relations lie buried."[3]

The petition addressed the continued insecurity of the We^{n}dat/Wa^{n}dat communities in the nineteenth century, as earlier issues persisted around the settler encroachment and colonial conquest that remained integral to the desires of the American and British colonial governments. Only a few decades later, the Ohio We^{n}dat/Wa^{n}dat, along with their Detroit River kin, would be forced to join the mass "Indian removal" project of President Andrew Jackson. The Indian Removal Act of 1830 authorized the President to renegotiate treaties to sever land titles in the eastern part of the US in return for lands west of the Mississippi River.[4] Perhaps the most well-known experience is the infamous Cherokee Trail of Tears, where approximately 20,000 Cherokees travelled west to Indian country (present-day Oklahoma). The circumstances were catastrophic and thousands of Cherokees lost their lives during the march.[5] The Cherokee were not alone, as many other Indigenous Nations had similar experiences.

The tumultuous years between the "Warriors and Women" petition and the We^{n}dat/Wa^{n}dat removal included the War of 1812 and the keen diplomacy of Chiefs Isadore Chesne and Adam Brown. While some We^{n}dat/Wa^{n}dat found refuge on British soil, others such as the Ohio We^{n}dat/Wa^{n}dat faced increased pressure to abandon their homes and move west like the Cherokee. By 1843, the warriors and women of the We^{n}dat/Wa^{n}dat Nations had gained little traction with their 1806 request to honour their established homelands in Michigan and Ohio. As a result, they, too, were forced to pack up their belongings and say goodbye to their villages and buried ancestors.[6] The Ohio We^{n}dat/Wa^{n}dat Chief Squire Grey Eyes reiterated the same attachment to the Ohio homeland as the warriors and women had in 1806. On the day of their departure, he outlined the devastating results of removal for his people. In his farewell speech, he said,

> My people, the time of departure is at hand … It remains only for me to say farewell. Yes, it is indeed farewell. No more shall we engage in the solemn feast, or the feast of rejoicing. No more shall Sandusky's Plains and forests echo to the voice of song and praise. No more shall we assemble in our Temple to sing the

> sacred songs and hear the story of the Cross. Here our dead are buried. We have placed fresh leaves and flowers upon their graves for the last time. No longer shall we visit them. Soon they shall be forgotten, for the onward march of the Strong White Man will not turn aside for Indian graves. Farewell – farewell Sandusky River. Farewell – farewell our hunting grounds and homes. Farewell to the stately trees and forests.[7]

Among the audience at Chief Grey Eyes's speech was his daughter, Margaret Grey Eyes Solomon. Born in 1816, this Chief's daughter had witnessed continued attacks on her people by colonial forces. She had survived the War of 1812 only to fall victim to the unavoidable loss of land and community through the Indian Removal Act. Following her father, she packed up her belongings and said goodbye to her home and ancestors.

This, however, was not the last that Ohio would see of Margaret. In 1865, she returned to Ohio and began her motherwork in earnest, as a public mother, eventually gaining the title "Mother Solomon." This reputation was inspired by not only her tireless daily care of children within the community but also her continued attempts to promote We^{n}dat/Wa^{n}dat heritage and culture in the area. Historian Lucy Murphy describes the emergence of midwestern public mothers like Margaret as a nineteenth-century phenomenon that derived from a need for mediation between settler and Indigenous groups. Indigenous women drew upon the common notions of womanhood to bridge cultural differences. Their public mothering focused on the greater good of the community, addressing social welfare issues and educational goals, as well as facilitating social control, inter-group diplomacy, and promoting peace. Public mothering, therefore, extended the roles and responsibilities of a mother to the entire community. Ultimately, this strategy tended to result in positive responses and an appreciation of Indigenous culture by settler outsiders, as well as the acculturation of newcomers into the community.[8] The fact that Margaret achieved the title "Mother" reflects the success of her work. Rather than "sister" or "auntie," Margaret received the highest recognition of kinship status within the community. Scholars have emphasized that "Mother" is bestowed on women who are generally honoured and highly respected.[9]

This kind of public respect garnered attention that gave her leverage to protect important heritage sites, such as the Wyandot Mission Church in Upper Sandusky, Ohio. Significantly, the church remains an enduring reminder of a We^{n}dat/Wa^{n}dat sacred place and homeland to this day because of Mother Solomon's work.

Despite popularity during her lifetime, there is very little published on her accomplishments outside of newspaper articles and minor references in local histories.[10] The exception is a sixty-page children's book published in 1984 and written by Thelma R. Marsh, an archivist for the Wyandot Mission Church. Marsh spent over thirty years compiling genealogical records pertaining to the Wyandot Nations.[11] This simple narrative describes Mother Solomon's childhood in significant detail and highlights important events such as her removal to Kansas and her return to Ohio. The book is grounded in an array of archival material, journal articles, and interviews with Mother Solomon's family members.[12] Marsh died in 1992 and is buried in the mission church cemetery. This chapter seeks to build on Marsh's book by connecting the details of Mother Solomon's life to a larger analysis of We^{n}dat/Wa^{n}dat motherwork.

FAMILY

The origin of the Grey Eyes family name (also recorded as Greyeyes and Grey-Eyes) was told to Mother Solomon by her uncle. According to their family's oral history, her paternal grandfather was part British, but was adopted into the Bear Clan. His eyes were grey and so he received the name "Grey Eyes Man" or "Tsoon-Dow-E-No" in Wa^{n}dat.[13] Eventually he became an important Chief among the Detroit River We^{n}dat/Wa^{n}dat and married a We^{n}dat/Wa^{n}dat woman of the Big Turtle Clan.[14] Together they had three sons: Lewis "Esquire" Grey Eyes, Matthew "Doctor" Grey Eyes, and Robert Grey Eyes.[15] The eldest would become Mother Solomon's father. Lewis acquired the nickname "Esquire," or sometimes "Squire," because he was one of the first We^{n}dat/Wa^{n}dat to become a fully licensed Methodist preacher in 1835. He would also follow in his father's footsteps and become a Chief of the Ohio We^{n}dat/Wa^{n}dat.[16]

Chief Lewis Grey Eyes married a We^{n}dat/Wa^{n}dat woman named Eliza who mothered five children including Margaret.[17] Margaret's siblings

John Hehn-toh Wesley Grey Eyes,[18] Silas M. Grey Eyes,[19] Theresa,[20] and Hannah[21] and her half-siblings Mary Grey Eyes[22] and Henry C. Grey Eyes[23] continued to maintain the bonds of kinship between the Detroit River We^{n}dat/Wa^{n}dat and the Ohio We^{n}dat/Wa^{n}dat communities. John, for instance, married Own-Di-Wis, the daughter of Charlotte Brown, descendant of Chief Adam Brown.[24] Similarly, Hannah married the "Michigan Wyandot" James Bluejacket.[25]

Margaret made similar decisions when it came to her own marriages. On 4 February 1883, Margaret married David Young, a Wyandot man by birth who had taken a Christian name when he became a Methodist preacher.[26] The couple were married by Reverend Thomas Simms at Wyandot Mission Church in Upper Sandusky, Ohio.[27] Together the couple had eight children, but none of them lived past childhood.[28] Young died in 1851, leaving Margaret a widow at the age of thirty-five. She did not remain alone, however, marrying the local sheriff John Solomon in 1860.[29] Their marriage lasted sixteen years until 1876 when Margaret once again became a widow, a status she kept for the remainder of her life.[30]

COMMUNITY

The We^{n}dat/Wa^{n}dat are a people accustomed to establishing multiple homelands. This tactic had even greater significance with the establishment of various colonial borders and powers in North America. It was a strategy that gained them geopolitical leverage as imperial wars raged and alliances, treaties, and losses were calculated. The foundation of a new village along the Upper Sandusky River was, therefore, a continuation of a successful approach to extend the We^{n}dat/Wa^{n}dat homeland from Detroit into the Ohio Valley. Further, it allowed the Ohio We^{n}dat/Wa^{n}dat to connect with other influential Indigenous groups, such as the Seneca, Mingo, Delaware, and Shawnee, and settlers, such as the Virginians and the Pennsylvanians. They used these networks to gain information and access to political, economic, and social capital that they then shared with their Detroit River kin.[31] It is said that during the initial period of Indigenous relocation to the Ohio River Valley, the We^{n}dat/Wa^{n}dat "spread a deer-skin for [their new neighbours] to sit down upon; signifying the allotment of a certain portion of their country, the boundary of which was designated by certain rivers, or points on certain lakes; and freely given for their use, without money and without price."[32] Thus, they provided space and engaged in protocols to redefine the boundaries in Ohio.

Margaret was born near Owl Creek, Ohio.[33] The family spent most of their time trading and hunting along the well-worn footpaths that connected their home to the larger We^{n}dat/Wa^{n}dat villages. When Margaret was four, her father took her to see the famous We^{n}dat/Wa^{n}dat caves or "Indian Caverns." Although the little girl was too afraid to enter the caves, she remembered vividly the importance of visiting these historic places where, for generations, We^{n}dat/Wa^{n}dat had held Councils and hid from enemies.[34] Her family moved permanently to Big Spring Reservation in 1822.[35] Big Spring was one of three reservations established for the Ohio We^{n}dat/Wa^{n}dat at the turn of the eighteenth century. The largest, with twelve square miles of land, was Grand Reservation, established in 1817. The reservation expanded one year later to include an additional seven miles on the eastern edge, making it the largest reservation in Ohio. Cranberry Reservation, the third, was the smallest. The US government gave the Ohio We^{n}dat/Wa^{n}dat $1,333.30. They used the funds to build a prayer house. In 1820, a sawmill and a gristmill were also built.[36]

Indigenous cultural practices, matricentric order, and an agrarian focus still informed the daily lives of these We^{n}dat/Wa^{n}dat.[37] Further, spiritual practice in Ohio had remained a syncretic system of Christian and Indigenous ceremony. Many We^{n}dat/Wa^{n}dat continued to follow the Catholic teachings of the Jesuits and looked for similar spiritual leadership for their Ohio community. The Jesuits, however, had no presence in the area; Methodist missionaries dominated this Christian work. As a result, the prayer house and subsequent mission in Ohio would begin a reorientation of We^{n}dat/Wa^{n}dat Christians as they adopted Methodist theological practices.[38] The prayer house was the first step in this process.

As much as Christian missionary work remained a part of Ohio We^{n}dat/Wa^{n}dat society, so too did their long-standing engagement with mission schools. Since the days of Cécile Gannendâris and the French Catholic seminaries, We^{n}dat/Wa^{n}dat had a long tradition of educating their children through European-style schooling.[39] Squire Grey Eyes,

Margaret's father, was at the forefront of the schoolhouse campaign. In late summer 1821, he and several other "Chiefs of the Wyandott Nation in Council Assembled at Upper Sandusky" sent a letter to the leaders of the Methodist Episcopal Church requesting a school. The letter read:

> We, your Wyandott brethren, acknowledge former favours thankfully, and wish peace and health to attend you all. We farther inform you that lately our council have resolved to admit a missionary school, to be established amongst us, at Upper Sandusky; and have selected a section of land for the purpose, at a place called Camp Meigs, where there is spring water and other conveniences; and all other necessary privileges that may be required for the furtherance of said school, shall be freely contributed, as far as our soil affords: Provided, the same does not intrude on any former improvements made by our own people, which are not to be intruded upon. Moreover, we will endeavor to supply the school with scholars of our own nation sufficient to keep it in action; and we will admit children of our white friends who live amongst us. As to the number of scholars our people will furnish the school to commence with, we cannot state. We are not sure the number.[40]

The Methodist Church received the request and complied immediately, referencing the treaty officially known as the "treaty with the Wyandots etc., 1817" as grounds to support a school for the Ohio We^{n}dat/Wa^{n}dat.[41] This made sense, as the treaty designated We^{n}dat/Wa^{n}dat territorial rights in Ohio and financial compensation for both land lost and loyalty to the American cause in the War of 1812. We^{n}dat/Wa^{n}dat drew upon their treaty rights to acquire support for land and money that would result in a mission school. Of particular note is that Catherine Jean's grandson Rontondee was among the key negotiators in the treaty.[42]

The governance and structure of the school was shaped by missionary and male leadership within the We^{n}dat/Wa^{n}dat community. The general requirements were outlined as follows: first, five We^{n}dat/Wa^{n}dat Chiefs, including Margaret's father, would form a committee to inspect the school. Secondly, the children could only attend full time; there were no part-time students. Third, no students could leave the school to return home without the permission of the missionary. Finally, all complaints from students and parents were to be investigated by the inspection committee of Chiefs before any action was taken.[43]

The school was popular from the very beginning. In the first week, five children attended, in the second week, eight, and by the third week, eighteen children were attending. One month later, the student population had risen to thirty-seven.[44] All the students boarded at the school, sleeping upstairs and attending school on the main floor. Classes ran from 9:00 a.m. to noon and from 2:30 to 4:00 p.m.[45] According to missionary records, approximately 7 per cent of the students could read, 22 per cent could write, and 25 per cent knew their alphabet. Almost half of the students had no knowledge of English before attending the school.[46] We^{n}dat/Wa^{n}dat interpreters were made available because most of the children still did not speak English.[47]

By 1825, We^{n}dat/Wa^{n}dat education and mission buildings included: a mission house; a double log cabin for the schoolchildren; a schoolhouse; a kitchen; a carpenter's shop; a chicken house; a stable; a brick milk house; a smokehouse; a wash house; a framed barn; two corn cribs; and a two-storey frame house.[48] By this time, there were thirty-four male students and twenty-two female students. One of the youngest students was Margaret's brother John Wesley Grey Eyes, age four; the eldest student was twenty-two-year-old George Clark.[49] Among Margaret's peers was her future husband, David Young.[50] The student body comprised mostly Ohio We^{n}dat/Wa^{n}dat, but included Detroit River We^{n}dat/Wa^{n}dat as well.[51]

Margaret was one of the first students to attend the school.[52] As a female student, she was expected to learn how to "read, write, spin, sew, knit, weave, cook, and do all sorts of house work necessary for comfortable living." The missionaries believed that this would lead female students to become "industrious and economical wives, submissive to their husbands, and affectionate parents."[53] Although the curriculum called for a clear adherence to patriarchal values, Margaret and other female students were not so explicitly constrained to European codes of conduct. Girls, for instance, were allowed to wear moccasins and leggings, just as the boys did, and they were allowed to pray in We^{n}dat/Wa^{n}dat rather than in English.[54] Boys experienced similar cultural hybridity, but were "to farm so that when they leave school they may be qualified to become industrious farmers, good citizens, intelligent men, tender parents, affectionate husbands, and obedient children, and thus people their nation with a generation equal, as men, citizens, or Christians, to any perhaps in the United States."[55]

The mission school and the church offer important insight into the Ohio We^{n}dat/Wa^{n}dat community. Far from an assimilated population of We^{n}dat/Wa^{n}dat refugees, they strategically acculturated Anglo-Christian traditions into their daily lives, while simultaneously preserving their Indigenous language and culture. The presence of missionaries among Ohio We^{n}dat/Wa^{n}dat did not alter their previous dedication to community well-being or ceremony. Children continued to speak their language and respect their traditions. This dynamic and prosperous community was, however, not to last. The stability that the reservations and mission were originally meant to sustain fell apart within a generation. Mission school graduates barely had time to begin their adult life when the US government, led by President Andrew Jackson, enforced the Indian Removal Act of 1830.

On 17 March 1842, We^{n}dat/Wa^{n}dat reluctantly signed a treaty for removal and joined thousands of Indigenous communities in a forced relocation west of the Mississippi. They had managed to secure land, purchasing 24,960 acres from the Delaware in what is now Kansas City, Kansas.[56] The decision was not easy. In fact, Squire Grey Eyes was publicly against the entire idea. It was not until a We^{n}dat/Wa^{n}dat council met and voted with two-thirds in favour of removal that he finally gave in and joined the majority in preparations to relocate.[57]

The mission church and school remained powerful cultural capital for the Ohio We^{n}dat/Wa^{n}dat. It was these material reminders that they aimed to preserve as they negotiated the terms of their removal. As a result, the We^{n}dat/Wa^{n}dat included a clause requiring the US government to agree that "the mission church and the ground around it containing the graves of its dead congregation should remain forever consecrated to the purpose for which it was originally designed."[58] With this peace of mind, the We^{n}dat/Wa^{n}dat began the final preparations for their journey. The scene upon departure was emotional. An observer recorded that

> the parting scenes at Upper Sandusky were most affecting. Consultations were held in the council house, and religious worship in the church, almost constantly for days before the final departure. Meanwhile, the remains of the chief, Summundewat, who was murdered by two white men in Wood Country, Ohio, in the fall of 1841, also those of the colored preacher, John Stewart, were brought hither and deposited in the burial group attached to their church. The last resting places of other loved ones were likewise tenderly cared for, and marked with stone or marble tablets.[59]

On 12 July 1843, approximately 664 We^{n}dat/Wa^{n}dat (55 from Detroit River and 609 from Ohio) gathered their belongings and began the long walk to their new home in Kansas.[60] There were, however, at least 50 We^{n}dat/Wa^{n}dat who managed to remain in Ohio and avoid the 1843 exodus.[61] Returning to Squire Grey Eyes's speech outlined in the introduction of this chapter, we see the severity of the pending relocation. Grey Eyes delivered a powerful speech to both settler neighbours and Indigenous kin and it is worth repeating here:

> It remains only for me to say farewell. Yes, it is indeed farewell. No more shall we engage in the solemn feast, or the feast of rejoicing. No more shall Sandusky's Plains and forests echo to the voice of song and praise. No more shall we assemble in our Temple to sing the sacred songs and hear the story of the Cross. Here our dead are buried. We have placed fresh leaves and flowers upon their graves for the last time. No longer shall we visit them. Soon they shall be forgotten, for the onward march of the strong White Man will not turn aside for Indian graves. Farewell – Farewell Sandusky River. Farewell – Farewell our hunting grounds and homes. Farewell to the wild creatures of the woods. Farewell to the Temple of the Great Spirit. Farewell to our White Brothers, and friends, and neighbours.[62]

Witnesses took in his sad lament, one of them describing the scene in the following way:

> In a most sublime and pathetic manner he discoursed upon all the familiar objects of a home – no longer theirs. He bade adieu to the Sandusky, on whose waters they had paddled the light bark canoe, and in whose pools they had fished, laved and sported. He saluted in his farewell the forests and the plains of Sandusky, where he and his ancestors had hunted, roved and dwelt for many generations. He bade farewell to their habitations, where they had dwelt for many years, and where they would still wish to dwell. With mournful strains and plaintiff voice he bade farewell to the graves of his ancestors, which now they were about to leave forever, probably to be encroached upon, ere the lapse of many years, by the avaricious tillage of some irreverent white man.[63]

The journey west took nineteen days. The We^{n}dat/Wa^{n}dat travelled by wagon, horse, and foot for the first week. On the seventh day they arrived in Cincinnati, where they left on two steamships via the Ohio, Mississippi, and Missouri rivers to Kansas.[64] The boats were named *Nodaway* and *Republic.* The departure and trip were nothing short of horrific. Before they had even boarded the boats, local whisky traders gathered and began threatening the worn-out travellers. No sooner had the passengers overcome the harassment from ashore than they lost two community members (one man fell overboard and drowned and a 105-year-old Elder woman passed away).[65] With no choice but to continue, they maintained their route only to find out that one of the passengers was infected with measles, which then spread to the majority of children onboard.[66]

Despite these hardships, a few hundred We^{n}dat/Wa^{n}dat arrived on 31 July 1843 at the mouth of the Kansas River, tired and unsure of their future. The uncertainty remained as survivors realized that the land originally reserved for them was no longer available. Consequently, We^{n}dat/Wa^{n}dat families were forced to camp in the lowlands where floods were frequent and often deadly. The floods were so extreme that observers noted buffalo carcasses rotting in the treetops after the water rush had subsided.[67] Further to floods, the Kansas We^{n}dat/Wa^{n}dat were hit with bouts of cholera and many suffered from inflammation of the eyes that led to blindness. This, they believed, was caused by the high winds and blowing sand of the new Kansas prairie landscape.[68] Bouts of incurable diarrhea were also widespread throughout the small community.[69] By 1844, there were 585 We^{n}dat/Wa^{n}dat living in Kansas – a loss of at least 18 per cent.[70]

Perhaps it is not surprising, then, that unlike in Ohio, the main fixture of the Kansas We^{n}dat/Wa^{n}dat community was not a mission church and school, but a cemetery for their dead.[71] Speaking of the unfortunate but frequent use of the so-called Huron Indian Cemetery, Lucy B. Armstrong, a member of the Kansas We^{n}dat/Wa^{n}dat, reported in 1890 that "to the best of my recollection and belief, I think that between the years of 1844 and 1855 there were at least four hundred internments there, and most of those graves are not perceptible and cannot be identified or even found. There were no tombstones placed there in all those years."[72] These burials, although full of sorrow, would have also instilled an immediate attachment to the new homeland. Similar to the burial grounds at the mission church in Ohio, this land become a sacred space for ceremony and ancestors from the very earliest days of We^{n}dat/Wa^{n}dat relocation.

The Kansas homeland did not present a secure situation for the We^{n}dat/Wa^{n}dat, however. Within a decade, the US government began to retract original agreements for land and annuities in Kansas. In 1855, the Kansas We^{n}dat/Wa^{n}dat were forced to sign another treaty that outlined their new relationship with the Kansas homeland and the US government. It stipulated that instead of being guaranteed land in Kansas, they would receive $380,000 in annual payments. The treaty also cancelled all previous annuity agreements and required all We^{n}dat/Wa^{n}dat who wished to maintain their tribal affiliation (rather than become US citizens) to move to Oklahoma and the last of Indian Territory.[73]

Margaret witnessed and experienced these series of traumatic events in their entirety. She and her husband David Young packed up their belongings and children to move west. Upon arrival, David worked as the ferryman and Margaret tried to heal and help her family after the devastating journey.[74] Life in Kansas was not easy. Margaret gave birth to a few more children, but none of them survived. On 11 September 1848, her two-year-old son died.[75] Three years later, the family had only three living children. In 1851, David died. The following year, another daughter died. Within a decade, Margaret would bury her entire family alongside each other in the Huron Indian Cemetery.[76] In this way, Kansas would forever hold special meaning for Margaret. Nonetheless, homesickness and loneliness plagued the widow in Kansas – a situation that led her to return to the Ohio homeland and start her motherwork.

MOTHERWORK

Margaret Grey Eyes Solomon's motherwork is grounded in a practice of public mothering. Left without any children of her own in the aftermath of the We^{n}dat/Wa^{n}dat Removal, she returned to Ohio not only to reconnect with her homeland but to reiterate to the Ohio community the long and sustained influence of the We^{n}dat/Wa^{n}dat in the area. Joined by a group of We^{n}dat/Wa^{n}dat, including her second husband, John Solomon, and nephew Jim Guyami, she returned to Upper Sandusky in 1865.[77] There was little left of the old reservation. Although the council house had burned down in 1851, the trail to it remained, as did a few unprotected grave sites, a few houses, and the mission church.[78]

Without children of her own, Mother Solomon sought out families that needed extra care. This gained her a respectable position within society and she used that to pass on We^{n}dat/Wa^{n}dat teachings for the greater good of the community. Many in the Ohio community viewed her as a mother. When she returned to the land of her birth, Margaret made it her mission to take care of the babies and growing children of the neighbourhood. According to her descendants, this became a source of pride for the entire community.[79] Indeed, many drew attention to the fact that they were "raised by her" and claimed this as a great honour.[80]

Mother Solomon retained the teachings of Elders who helped situate the We^{n}dat/Wa^{n}dat in the long history of North America. She passed these teachings on in order to help remind younger generations of the links between their ancestors and contemporary We^{n}dat/Wa^{n}dat. Her uncle, for instance, relayed the We^{n}dat/Wa^{n}dat migration story to her when she was a child. She gathered with a group to listen to her uncle, Chief Warpole, outline the origins "from the north" and the subsequent relocations to Michilimackinac, Detroit, and Upper Sandusky. He emphasized the importance of maintaining We^{n}dat/Wa^{n}dat culture and heritage, telling the children, "We are the Wyandott-Huron, sometimes called the Tobacco Nation, for long ago in Canada we grew tobacco which we traded with other tribes for them to have to smoke."[81]

Other We^{n}dat/Wa^{n}dat affirmed these oral traditions and Margaret was a keen listener. Warpole made sure to remind his community, "We lived in Canada."[82] He further explained that there "are very ancient customs among us, which we think of great importance, and lawful."[83] Included in this list of customs were the War Dance, the Green Corn Feast, and lacrosse.[84]

Margaret Grey Eyes preserved the We^{n}dat/Wa^{n}dat language as much as We^{n}dat/Wa^{n}dat stories. Despite the fact that she attended the mission school and learned English, she never stopped speaking her mother tongue. Her family continued to speak Wa^{n}dat at home, and as a child Margaret would recount We^{n}dat/Wa^{n}dat teachings to her dolls in the language.[85] It is likely that she continued this practice once she returned to Ohio. We know for certain that she continued to share the Wa^{n}dat language in public presentations and community gatherings.[86] Language and culture cannot be separated. Language is the window into world views and ways of knowing. It is the basis for cultural context and connections to place-based teachings.[87] By continuing to speak the language, Mother Solomon simultaneously provided insight into uniquely We^{n}dat/Wa^{n}dat perspectives and history.

The motherwork of Mother Solomon extended beyond the acts of caring for and teaching the children of the community. This same kind of public mothering informed her advocacy for the mission church as well. The mission church, much like We^{n}dat/Wa^{n}dat oral traditions and language, remained an important reference to We^{n}dat/Wa^{n}dat history and culture. Margaret called upon the community to restore and preserve the mission as a means to maintain a We^{n}dat/Wa^{n}dat presence in Ohio. Since the We^{n}dat/Wa^{n}dat departure, the mission church had fallen into disrepair. Some of the graves were tended to, but the building's roof and walls had begun to crumble from neglect. In 1888, the general conference of the Methodist Episcopal Church agreed to allot $2,000 for the restoration of the structure.[88] In the autumn of 1889, during the church's central Ohio conference, the mission officially received a dedication and was restored – nearly fifty years after the We^{n}dat/Wa^{n}dat Removal. Many people attended the ceremony. Various ministers gave speeches and Rev. N.B.C. Love provided a historical sketch of the building.[89] Mother Solomon had a key role in the event, as she was the only surviving student or congregation member from the earlier days.[90]

Margaret, at the age of seventy-three, took centre stage, delighting the audience with a hymn she had learned at the church as a child. Her decision to sing the hymn in Wa^{n}dat did not go without comment. Many were struck by the beauty of the language and Margaret's keen ability to bridge European Christian and We^{n}dat/Wa^{n}dat traditions. The hymn, "Come Thou Fount of Every Blessing," was fitting. It was infused with notions of wandering, loss, and loneliness, while maintaining that despite these human experiences, salvation and support were achievable through the Christian faith.[91] The last lines state:

> Prone to wander, Lord, I feel it;
> Prone to leave the God I love:
> Take my heart, oh, take and seal it
> With Thy Spirit from above.
> Rescued thus from sin and danger,
> Purchased by the Saviour's blood,
> May I walk on earth a stranger,
> As a son and heir of God.[92]

In many ways, the hymn provided context for the Ohio We^{n}dat/Wa^{n}dat history, as well as the personal history of Mother Solomon. Many We^{n}dat/Wa^{n}dat were forced to wander from their mission, reservation, and homeland in the 1840s, but they never relinquished their desire to return to the place that gave them strength.

With the dedication of 1889 complete, the mission church remained a place of spiritual, cultural, and ancestral significance for the We^{n}dat/Wa^{n}dat. In 1890, Jim Guyami's father and Mother Solomon's relative became the first We^{n}dat/Wa^{n}dat to receive burial in the church cemetery since the We^{n}dat/Wa^{n}dat Removal.[93] Through this act, We^{n}dat/Wa^{n}dat descendants maintained their connection to this sacred and traditional space. They joined notable We^{n}dat/Wa^{n}dat leaders, such as Chiefs Between-the-Logs and Summundewat.[94] In addition, at least two of Mother Solomon's children were buried on these grounds.[95] Mother Solomon joined these relatives after her passing on 18 August 1890. She was buried in a fenced plot behind the church two days later.[96] The funeral took place in the mission church and although there was a heavy rain, the church overflowed with people who wanted to pay their respects.[97]

Rev. Lease presided over the Christian ceremony, making sure to acknowledge Mother Solomon's "nobleness and true womanhood."[98] The event was covered widely by local newspapers. In these reports, Margaret was repeatedly recorded as the daughter of a famous Chief, and one of the first students at the Wyandot Mission School. Articles also made sure to mention the We^{n}dat/Wa^{n}dat Removal and emphasize the importance of Mother Solomon's return to Ohio and her established reputation as a public mother.[99] The *Daily Herald* published the following:

> Upper Sandusky, O. Aug. 19 – Margaret Solomon, better known as "Mother Solomon," the last of the tribe of the Wyandot Indians, died yesterday in her humble home north of this city, on the banks of the Indians' beloved Sandusky river. She was a full-blooded Wyandot Indian, the daughter of John Grey Eyes, a noted Chief. She was born in 1816, and when in 1821 Rev. Finley opened his mission school Margaret Grey Eyes was the first little maiden who was brought to be taught.
>
> When the Indians went west in 1843 she went with them, but some years ago after her husband, John Solomon, died, she returned and bought the home where she lived quietly and alone. Of all the Indians who parted from their beloved church in 1843 she was the only one who was present at its restoration; being the only one of the tribe living in Ohio – the last of the Wyandots.[100]

While the public recognition of Mother Solomon served as a momentary acknowledgment of We^{n}dat/Wa^{n}dat resilience in Ohio, the repeated false declaration stating that Margaret was "the last of the Wyandots" reflects a continued attempt to remove the We^{n}dat/Wa^{n}dat from Ohio. This was not unique, but part of a widespread "vanishing Indian" myth, rooted in nineteenth-century settler-American notions of manifest destiny and the colonization of the Americas.[101] It was much easier to romanticize the loss of a civilization than take responsibility for the targeted genocide of Indigenous communities across the North American continent. Ohio was no exception to this process. While it had been a generation since the forced removal of We^{n}dat/Wa^{n}dat from Ohio territory, the return of Mother Solomon and other kin in the 1860s threatened the stability of settler society. Put another way, the recognition of We^{n}dat/Wa^{n}dat residing in Ohio post-1843 would have unravelled an established US policy of erasing Indigenous Peoples from the landscape, especially east of the Mississippi. Still, Mother Solomon's motherwork outlasted this popular and persisting myth. Her notoriety due to significant public mothering gained support for the preservation of the Wyandot Mission Church, a symbol of We^{n}dat/Wa^{n}dat heritage and culture for future generations.

LEGACY

The legacy of Mother Solomon's work rests within the renovated walls of the Wyandot Mission Church, renamed the John Stewart United Methodist Church (JSUMC). It has been preserved as a historic site and is used as a pilgrimage destination for many We^{n}dat/Wa^{n}dat retracing the steps of their ancestors who were forced to leave Ohio in 1843. "Wyandots return each year and visit their ancestral homeland," says JSUMC staff records and history committee member Betsy Bowen. "They stand near the graves of their ancestors and try to imagine what it was like then. The peaceful little cemetery is filled with large oak trees that may have been standing so many years ago."[102] In 2010, the Wyandotte Nation (Oklahoma) began a series of high school and college internships. This program included retracing the We^{n}dat/Wa^{n}dat migrations to Detroit, Ohio, Kansas, and Oklahoma. Fundamental to this experience was visiting the JSUMC, where so many of their ancestors lived.[103]

Several events and commemorations have taken place to continue Mother Solomon's work, reminding both We^{n}dat/Wa^{n}dat and the larger public about the We^{n}dat/Wa^{n}dat presence in Ohio. In October 2016, the JSUMC hosted a celebration recognizing the two hundredth anniversary of the Methodist missionary John Stewart coming to the We^{n}dat/Wa^{n}dat community. Representatives from the modern We^{n}dat/Wa^{n}dat included Catherine Jean's descendant Chief Billy Friend (Wyandotte Nation), Chief Janith English (Wyandot Nation of Kansas), Chief Ted Roll (Wyandot of Anderdon Nation), and Second Chief D'Arcy Tammaro

(Wyandot of Anderdon Nation). The Chiefs took the opportunity to educate hundreds of people in attendance about their history in the area. Much like Mother Solomon, these We^{n}dat/Wa^{n}dat leaders used the church as a platform to call attention to We^{n}dat/Wa^{n}dat history and struggles. The event took place over four days and began with opening remarks by the Chiefs. They shared stories about the history of their communities as well as their current circumstances. Roughly eighty-five people were in attendance. The next day, 192 people took part in a tour of the sacred burial ground still preserved on the church property. The day was cold, but this did not deter participants who gathered outside on the frosted ground to hear the histories of those buried in the cemetery, including the story of Margaret Grey Eyes.[104]

Education remains at the forefront of We^{n}dat/Wa^{n}dat involvement with the JSUMC. The 2016 event included education and cultural stations that attracted members of the congregation, as well as local schoolchildren. The first station featured a short play about the life of John Stewart. The second workshop was run by fancy shawl dancer Sara Wright (Wyandotte Nation). Chiefs Roll and Tammaro led the third stop, providing information on the cultural and spiritual significance of the drum. Other stations covered topics such as We^{n}dat/Wa^{n}dat language, lacrosse, and artifacts. The final station, "The Wyandot Today," was led by Chief Friend.

The 2016 event was a tremendous success, leading to a similar event two years later. Rather than focusing on the JSUMC itself, this gathering sought to highlight We^{n}dat/Wa^{n}dat history specifically. The date 15 July 2018 marked the 175th anniversary of the We^{n}dat/Wa^{n}dat Removal. Once again, Chiefs returned to Ohio to share in the commemoration. Chief Janith English and Second Chief Norman Hildebrand Jr (Wyandotte Nation) attended.[105] The service began with the Chiefs' presentations about their ancestors' work at the mission. The sermon focused on the removal of the Ohio We^{n}dat/Wa^{n}dat in 1843. Service concluded with a re-reading of the famous farewell speech by Squire Grey Eyes.[106] Perhaps more appropriate would have been the hymn "Come Thou Fount of Every Blessing," sung by Mother Solomon in 1889. Grey Eyes's speech indicates a devastating conclusion to the We^{n}dat/Wa^{n}dat in Ohio, while the return of his daughter to that same place serves as a reminder that some We^{n}dat/Wa^{n}dat did not vanish after the fact. Further, it emphasizes the significant history of the We^{n}dat/Wa^{n}dat in Ohio – a history preserved by Mother Solomon.

The deep attachment held by We^{n}dat/Wa^{n}dat to the JSUMC is easily explained. Little has changed since 1806. Ohio continues to be "the place where [they] were born, where [their] ancestors were born; and where they, and many of [their] relations lie buried."[107] The JSUMC is a symbol of "this place" and We^{n}dat/Wa^{n}dat continue to draw upon its cultural significance. This love for the historic homeland has inspired settlers to join the preservation project as well, demonstrating that they, too, "hold this place in [their] hearts as the Wyandots do."[108]

CHAPTER 4

Mary McKee (1838–1922)

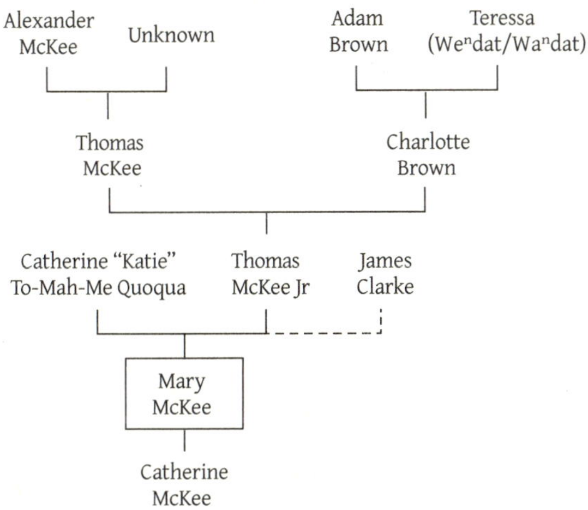

INTRODUCTION

On 14 May 1790, Alexander McKee, the British Deputy Indian Agent at Detroit and the son of an Irish fur trader and Shawnee woman, speculated that "the purchase from the Indians would probably be completed within a few days."[1] Five days later, the We^{n}dat/Wa^{n}dat (as well as the Odawa, Ojibwe, and Potawatomi) signed the so-called McKee Treaty. Negotiations had been contentious as both colonial officials and Indigenous diplomats attempted to re-map the Detroit River settlements. The aftermath of the Seven Years' War and the American War of

Independence had re-shaped the community around Detroit. European colonial powers pushed their way into We^{n}dat/Wa^{n}dat settlements, forcing Indigenous peoples to redefine their home territory in order to protect it from settler encroachment.[2] Despite almost a century of occupation and after successfully avoiding the relocation to Upper Sandusky, Ohio, the remaining 1,500 Detroit River We^{n}dat/Wa^{n}dat continued their struggle to stay.

By the end of the eighteenth century, We^{n}dat/Wa^{n}dat occupied several villages in the area, including one directly across the river from Detroit, Amherstburg. To the south, they also occupied the mouth of the Rivière-aux-Canards, in what is now the hamlet of River Canard at the north end of Amherstburg. They also had a significant presence on the west side of the river with the villages of Maguagua, in what is today Trenton, Michigan, and Brownstown, about twelve kilometres south of Detroit.[3] The British had allocated much of the area under the administration of the District of Hesse and were eager to sell portions of it to British loyalists in return for their service to the Crown. The Mckee Treaty became integral to this process as the Royal Proclamation of 1763 had outlined that no land could be acquired by settlers without negotiating a treaty with the Indigenous people of the area. Thus, McKee was charged with the task of selling We^{n}dat/Wa^{n}dat land, while also providing provisions for its protection.

Upon the conclusion of negotiations, the 1790 agreement confirmed the sale of 5,440 square kilometres of land in return for 1,200 Quebec Currency. In addition, two "Huron Reserves" were established.[4] McKee died nine years later, but his initiative to carve out We^{n}dat/Wa^{n}dat land did not die with him. His great-granddaughter Mary McKee (1838–1922) was among the future generations of We^{n}dat/Wa^{n}dat who, one hundred years later, sought to keep the land he had negotiated for in 1790.

Scholars have taken note of the important relationships between Indigenous Peoples, land, community, and identity.[5] Indigenous peoples view landscapes as archives that provide crucial scientific, historical, and ethical knowledge.[6] Further, arguments can be made in regard to the specific relationship between Indigenous women and land. For centuries, societies across the North American continent have acknowledged that the relationship between women and the land is unique. For many societies this means paying special attention to how women have historically been stewards of the land and guardians of the processes in which people use the land.[7] We^{n}dat/Wa^{n}dat women, as "farmers of the north," have a long history of cultivating the land and incorporating it into their cultural practices. Without the land, connections to history, language, and sacred spaces often run the risk of being lost.[8] It is reasonable to assume then that the protection of We^{n}dat/Wa^{n}dat land is an essential aspect of We^{n}dat/Wa^{n}dat motherwork, especially for a society that holds a strong tradition of matricentric agricultural lifeways.

The Indian agent Alexander McKee's great-granddaughter Mary McKee reflects this kind of motherwork. Her tombstone states that she was a "keeper of traditions." Traditions, in her case, have often been associated with public contributions and her work with the famous anthropologist Marius Barbeau. Acting as what Barbeau called an informant, Mary shared We^{n}dat/Wa^{n}dat traditional knowledge, including artifacts such as material culture, songs, and oral histories.[9] This important initiative has overshadowed, however, her seemingly independent struggle to maintain We^{n}dat/Wa^{n}dat land rights.[10] This chapter connects these initiatives and argues that for Mary McKee, although her ethnographic work remains invaluable, a history of her motherwork is incomplete without incorporating her acquisition of land for the Detroit River We^{n}dat/Wa^{n}dat. Further, this was not a private endeavour, but rather inspired by We^{n}dat/Wa^{n}dat practices of communal land ownership. Her drive to maintain this practice, therefore, cannot be separated from her other motherwork – and perhaps is integral to it.

FAMILY

Mary McKee came from a long line of influential figures. Her paternal lineage is filled with We^{n}dat/Wa^{n}dat allies for generations. Her great-grandfather was Alexander McKee (1735–1799), the Indian agent who negotiated several treaties on behalf of the British Crown in southwestern Ontario, including the 1790 McKee Treaty. In many ways Alexander McKee was the ideal man to fill the post of Deputy Indian Agent. Born to a Shawnee mother, McKee was raised in the interior and educated in the ways of his mother's people.[11] One of the most politically active and important people in the upper Great Lakes, McKee held notable positions, such as the Keeper of the Belts of the Western Confederacy (led by the famous Tecumseh). This was complemented by the education he received as a result of his Scots-Irish father, Thomas McKee. Records indicate that a tutor was retained to teach the young McKee in a number of subjects that would later allow him to operate in the highest circles of colonial society.[12] In addition, McKee had also been afforded a first-class education in the arts of diplomacy. Working alongside his father at his trading post from a young age, McKee learned the ways of Indigenous diplomacy from a well-loved expert. Accounts suggest that Indigenous people from a variety of Nations made detours off the most direct routes to their destinations to visit Thomas McKee's post. Indeed, there are a couple of instances of Indigenous people having taken the elder McKee's name as a mark of respect. Throughout his adult life, Alexander McKee spent his time living and working amongst the people of the Indigenous communities of the area, making his home at "McKee's Town" in the heart of "Indian country" rather than in colonial Detroit.[13] Alexander McKee became an accomplished diplomat and eventually rose to the ranks of deputy superintendent general of Indian Affairs.[14]

McKee had several children who, historians have claimed, are of Indigenous ancestry. In 1770, before the American War of Independence, McKee had a son he named Thomas. Thomas became a lieutenant in the British army in 1795, and captain a year later. He was appointed deputy superintendent for the western Indians in 1799 and later he became deputy superintendent general. When war broke out again in 1812, between the British and the Americans, Thomas took up arms as a major for the Second Regiment of Essex Militia. As an active member of Detroit-area society, Thomas McKee had the opportunity to meet a wide range of people. Relationships were both intimate and necessary to survive these war-torn years. Of particular advantage was his first marriage to Charlotte Brown (1781–1855), the daughter of We^{n}dat/Wa^{n}dat Chief Adam Brown (c. 1743–1823). This union led to a son, Thomas McKee Jr, in 1800.[15]

Unlike his father, Thomas McKee Jr rejected the call to engage with colonial administration; rather, he spent most of his time with his We^{n}dat/Wa^{n}dat kin. Educated in both We^{n}dat/Wa^{n}dat- and European-style schooling, Thomas Jr was an early pupil at the Wyandot Mission School in Ohio at the age of seventeen. There, he would have been exposed to the same regimen and training as his peer Margaret Grey Eyes, who would have been thirteen at the time.[16] This would have meant accompanying his family on trips to visit the Ohio We^{n}dat/Wa^{n}dat in order to conduct trade and maintain alliances. It was through this networking that he met and married Catherine (Katie) To-Mah-Me Quoqua (1806–c. 1876), the daughter of We^{n}dat/Wa^{n}dat war Chief Quoqua and a member of the Bear Clan.[17]

Born shortly before the War of 1812 in a log cabin built by her father near Fort Recovery, Ohio, Katie spent her early years among the Ohio We^{n}dat/Wa^{n}dat.[18] After the war, however, she and her father moved farther north along the Huron River and established a new residence at Brownstown, Michigan, where Thomas McKee Jr lived.[19] Both children would have been at the centre of We^{n}dat/Wa^{n}dat society during their formative years. As the descendants of We^{n}dat/Wa^{n}dat Chiefs, they had lineages that fostered attention within their community. Katie, for instance, had a reputation as a lively socialite, and reportedly was the "belle of bowery dances."[20] She was baptized as a Catholic in what is now Sandwich, Ontario. Most likely this took place at Ste Anne's Church.[21] As an adult, Katie filled her role as an important Clan Mother. Her death was recorded by a local newspaper – *The Amherstburg Echo* – with the observation that she had become "widely known and noted for her skill in the healing art with roots and herbs, which she gathered with her own hands, from the wilds of Michigan and there still live far and near, many who were cured under her treatment, that will testify to the efficacy of the powerful medicinal roots she used in the preparations."[22]

It is unclear the nature of the complex relationship between Thomas Jr and Katie. Scholars speculate that the two had a heated relationship and often avoided each other altogether.[23] Yet, despite this noted animosity, records indicate that they married in 1837.[24] One year later, in the spring of 1838, Katie gave birth to a daughter in Chief Quoqua's old log cabin.[25] The baby received both a Christian name, Mary, and a We^{n}dat/Wa^{n}dat name, Tarema, which can be translated to "Carrying a Lake."[26] The family did not remain together for very long, however. They, like Margaret Grey Eyes Solomon and the Ohio We^{n}dat/Wa^{n}dat, were subject to the Indian Removal Act of 1830. Many Michigan We^{n}dat/Wa^{n}dat were forced to abandon their homes and relocate to Indian Country. In 1843, the family separated. Thomas Jr went west to Kansas and caught one of the many illnesses that ravaged the We^{n}dat/Wa^{n}dat community there. Records indicate that he died when Mary was five years old.[27] Katie and Mary remained closer to home and avoided the American removals by relocating to the British We^{n}dat/Wa^{n}dat reserve near Detroit, in what is now Ontario.[28]

Katie later married the We^{n}dat/Wa^{n}dat man James Clarke (1804–1895), who would eventually become Chief in 1886. Clarke came from a well-known We^{n}dat/Wa^{n}dat family. Mary became close with her stepfather's family. The Clarkes had a reputation for maintaining tradition and We^{n}dat/Wa^{n}dat ways of life. In particular, James Clarke's brother, Peter Dooyentate Clarke, published the teachings he received from Elder Therese Hunt in order to outline the long history of the We^{n}dat/Wa^{n}dat from their origins along the St Lawrence River to their relocation to Detroit.[29] James and Peter Clarke's mother was the daughter of Chief Adam Brown and their father was a settler born in Pennsylvania. Their father worked for the Indian Department of Western Canada and as an interpreter before the War of 1812.[30] This familial connection remained after Katie died in 1876, as Mary had James Clarke live with her until his death in 1895.[31]

Mary never married, although there were opportunities. According to one source, Katie tried to take the lead and offered "a half a bushel of silver dollars to any white man who would marry [her daughter]."[32] This seems an odd approach, however, considering that Mary was often described as "an accomplished and charming young woman."[33] Indeed, there still exists a rare ambrotype photograph of Mary at age 18 that depicts a striking young woman, well dressed and inquisitive.[34] It was perhaps due to these striking features that Mary would have come to know her fiancé, an unnamed German man living among the Kansas We^{n}dat/Wa^{n}dat. Despite the couple's wishes, the wedding never took place; Mary's future in-laws disapproved of her We^{n}dat/Wa^{n}dat ancestry.[35] Whether the union was legalized or not, the relationship resulted in a daughter. Born circa 1857, Catherine McKee was Mary McKee's only child. Catherine was raised among her We^{n}dat/Wa^{n}dat family and, in particular, her mother and maternal grandmother, whom she was named after. Catherine would have been about twenty years old at the time of Katie's death. There is little else known about Catherine, except that she lived with her mother for most of her life.[36] In the We^{n}dat/Wa^{n}dat tribal roll of 1867, both she and Mary are described as living in "destitute" circumstances.[37] It is clear that Mary overcame these "destitute" circumstances, but did her daughter? Records indicate that Catherine remained alive at least until the passing of her maternal grandmother in 1876. Mary McKee died at the age of eighty-five on 11 June 1922. Although surrounded by friends and family, there is no mention of any surviving children.[38]

COMMUNITY

Mary had connections to several We^{n}dat/Wa^{n}dat communities throughout the We^{n}dat/Wa^{n}dat diaspora. Much like Margaret Grey Eyes Solomon, Mary's community of birth provided the most profound sense of homeland. Born along the banks of the Detroit River, Mary lived among the Detroit River We^{n}dat/Wa^{n}dat – the same community that Catherine Jean dit Vien called home. The generational gap between Catherine and Mary demonstrates both consistency and change for the community. Culturally, they continued to adapt to colonial customs, while also maintaining We^{n}dat/Wa^{n}dat traditions. Peter Jones, a Methodist minister who visited the area in 1828, made note of their religious convictions. The Detroit River We^{n}dat/Wa^{n}dat, he observed, were mostly Catholic, although there were a few Methodist families as well.[39] Still, just as the Ohio We^{n}dat/Wa^{n}dat were baptized and retained their Indigenous cultural practices, so too were the Detroit River We^{n}dat/Wa^{n}dat.[40]

Mary McKee's life spans most of what might be termed the "reservation period" for this community.[41] In 1790, the We^{n}dat/Wa^{n}dat signed the McKee Treaty with the British Crown that designated two "Huron reserves." These reserves eventually became known collectively as the Anderdon Reserve.[42] We^{n}dat/Wa^{n}dat also lived on the American side of the border. In 1820, the territorial governor of Michigan assigned land to each We^{n}dat/Wa^{n}dat family for fifty years based on occupancy, not possession. Mary's grandfather, Chief Quoqua, received this land and proceeded to build a "substantial log cabin" for his family.[43] In 1829, the We^{n}dat/Wa^{n}dat faced Chippewa, Odawa, and Potawatomi claims on their lands, based on joint treaties between these tribes and the We^{n}dat/Wa^{n}dat.[44] Sir John Colborne's decision of the same year favoured the We^{n}dat/Wa^{n}dat and did not affect the size of the Huron Reserve. However, in 1835, when Sir Francis Bond Head replaced Colborne as Lt Governor of Upper Canada, the claim was renewed and Bond Head "resolved the matter by reducing the size of the We^{n}dat/Wa^{n}dat holdings to about a third" under Treaty 46.[45] In 1836, the We^{n}dat/Wa^{n}dat Chief Joseph Warrow resolved that after many negotiations "there was no alternative but to surrender or treaty."[46] Ultimately, the original 23,2230 acres were reduced to 7,770 acres.

It was under these circumstance that Mary was born in 1838. Eight years later, in 1846, Katie was forced to abandon her father's log cabin, receiving some financial compensation for the surrender of Chief Quoqua's fifty-year lease of land.[47] In return, Katie gained property on the third concession of the Anderdon Reserve, next to the lands held by Chief James Clarke. The Detroit River We^{n}dat/Wa^{n}dat – and their descendants, the Anderdon We^{n}dat/Wa^{n}dat – continued to struggle to maintain their land holdings in the wake of Canadian and American encroachment for the remainder of Mary's life. By 1892, the Anderdon Reserve had ceased to exist, and by 1914, the majority of Anderdon We^{n}dat/Wa^{n}dat were forced to enfranchise.[48] The only remaining territory was the cemetery that is held in trust with the Canadian government to this day. Mary lived in Anderdon with her mother from 1838 to 1853 and then again from 1867 to 1918 – approximately fifty-five years of her life.

Mary's sense of community expanded geographically with the American Indian Removal Act of 1830. Although she and her mother remained on the Anderdon Reserve and did not join her father, Thomas Jr, in the immediate relocation to Kansas in 1843, Mary did eventually move to Kansas.[49] In 1853, at the age of fifteen, Mary left her mother to live with her aunt Mary Williams (1830–1915) and uncle Isaiah Walker (1826–1886), among the We^{n}dat/Wa^{n}dat of Kansas.[50] There she attended school with other We^{n}dat/Wa^{n}dat children and reconnected with her extended We^{n}dat/Wa^{n}dat family.[51] Roughly a decade after the traumatic events that encompassed the relocation west, the Kansas We^{n}dat/Wa^{n}dat had found the energy to re-establish themselves within their new homeland. Mary's uncle and aunt built a three-storey brick mansion, named "Turtle Hill" after their Clan affiliation. The Walker mansion was significant in that it was possibly the first brick house built in "Indian Territory." In addition, it had the first grand piano to cross the Missouri River.[52] It was also in this Kansas home in 1857 that Mary gave birth to her daughter Catherine and raised her for the first ten years of her life.

Due to her sustained residence out west, Mary received an allotment of land in Kansas when the tribal lands were distributed to individuals. This was not to last, however. The complicated aftermath of the American Civil War left We^{n}dat/Wa^{n}dat at a disadvantage. Mary, like Margaret Grey Eyes Solomon, witnessed a "choice" given to her Kansas kin: enfranchise and become American citizens or move to Oklahoma (the new Indian Territory) and retain their We^{n}dat/Wa^{n}dat status. The Kansas We^{n}dat/Wa^{n}dat community was divided. Some chose to stay, while others, like the Walkers, packed up their belongings and found refuge among the Seneca to the south. Eventually the We^{n}dat/Wa^{n}dat were granted a part of the Seneca reservation, which became the Wyandotte Tribe of Oklahoma Reservation. In 1867, the British relinquished their hold on North America and Canada became a nation-state. Taking these geopolitical circumstances as a whole, Mary made the decision to return to her place of birth and rejoin her mother in Anderdon.[53]

Mary maintained her home among the Anderdon We^{n}dat/Wa^{n}dat until 1918, when she could no longer take care of herself. It was then, at the age of seventy, that she moved south to live with her relatives in Oklahoma. The Walkers had moved there in 1874 and built a new home. Their son Bertrand Nicholas Oliver (B.N.O.) Walker had become head of the household and welcomed Mary to the Oklahoma residence known affectionately as "Last Chance."[54] While there, Mary received care primarily from her second cousin Cecile Wallace (Shundiahwah), the niece of Bertrand Walker. Cecile nursed Mary for roughly two years. She remembered that Mary passed her time quilting and that near the end of her life she suffered greatly from stomach pain.[55] Mary is buried at the Walker Family Cemetery near Wyandotte, Oklahoma. Her tombstone reads, "Mary was a keeper of traditions during turbulent times."[56]

Combined, Anderdon, Kansas, and Oklahoma each presented unique community experiences for Mary. While she spent most of her life in Anderdon among the Detroit River We^{n}dat/Wa^{n}dat, she held strong connections to We^{n}dat/Wa^{n}dat settlements farther west. None of these homelands were predetermined. Rather, they reflect her own conscious decision as well as that of her mother, who sent her to Kansas originally. Katie Quoqua Clarke chose to remain in Anderdon instead of moving to Kansas, a decision that might have saved Mary's life as it excluded her from the treacherous relocation and the illness that killed her father

Thomas McKee Jr. Still, while remaining in Anderdon, the McKees were not isolated from their extended We^{n}dat/Wa^{n}dat kin. When opportunities for schooling arose in Kansas, Mary drew upon We^{n}dat/Wa^{n}dat aunts and uncles to take advantage of the growing community of Kansas We^{n}dat/Wa^{n}dat. Later in life, the same extended network would serve to support Mary in the final years of her life. Community, therefore, continued to intersect between local levels of significance and attachment to greater networks of We^{n}dat/Wa^{n}dat diaspora identity, culture, and kinship.

MOTHERWORK

Family and community inspired Mary McKee's motherwork. As a young girl, she received teachings on We^{n}dat/Wa^{n}dat customs and history. As an adult, she took it upon herself to preserve those teachings for future generations. When the ethnographer Marius Barbeau visited Anderdon in 1911, he found "a refined half-breed Wyandot, aged 73" who "was one of the very last to speak the language of her nation on the Detroit River."[57] Mary agreed to contribute to Barbeau's project, which focused on documenting We^{n}dat/Wa^{n}dat culture. In short, he wanted to "save these authentic materials from oblivion."[58] Mary joined roughly eighteen other We^{n}dat/Wa^{n}dat teachers that Barbeau referred to as "informants." In his system, Mary was ranked fifth in order of importance.[59]

Mary contributed to Barbeau's project in three main ways. First, she allowed herself to be recorded. Barbeau believed that she was the "only informant to be found in Anderdon reservation" and one of the last to speak the We^{n}dat/Wa^{n}dat language before it became "extinct."[60] Mary also sold Barbeau We^{n}dat/Wa^{n}dat artifacts that were in her possession. These were given to the Canadian Museum of History and remain there to this day. Items included material culture made both by herself and by other We^{n}dat/Wa^{n}dat (mostly women). For instance, part of the collection included "a piece of leather" measuring 32 × 27 cm. The description reads that Mary's mother had created the piece using the "ancient wind method" for tanning.[61] Other artifacts had belonged to Mary's mother, but were not made by her. An elm bark tray made by Mary Grey Eyes for preparing dried corn and other food was one such item.[62] Mary McKee's own work included a pair of ornamental leggings, as well as several bundles of plants including tobacco, "Indian hemp," spicebush twigs, and basswood bark.[63]

Finally, the most well known of her contributions was her dissemination of We^{n}dat/Wa^{n}dat legends and histories. Mary gave Barbeau permission to publish these for preservation and widespread dissemination. The information was recorded in We^{n}dat/Wa^{n}dat and then translated by Barbeau into English.[64] Mary authored information about winter storytelling practices as well as details concerning the origin story "The Woman Who Fell from the Sky," as well as other stories such as "The Origin of the Stars," "How Famine Was Ended," and "The White Man and the Indian."[65] Through these recountings, Mary passed on ancient knowledge and customs of her ancestors. At the time, there was speculation that We^{n}dat/Wa^{n}dat culture and language (perhaps even the people) were disappearing, assimilating into settler society. Anxiety over losing key histories and frameworks of a vanishing race were central to Barbeau's motivations. For Mary, Barbeau represented a means to preserve the teachings for future generations by publishing them and placing them within museum archives.

The artifacts and stories collected by Barbeau are traditions that connect We^{n}dat/Wa^{n}dat people to their culture, a culture predicated on the relationship between people and place. The origin story, for instance, explains in detail the "beginning of the world." Mary said, "The way I heard it was: the toad dived twice or thrice, and when she picked up some earth, she brought it up to the enlarged island," creating the We^{n}dat/Wa^{n}dat world.[66] In her account of "The White Man and the Indian," Mary described the history of colonial settlement for the We^{n}dat/Wa^{n}dat through a parable. She related, "In the beginning the white man came to speak to the Indian, who was sitting on the log. 'Sit over!' said the white man. So the Indian allowed the stranger to sit on the log. But the other fellow kept pushing him and repeating, 'Sit over! Sit over!' Until the Indian found himself at the other end of the log. And then the white man said, 'Now all this log is mine.'"[67]

This story depicts both the larger colonial narratives and the local Anderdon history. Although new to the area in 1701, the We^{n}dat/Wa^{n}dat had made the Detroit River their home for centuries by the time Barbeau and Mary McKee met in the early 1900s. We^{n}dat/Wa^{n}dat created and maintained a diaspora homeland that incorporated numerous locations throughout North America. Anderdon was one such place, and while the We^{n}dat/Wa^{n}dat and other Indigenous nations of the area tried to hold their seat on the metaphorical log, settlers continued to demand that they "sit over!" Mary understood this situation all too well as she had personally been pushed off the log when she left for Kansas. When she returned to Anderdon in 1867, she consciously pushed back and petitioned the Canadian government for land owed to her.

The process undertaken by Mary to maintain land in Anderdon represents her motherwork as a keeper of traditions. Mary understood her rights within colonial society as well as her customary role as a We^{n}dat/Wa^{n}dat woman. Land was central in both cases. As a status member of the We^{n}dat/Wa^{n}dat of Anderdon Band residing within the newly formed Canadian nation-state, Mary was subject to colonial laws and practices. Mary was aware of her treaty rights and British legislation as well.

In 1790, Alexander McKee declared that he "found it impracticable to obtain so extensive a Tract without paying some attention to the claims of the Indians."[68] It was through this "attention" by Mary's great-grandfather and the sage diplomacy of the Indigenous signatories that lands reserved for Indigenous people were negotiated and protected against settler encroachment. In sum, the Crown purchased ownership of the land and usage rights to the land specified, totalling approximately 5,440 square kilometres, from the "Chiefs of the Ottawa, Chippawa, Pottowatomy and Huron Indians Nations of Detroit for 1,200 Quebec Currency in assorted goods."[69] In addition, within the written document, the McKee Treaty of 1790 included two tracts of land reserved for the "Indians."[70] The McKee Treaty, therefore, secured specific tracts of land in the Detroit River area that were to be preserved for the We^{n}dat/Wa^{n}dat and their descendants, land that would become known as the Anderdon Reserve.

Mary's rights as an Indigenous woman within a colonial system were also subject to the British – and later, Canadian – Indian Act (1851 and 1876). The "rights" under the Act were minimal, which made enfranchisement appealing to those We^{n}dat/Wa^{n}dat who sought to gain access to the privileges garnered from settler society and refused to be "Status Indians." In 1873, a number of We^{n}dat/Wa^{n}dat, including Grand Chief Joseph White, recognized the advantages of enfranchisement and suggested that they trade their "Indian Status" for the sale of the reserve "to secure to each of our male members one hundred acres of land, and twenty-five acres for the females, as well as a division of all monies as soon as may appear practical."[71] In contrast, We^{n}dat/Wa^{n}dat families in favour of maintaining the communal land wrote to the Canadian government a year later explaining that they were "decidedly opposed to having the 'residue' of our lands 'sold en bloc' to any individual or company for speculation."[72] These We^{n}dat/Wa^{n}dat included Peter D. Clarke, Joseph Warrow, and James Clarke. Indeed, a number of We^{n}dat/Wa^{n}dat did not enfranchise, or did so much later.

Combined, the treaties and the Indian Act guaranteed We^{n}dat/Wa^{n}dat like Mary McKee certain rights. These included annuities as well as land. Throughout the nineteenth century, the Canadian government and Detroit River We^{n}dat/Wa^{n}dat negotiated further land sales and eventually dissolved the final tracts of the "Huron Reserves" designated in 1790. Part of the negotiations included the allocation of allotments to We^{n}dat/Wa^{n}dat individuals. As a result, Katie Quoqua Clarke received fifty acres and Mary's step-father James Clarke received 100 acres, land that the recipients had already been living on for most of their lives.[73] Mary did not receive any land during those years as she was away in Kansas and absent from the negotiations. Upon her return, however, she discovered that her Anderdon membership had been revoked, disqualifying both herself and her daughter from any personal land allotment.

Aside from the obvious injustice and frustration surrounding her inability to acquire land in accordance with her treaty rights, Mary also had the added pressure of not being able to fulfill her responsibility, as a We^{n}dat/Wa^{n}dat woman, to protect and nurture We^{n}dat/Wa^{n}dat land for her ancestors and future generations. Her mother had instilled in Mary a multitude of We^{n}dat/Wa^{n}dat traditions, including the importance of land. Katie, for instance, had protected her father's cabin at gunpoint to fend off settler invaders. Later, she fought for Mary's right to land while Mary was away in Kansas. Mary watched her mother's dedication to protecting We^{n}dat/Wa^{n}dat land. Government officials observed that Mary "ha[d] … been clamorous in assertion of her 'rights,' and her mother, at every pay-time … made a great disturbance on her behalf."[74]

Embedded in this relationship and responsibility was the idea of collective cultural survival. Land was a critical aspect of this and was, according to We^{n}dat/Wa^{n}dat customs, meant to be communal. Concepts of communal property were also affirmed by Weⁿdat/Waⁿdat leadership throughout the eighteenth and nineteenth centuries. At Fort Stanwix in 1784, Mohawk Chief Joseph Brant (ally to and perhaps relative of the Weⁿdat/Waⁿdat) stated, "We must observe to you, that we are sent in order to make peace." He added, "We are not authorized, to stipulate any particular cession of lands."[75] Indigenous people who opposed these land cessions did so on the basis that they had come for the purpose of negotiating peace, not land surrender. They did not have the authority from their respective communities to negotiate territorial surrenders.

Consequently, the concept of universal ownership was formalized at a later Council in 1786. At the Weⁿdat/Waⁿdat village of Brownstown, Weⁿdat/Waⁿdat and allied nations explained it thusly to Mary's great-grandfather Alexander McKee:

> Take but a cursory view of that large tract of Country between our present habitations & the Salt water, inhabited by the Christians; and consider the reason why it is not still inhabited by our own colour – It is certain that before Christian Nations visited this Continent, we were the Sole Lords of the Said? *We* were the Lords of the Said, the great Spirit placed us there! and what is the reason, why we are not still in possession of our forefathers birth Rights? you may safely say because they wanted that unanimity which we now so Strongly and repeatedly recommend to you.[76]

They therefore proposed that the Weⁿdat/Waⁿdat and their Indigenous allies have "unanimity in our Councils on matters that concern us all, if we make a war with any Nation, let it result from the great Council fire, if we make peace, let it also proceed from our unanimous councils but whilst we remain disunited, every inconvenience attends us. The Interests of Any One Nation should be the interests of us all the welfare of the One should be the welfare of all the others."[77]

Ultimately the Council adopted the suggestion that all Weⁿdat/Waⁿdat and their allies – not just the people who occupied a particular parcel of land – had to consent to ceding the land. The effect was that they asserted a principle of common ownership of all Indigenous lands. This did not mean that they understood everyone's stake in all the territory to be the same. They continued to recognize different rights of use applied to specific lands held by different communities. Rather, independently of rights of use and occupation belonging to individuals or communities, the We^{n}dat/Wa^{n}dat and allied Nations at large held an interest in *all* Indigenous lands.[78]

A similar kind of discussion took place during Treaty 46 negotiations in 1836. This treaty focused specifically on the "We^{n}dat/Wa^{n}dat Tribe" as the British tried to purchase the remainder of Anderdon Reserve.[79] There, We^{n}dat/Wa^{n}dat leaders once again contrasted the advantages and disadvantages of communal land versus private property. In the end, the majority of Wa^{n}dat signed Treaty 46 despite a strong opposition towards transitioning to private ownership. Chief Joseph Warrow justified the action as he believed "there was no alternative but to surrender or treaty."[80] Others maintained their stance. Chief Splitlog, for instance, refused to sign and was witnessed stomping his foot and saying "I will not!" In the end, Treaty 46 reduced Anderdon Reserve by over half.[81]

Taken together, Mary McKee's motivations to acquire land among the Detroit River We^{n}dat/Wa^{n}dat found justification on both legal and cultural grounds. In addition to her "clamorous agitation for rights" at meetings with Indian agents, in 1877 Mary made her case in writing:

> To the Honourable, the Minister of the Interior, *Ottawa*
>
> The Petition of the undersigned, a daughter, of the late Kitee Clark, wife of James Clark, one of the Wyandotte band of Indians in the Township of Anderdon in the County of Essex; Humbly, sheweth that her Mother departed this life on the 7th day of September last year, at her late residence in the Township of Anderdon, and before her death she requested all her worldly goods should be allowed to me, her only child; that I have lived with my Mother, and taken care of her for the last nine years at her late home on the Wyandotte Reserve; that, when young, I left home with an Aunt of mine, and lived with her in Kansas, the U.S., and returned to the Wyandotte Reserve in the year 1867, and has lived with my Mother ever since up to the time of her death; that I did not leave my Mother, nor go to the United States, for the purpose of leaving the Wyandotte tribe, or band, for it was understood by my Aunt and Mother that I was to return to her, my Mother, after I had been done with my school, which I did, and as the

> Wyandotte Tribe has not since my return from the United States readmitted me into the Band, for what reason I cannot tell, nor have they in any way made provision for me in the distribution of the reserve, to which I am entitled, but they at different times have offered me half share, which I always refused, at one time since my return the Band paid me one full share amounting to $21.00 this was about two year ago.
>
> I would further state that I am full bred Wyandotte, that my father, and Mother, was full bred Wyandotte, and with the exception of Mr. and Mrs. Diver, I know no other in the band.
>
> My Mother's father, Chief Quoqua, was Loyal to the British Crown, and during the War of 1812, fought on the side of Canada, and the British forces.
>
> I would further state that our family has been living on two hundred acres, known as Lot Number Seven, in the Third Concession of the Township of Anderdon, in the Indian Reserve, for the last (30) Thirty years, and that we have been to great expense, and labor, in fencing, and other improvements, on said Land.
>
> And your petitioner would Humbly pray that she may be allowed her fair share of the Reserve, to which she is duly and lawfully entitled to, and be placed on the same footing as the other Members of the Wyandotte Tribe or Band of Indians, of the said Township of Anderdon, in addition to, any with the land that was allotted to my Mother in her lifetime, and that the two Hundred Acres may be left to my stepfather James Clarke, and myself, that is one hundred acres to Mr. Clarke, fifty that was allotted to my Mother, and fifty my own just share, making two hundred acres, which would leave the land held by our family for the last thirty years in our rights, and which is now in our possession.
>
> And now your petitioner as in duty bound will ever pray.[82]

In sum, Mary outlined her case for land. Essentially her argument rested on four main pieces of evidence: her loyalty to the crown; her ancestors were We^{n}dat/Wa^{n}dat; she was not there when the allotments were made; and her mother had died.

Family members also wrote in support of her case. In particular, her step-uncle Peter Clarke reiterated Mary's petition in 1884 by stating, "I beg leave to remind you of Mr. Mills [Minister of the Interior], opinions in regard to Mary McKee's claim to her deceased mother's fifty acres … Wyandott lands of Anderdon which Mary McKee now occupy … Mr. Mills said to me … that the said Mary McKee ought to have her mother's fifty acres."[83] Again in 1877, Clarke continued his letter-writing campaign, this time drawing on more substantial arguments: "Not only do I believe that she is justly entitled to her deceased mother's fifty acres of land, but I think the Department will agree with me, when I say that it would be nothing more than right and just to have her name put on the Wyandott pay-roll, at once."[84] He went on to say that optics should play a role in the government's decision concerning McKee. He said,

> It looks hard, indeed, to see this Wyandott woman, by blood among the assembled Band before Mr. Mackenzie, unjustly deprived, for all time, of her rights – quite young, she was [unwittingly?] forfeited her rights here, when persuaded (as stated in her petition by her aunt to leave this country) and join her people in the west. Therefore, she is excusable, and can be looked over by the Department, for she was not to be blamed. I respect it looks hard – to see her kept out of the Band now, her deceased mother's home – to whom she was ever kind and faithful in her home now, and while she lives.[85]

Clarke concluded the letter by stating, "Individually, and as a Wyandott by blood, her rights to the land and money, here now, is clear as can be."[86]

McKee's case found backing from notable We^{n}dat/Wa^{n}dat leaders. Chief Joseph Warrow reminded Mary of his personal support in a letter he wrote in 1895. He recalled: "I stood by you like a man and worked hard to get you what you now have and enjoy … I took up your case and … we set to work to get you your rights for three long years with united effort and hard work and … writing the department to except a surrender in your favor."[87]

The struggle was long, but successful in the end. Eventually, Mary was granted the land by the Canadian government. Indian agent Robert Mckenzie wrote to this effect, stating, "Mary McKee ought to be readmitted to the Band and have admitted to her the 50 acres of Land which her mother would have been allotted had she been alive at the time the allotments were made."[88]

The legal and final notification was outlined in a deed dated 24 February 1887, decades after McKee's initial battle had begun. The deed confirms the "absolute purchase of the 50 acre tract in Anderdon Township to one Mary McKee, for the consideration of one dollar." It also included a "peculiar clause," according to lawyers familiar with property and estate work, which read, "To have and to hold the said parcel or tract of land hereby granted unto the said Mary McKee, her heirs and assigns for ever … reserving nevertheless unto us, our heirs and successors, the free use, passage and enjoyment of, In over and upon all navigatible waters that shall or may be hereafter found on or under or flowing through or upon any party of the said parcel."[89] The home was affectionately called "Walnut Hill" and was the "last 50 acres of ground originally set aside for the … Wyandott Indians who made their home in Anderdon"[90]

It is in this way that Mary completed her motherwork, safeguarding fifty acres of We^{n}dat/Wa^{n}dat land not for herself, but for the We^{n}dat/Wa^{n}dat at large and the generations to come.

LEGACY

The legacy of Mary McKee's motherwork is both obvious and obscure. The most obvious is the way in which We^{n}dat/Wa^{n}dat culture has been preserved through her work with Marius Barbeau. The documents, recordings, and material artifacts can be found at the Canadian Museum of History (CMH) in Gatineau, Quebec. There is public access to the collection, and at times some of the items have been put on display. The location, however, is far from any modern We^{n}dat/Wa^{n}dat community. Perhaps as a means to address this issue, the CMH negotiated a loan of over fifty Barbeau artifacts and twenty-nine photographs and original recordings to the Sam Noble Oklahoma Museum of Natural History in Norman, Oklahoma, in 2012. The site was the location of a celebration that included a special exhibit titled "The Gathering of Traditions: A Centennial Celebration of Dr. Charles Marius Barbeau in Oklahoma." Among the items were the artifacts that Mary McKee sold to Barbeau – preserved for decades within the museum's archives. The exhibit lasted two and a half months.[91]

Barbeau's preservation of Mary's songs and stories have further served as a source for language revitalization among the modern We^{n}dat/Wa^{n}dat diaspora. In her home community of Anderdon, the annual Green Corn Feast has incorporated We^{n}dat/Wa^{n}dat words since 2014. According to We^{n}dat/Wa^{n}dat cultural keeper Richard Zane Smith, although We^{n}dat/Wa^{n}dat are using a number of sources, "Barbeau's work is central, actually it's some of the most 'recent' working with speakers."[92] Smith's language work is a testament that Barbeau's fear that the We^{n}dat/Wa^{n}dat language was doomed to oblivion never came to fruition. It also counters the declensionist observations made by many, including Louis Goulet who, in 1925, declared that there was no hope "of the language ever being restored to practical use in living humanity again."[93]

Beyond Barbeau, Mary's ability to affirm sustained relationships with land highlights a lesser known but equally critical aspect of her attempt to keep We^{n}dat/Wa^{n}dat traditions alive. She created a common and collective space for future generations. Her deed includes a stipulation that the land remain for "her heirs and assigns forever." Records indicate that this worked for roughly one hundred years.

In 1913, Mary sold her tract of land to Annie Splitlog, a descendant of Chief Splitlog, who had originally refused to surrender a portion of the reserve in the Treaty of 1836. This transfer of land was a conscious effort to maintain traditional We^{n}dat/Wa^{n}dat land practices. While Mary could no longer live on her own in Anderdon due to poor health, she created a plan before moving to Oklahoma. The arguments that had engulfed the 1836 deliberations continued to shape the We^{n}dat/Wa^{n}dat of Anderdon community. Families were divided on the ways We^{n}dat/Wa^{n}dat land could and should be used. The Splitlogs maintained their reputation as "traditionalists" and favoured communal land ownership. The McKee family also continued to support this approach, as did the Clarkes and Warrows.[94] In addition, Annie Splitlog was a We^{n}dat/Wa^{n}dat *woman*. These two factors likely played a role in Mary McKee's selection. Mary's relationship to Annie was not one of particular significance. Annie's son did observe, however, that his "mother and Mary

McKee were close relatives."[95] Relatives and politics had shaped most of Mary's actions in life. Generational legacies also played a part. By passing her land to a We^{n}dat/Wa^{n}dat woman whose family had a long history of supporting community and attempts to maintain We^{n}dat/Wa^{n}dat land, McKee was actively and consciously preserving We^{n}dat/Wa^{n}dat land practices. Annie was also known as one of the few We^{n}dat/Wa^{n}dat who still understood the old teachings and ways of life. She had a reputation within the community as such and was deemed "one of the few local survivors of the Wyandotte Indian Band."[96]

Subsequently, Annie lived on Walnut Hill for sixteen years. Annie kept the property in the We^{n}dat/Wa^{n}dat family and granted her son, Norman Gibbs, ownership after her death in 1928.[97] Although Gibbs was not educated in the ways of his We^{n}dat/Wa^{n}dat ancestors, he recognized the importance of being one of the last We^{n}dat/Wa^{n}dat descendants to maintain property in what had been the Anderdon Reserve. In fact, by 1949 he believed he was the "only one left in the [Anderdon] township."[98] Notwithstanding this significance alone, he also drew attention to the history and value of the property he inherited. In an interview with the *Windsor Daily Star* he highlighted the fact that the "house in which I live was built by the Indians." He provided further details on Mary McKee and her struggle to maintain the home. This was reinforced by the fact that he kept a framed copy of the McKee deed on his wall.[99] It remained there until his death in 1975.

It seems that Gibbs did not understand, however, the importance of maintaining Walnut Hill for future We^{n}dat/Wa^{n}dat generations. In 1976, the house and property were sold to Mrs. Lorette Renaud, a friend of Norman Gibbs. Since that time, the copy of the deed has been lost.[100] After one hundred years, Mary McKee's initiative had come to an end.

While We^{n}dat/Wa^{n}dat have continued to live near and around the old Anderdon Reserve, their 1790 land base had finally dissolved into private property. Much like the language initiative, however, the modern Anderdon We^{n}dat/Wa^{n}dat have made attempts to reclaim their focus on communal land for collective cultural survival. In 2015, the Wyandot of Anderdon Nation, with support from the Wyandotte Nation (Oklahoma) and the University of Michigan, purchased fifteen acres of land in Gibraltar, Michigan. The tract is situated on a historic We^{n}dat/Wa^{n}dat village site established by Chief Adam Brown (Mary McKee's great-great-grandfather).[101] According to the modern We^{n}dat/Wa^{n}dat of Anderdon Nation, this land, called "Six Points Village," includes

> 7 ½ acres [that] are considered uplands, or "buildable" on which will be the site of our planned Longhouses and other buildings. These will be featured as community, ceremonial spaces for members and separate visitors spaces. The remaining acreage encompasses wetlands which is where our beloved Turtle pond is located. We hope that the building of the traditional Wyandot Longhouses, Museum, Visitors Center and other features, will help us to teach our non-Indigenous guests about our history and our contemporary organization. This land also contains a sacred Ancestral space, which is the most significant reason for choosing this location. We honour our Ancestors![102]

Indeed, this initiative recalls the goals of Mary McKee entirely. It seeks to provide an exceptional space for a multitude of We^{n}dat/Wa^{n}dat cultural practices. It also reflects McKee's "peculiar" clause in that it does not preclude use by non-Indigenous people and in fact welcomes outsiders to share in the use of the land and We^{n}dat/Wa^{n}dat ways. The community believes that "this land was lost to us over 200 years ago, but our ties to it have never been broken. Our Nation has proudly regained this land and is reclaiming our heritage in hopes of educating our children and grand children, and making our presence known to the world."[103] Certainly this final statement by Mary's relatives indicate that she was not the last of the We^{n}dat/Wa^{n}dat, nor was her fifty-acre lot the last We^{n}dat/Wa^{n}dat land in the Detroit area. Much like the language and cultural teachings preserved by Mary through Barbeau, the importance of land and territorial traditions have remained within the community.

CHAPTER 5

Eliza Burton Conley Jr (1869–1946)

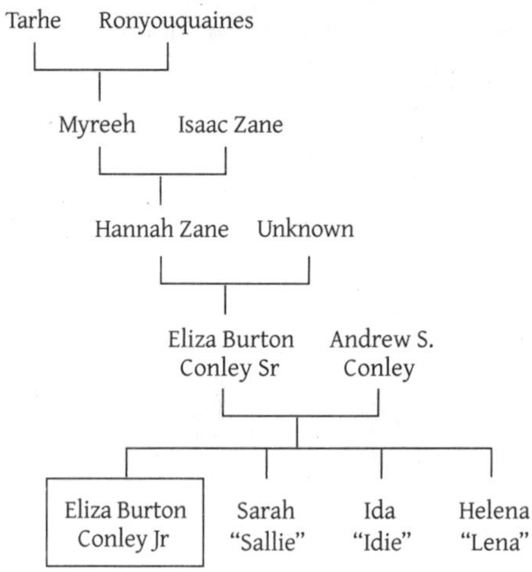

INTRODUCTION

On 31 January 1855, We^{n}dat/Wa^{n}dat Chiefs made special provisions, through treaty negotiations, for the protection of their sacred burial grounds in Kansas. Upon conclusion, Chiefs Silas Armstrong Sr, George I. Clark, Joel Walker, John Hicks, Tauromee, and Matthew Mudeater signed a treaty with the understanding that the "question of the permanency of the burying ground was settled for all time."[1] Thirty-five years later, Mother Grey Eyes Solomon signed another document, indicating her clear objection to the removal in 1890 of remains from the Kansas Huron Cemetery, the burial ground that held her late husband David Young and several children.[2] This act of protest indicates that the provisions of the

1855 document had not been "settled for all time." Mother Solomon and other Kansas We^{n}dat/Wa^{n}dat had to continuously prove the importance and legitimacy of their cemetery as their legal status fluctuated in the wake of Indian Removal and forced enfranchisement. Thus, as settlers arrived and Kansas City became a colonial stronghold rather than an Indigenous refuge, it would seem that the 1855 treaty had had little effect.

Letter writing and petitions remained useful strategies in this struggle. Much like Mary McKee and the Detroit River We^{n}dat/Wa^{n}dat, the Kansas community engaged with colonial systems of education and politics, experiences that they used to navigate American society to preserve their way of life. Their battle over the preservation of the Kansas Huron Cemetery received similar attention. It was within this context that Eliza (Lyda) Burton Conley Jr took the initiative to go beyond the written word by presenting a public protest through legal action. Officially the first Indigenous woman to argue a case before the US Supreme Court, Conley's motherwork rested in both her power as an attorney and her desire to honour the ancient teachings of her We^{n}dat/Wa^{n}dat ancestors concerning sacred spaces and burial practices.[3]

We^{n}dat/Wa^{n}dat cemeteries, or burial grounds, have historically been some of the most important locales for maintaining and affirming communal identity and culture. These sacred spaces are classified as cultural landscapes that We^{n}dat/Wa^{n}dat have traditionally maintained through modifying, connecting, and creating relationships with the land. By modifying and actively living and dying there, We^{n}dat/Wa^{n}dat solidified their relationships with their homelands. Burial practices and spaces represent an important feature of this relationship-building because they encompass all aspects of what constitutes a cultural landscape, incorporating songs, dance, elaborate feasting, and physical modification of the ground for the interment of bones. As a result, burials solidify their relationship with the living world and the Land of the Souls through a physical and metaphoric contract to maintain and actively protect these spaces.[4]

Scholars have recognized the importance of burial spaces and ceremonies for the We^{n}dat/Wa^{n}dat.[5] Before Europeans arrived, their most important ceremony was the Feast of Souls. Commenting on the significance of this burial ritual in the seventeenth-century, Jesuit Jérôme Lalement explained that it was "the oil of their ointments … the honey of their medicines, the preparations of their hardships, a star for their guidance … the spring of their activities … in short, the general instrument or condition without which nothing is done."[6] Although the Feast of Souls had lost popularity over the years and was no longer practised by the time the Kansas Huron Cemetery was established, the significance of We^{n}dat/Wa^{n}dat burial practices had not diminished. Post-dispersal We^{n}dat/Wa^{n}dat incorporated a syncretic approach to burials, allowing for both Christian and Indigenous traditions. This acculturated custom ensured that deathways continued to be "star[s] for their guidance." Nineteenth-century We^{n}dat/Wa^{n}dat cemeteries held the same meaning as their pre-contact ossuary pits. Within this continuum, women have consistently held a position of unique importance in We^{n}dat/Wa^{n}dat burial practices. As both the givers of life and the overseers of death, We^{n}dat/Wa^{n}dat women controlled these spaces even after colonial systems of patriarchy devalued and diminished many other aspects of their daily lives.

Lyda Conley's motherwork, in relation to the Kansas Huron Cemetery, can be seen as an extension of these ancient practices into modern times. Her court case and protests represent important innovations to the ways in which We^{n}dat/Wa^{n}dat women continued to manage and defend We^{n}dat/Wa^{n}dat sacred spaces. Lyda received notable interest from both the We^{n}dat/Wa^{n}dat community and the public because of her unique motherwork. Local and regional newspapers drew attention to her cause, conducting interviews and reprinting her story for over fifty years.[7] Despite this attention and display of We^{n}dat/Wa^{n}dat agency, histories of Lyda Conley are limited. Woven into larger narratives of Kansas and the Wyandot, few scholars have situated her centrally in their research.[8] Consequently, this chapter describes Lyda Conley within larger historical processes of colonialism, while simultaneously forefronting her agency as a means to understand the ways We^{n}dat/Wa^{n}dat women have continued to create and care for their sacred spaces.

FAMILY

Eliza (Lyda) Burton Conley Jr (1869–1946) was the youngest daughter of Andrew S. Conley (1835–1885) and Eliza B. Conley Sr (1838–1879). She had three sisters: Sarah (Sallie, b. 1861), Ida (Idie, b. 1859), and Helena (Lena,

b. 1858).[9] Her We^{n}dat/Wa^{n}dat heritage came from her mother's side, as Eliza Sr was the granddaughter of Isaac Zane and Myreeh, the daughter of Chief Tarhe (1742–1816).[10] Tarhe ("the crane") of the Porcupine Clan was born among the Detroit River We^{n}dat/Wa^{n}dat. Later he became an important leader of the Ohio We^{n}dat/Wa^{n}dat during Pontiac's War and the American Revolution. Colonial officials also recognized his importance, taking note of his eloquent and determined diplomacy. In 1795, for instance, witnesses recorded the following speech:

> *Elder brother!* Now listen to us. The Great Spirit above has appointed this day for us to meet together. I shall now deliver my sentiments to you, the fifteen fires. I view you, lying in a gore of blood. It is me, an Indian, who has caused it. Our tomahawk yet remains in your head – the English gave it to me to place there.
>
> *Elder brother!* I now take the tomahawk out of your head; but with so much care you shall not feel pain, or injury. I will now tear a big tree up by the roots, and throw the hatchet into the cavity which they occupy; where the waters will wash it away, to where it can never be found. Now, I have buried the hatchet, and I expect that none of my color, will ever again find it out. I now tell you, that none in particular can justly claim this ground – it belongs, in common, to all. No earthly being has an exclusive right to it … [Spoken on a blue belt.]
>
> *Brothers, the fifteen fires, listen!* You now see that we have buried the hatchet. We still see blood around; and in order to clear away all grief, we now wipe away the blood from around you, which together with the dirt that comes away from it, we bury with the hatchet, in the hole we have made for them; and replace the great tree, as it stood before; so that neither our children, nor our children's children can ever again discover it. [Spoken on a blue string attached, and both delivered.]
>
> *Brothers, listen!* I now wipe your body clean from all blood, with this white, soft linen (a white wampum) and I do it with as much tenderness as I am capable of. You have appointed this house for the chiefs of the different tribes to sit in with you, and none but good words ought to be spoken in it. I have swept it clean – nothing impure remains in it.

Brothers, listen! We are both placed on this ground. I now wipe the tears from your eyes, and open your ears. I see your throat is so stopped that you are nearly suffocated – I now open your throat, and make it quite clean, that whatever the Great Spirit may think proper for you to swallow, may go down, without any obstruction. I see also, that your heart is not in its true situation – I now place it in its proper position, that anything you may hear from us, your brothers, may descend directly to it; and what you shall say, may come with truth and ease from it.

Brother! I clear away yon hovering clouds, that we may enjoy a clear, bright day; and easily see the sun, which the Great Spirit has bestowed on us, to rise and set, continually. [A white string.]

Brother! Listen to us, Indians, who now speak to you. The bones which lie scattered, of your ancient warriors, who fell in defense of the present cause, we gather all together, and bury them now, and place this white board over them, that they may never again be seen by our posterity. [A white and blue belt and string.]

Brother warrior! Listen to us! The great chiefs are about to speak to you. You chiefs and warriors present, listen also!

Brother! We speak not from our lips, but from our hearts, when we are resolved upon good works. I always told you that I never intended to deceive you, when we entered upon this business. It was never the intention of us Indians, to do so. I speak from my heart what I now say to you. The Great Spirit is now viewing us, and did he discover any baseness or treachery, it would excite his just anger against us.

Brother! Listen to me. We are all of one mind, who are here assembled. This is a business not to be trifled with – it is a matter of the utmost concern to us. We happily so far agree in handling our ancestors' records, who always worked for peace.

Brother! You have proposed to us to build our good work on the treaty of Muskingum. That treaty, I have always considered as formed upon the fairest principles. You took pity on us Indians – you did not do as our fathers, the British, agreed you should. You might by that agreement, have taken all our lands; but you pitied us, and let us hold part. I always looked upon that treaty to be binding upon the United States, and us Indians.

> *Brother!* Listen to us Indians – I told you just now, that we were upon business of the greatest moment. I now conclude the great work we have been employed in; and with *this*, I cover the whole earth, that it may appear white, and shine all over the world. I hope the Great Spirit will have pity on us, and make this work lasting. [Four large mixed belts presented.]
>
> *Brother!* I am going to relate to you the treaty made at Muskingum, in a few words. I have not forgotten that treaty; neither have you. At that time we settled a peace, between the Delawares, Six Nations, Ottawas, Chippeways, Pottawattamies, and us Wyandots. It is very true there were not so many different nations then assembled, as are now present. We now establish a general, permanent, and lasting peace, forever.
>
> *Brothers!* We are all sensible that when you struck the boundary, at that time, it ran from Tuscarawas to a little way below Loramies, where the fort stood, which was destroyed in 1752. I understand the line has since been moved, a little towards us. Be strong, brothers, and fulfill your engagements.
>
> *Brothers, listen!* I have told you that I speak from my heart – you see the speeches I have delivered. Peruse them and see whether or not I have spoken with sincerity. This is all your brothers of the different nations present have this day to say to you.[11]

Speeches such as this became notorious and Tarhe's public fights against settler encroachment onto We^{n}dat/Wa^{n}dat lands gained significant attention. Eventually, Tarhe took up the role of Sasteretsi, the Grand Chief of the We^{n}dat/Wa^{n}dat, in 1788. This position had never been filled by a member of the Porcupine Clan and is evidence of Tarhe's important role within the We^{n}dat/Wa^{n}dat community.

Myreeh was the only daughter of Tarhe and Ronyouquaines (whose last name may have been LaDurant).[12] Myreeh followed in a long line of Porcupine Clan women, likely taking her name from Tarhe's grandmother.[13] Her family's protests continued for generations. Myreeh's daughter Hannah Zane (Lyda's grandmother), for instance, refused to enfranchise and give up her We^{n}dat/Wa^{n}dat status.[14] Likewise, Eliza Sr followed her mother's lead and in 1867 requested that her family retain their tribal status.[15] Indian Affairs made note of her desires, recording that "Eliza wishes herself and family placed on Indian list."[16] Eliza Sr became a highly respected member of We^{n}dat/Wa^{n}dat society and an advocate for We^{n}dat/Wa^{n}dat cultural preservation. Her obituary read, "The deceased was a member of the Wyandott Nation and was highly esteemed by her neighbours and acquaintances."[17] Generations of activist ancestors had not faded from the We^{n}dat/Wa^{n}dat collective memory and their goals for maintaining We^{n}dat/Wa^{n}dat territory, culture, and community continued to dominate their protests in Kansas.

In this way, the intersection between past familial strategies to counter colonial conquest and contemporary sites of contest find particular meaning with Lyda Conley. Similar to Mother Solomon, Lyda's connection to the Huron Cemetery was intimate. Her mother, Eliza Sr, was buried there in 1879, as was her little sister Sarah, who died when Lyda was eleven years old.[18] Her activism was, therefore, grounded in customary We^{n}dat/Wa^{n}dat practices, honouring the connection between the land and people through burials and ceremony. The threat of removing these ancestors and relinquishing the land would have, in effect, shattered this contract for future generations. Family, therefore, provided critical inspiration for Lyda's motherwork as she endeavoured to maintain a sacred space for We^{n}dat/Wa^{n}dat souls both past and present.

COMMUNITY

Lyda's family was among the refugees who relocated to Kansas following the Indian Removal Act of 1830. The reality of the devastation experienced in the first few years of this relocation would have been relayed to Lyda as her family tried to carve out a new homeland in the west. This was not the first time a We^{n}dat/Wa^{n}dat community had faced forced relocation, and as a diasporic people, the Kansas We^{n}dat/Wa^{n}dat drew upon past practices to familiarize themselves with the land and the people.

Initially, the Kansas We^{n}dat/Wa^{n}dat maintained two historic towns in Kansas. The first was 540 acres bought for $46,080 from the Delaware in 1843 and sanctioned by Congress in 1848.[19] This would eventually become Wyandotte City (later Kansas City, Kansas), which was incorporated in 1851. As a busy economic and political centre, Wyandotte City attracted a variety of people, Indigenous and non-Indigenous alike. Still, the early years were a time marked predominantly by the We^{n}dat/Wa^{n}dat – a people who transformed the landscapes to meet their needs. In addition to the immediate establishment of a cemetery for their dead, the We^{n}dat/Wa^{n}dat refugees carved out a city landscape. Streets, for instance, were named after prominent We^{n}dat/Wa^{n}dat families such as Armstrong, Tauromee, and Northrup.[20] The first house was built in December 1843 and belonged to We^{n}dat/Wa^{n}dat leader John Armstrong, and a church was built the same year.[21]

The We^{n}dat/Wa^{n}dat established a second settlement in 1851 called Quindaro.[22] Pressures rose from the American pro- and anti-slavery movements and the Kansas Wyandot were not isolated from these heated controversies. Quindaro was a key site for the anti-slavery movement and a stop on the Underground Railroad.[23] Its popularity grew quickly. The local newspaper, the *Chindowan*, reported that by May 1857 the town included approximately thirty-five houses, a schoolhouse, which also served as a church, and sixteen business houses that "were in the process of erection."[24] The town also held the second-largest hotel in the territory, the Quindaro House. According to the report, the town was "well supplied with two hotels, two commission houses, a sawmill of 5,000 feet per day capacity (later 20,000), a stoneyard, carpenter shop, land agencies, surveyor, builders, cabinetmakers, blacksmiths and a cemetery."[25] Lyda's family purchased eighty-five acres of farmland within the town's jurisdiction.[26] The We^{n}dat/Wa^{n}dat presence in Quindaro was not to last, however; the legislature of 1862 repealed the act incorporating Quindaro, and the town company officially went out of business.[27]

Woven throughout the history of both Quindaro and Wyandotte City is the controversial battle over We^{n}dat/Wa^{n}dat identity, community, and Indigenous rights in the American West. The loss of their short-lived townsite of Quindaro marked another era of removal and erasure for the Kansas We^{n}dat/Wa^{n}dat. In 1855, the We^{n}dat/Wa^{n}dat took part in yet another round of treaty negotiations with the US government. It was then that they were pressured into declaring American citizenship, as the dissolution of tribal status became inevitable. In return, they would be given private ownership of certain lands while surrendering the largest portions of the 1843 purchase. This process resulted in the tribe losing their federal status and their rights to the Kansas homeland.[28]

We^{n}dat/Wa^{n}dat were given the option to request exemption from the citizen roll of 1855, but records indicate that only forty-six individuals made this application. The reasoning behind this does not reflect the general desires of the community. According to John Grey-Eyes, the commissioners chose to accept applications for exemption in October 1855 at a meeting held by the Wyandot Council to deal with some "ordinary business of the tribe. There was but few of the tribe present, as it was not known before that this particular business would be transacted on this particular day." Moreover, the commissioners provided a mere two hours to complete the task. As a result, many We^{n}dat/Wa^{n}dat were absent or unaware of the council's proceedings and the serious ramifications of their disengagement.[29]

Tensions grew within the We^{n}dat/Wa^{n}dat Kansas community, as they lived in the centre of escalating controversies over slavery and civil war that threatened the free-state movement in Kansas. In 1856, both the Methodist Episcopal and the Methodist Episcopal South churches were deliberately destroyed by fire. The culprits were never caught, and their actions reflected the growing divides between pro- and anti-slavery factions within the community. Struggles did not wane after the Civil War. The 1855 treaty and termination of the Wyandot Nation of Kansas did not solve the need for settler land in Kansas. In 1867, the We^{n}dat/Wa^{n}dat negotiated the establishment of a 20,000-acre reservation on the Seneca reservation in Oklahoma. This land would be for the sole use of the newly resurrected "Wyandotte Tribe of Indians."[30] This federal regulation of tribal identity and culture was a continued attempt to erase the We^{n}dat/Wa^{n}dat from the land and complete the settler colonial conquest of the west. While a number of We^{n}dat/Wa^{n}dat chose to move south to Oklahoma and regain their federal tribal status, there were many who remained in the Kansas City area, including the Conley family.[31]

Perhaps one of the greatest inspirations for staying was the We^{n}dat/Wa^{n}dat cemetery, a two-acre space located in the heart of Kansas City, Kansas.[32] In 1890, Lucy B. Armstrong, the wife of We^{n}dat/Wa^{n}dat John

McIntire Armstrong, observed, "It is an interesting thought that in that place are buried the people who made the first history of Kansas and of their country and city. It is pleasantly shaded with natural forest trees, such as black walnut, elm and oak. Some of the smaller trees are covered with wild grape vines, and the place, in its neglected condition, has the appearance of a primeval forest. It is picturesque, and, on account of its elevation, commands a good view of the surrounding city."[33]

With the termination of Quindaro, and the relocation of We^{n}dat/Wa^{n}dat to Oklahoma, this burial ground was the last piece of territory under We^{n}dat/Wa^{n}dat jurisdiction in Kansas. Further to this, it represented a sacred space for hundreds of We^{n}dat/Wa^{n}dat souls that lay in contract with the We^{n}dat/Wa^{n}dat people and the Kansas homeland.[34] The burial ground was where eleven-year-old Lyda Conley buried her parents and little sister. With both parents dead, the surviving siblings had to fend for themselves. Ida, being the oldest, took on the housekeeping responsibilities while the other two completed school. Eventually Lyda graduated from Park College, Missouri, paddling to school by crossing the Missouri River. Later, the sisters relocated to town to have better access to jobs, taking up residence in a "modest" home in Kansas City, Kansas. There, they survived but struggled to make ends meet; they used a cook stove for heat and newspaper to cover the floors and windows for insulation.[35] Because of these circumstances, the Conley sisters had no choice but to enter the workforce as soon as possible. Lyda trained as a telegraph operator and became an instructor at Spaulding Business College in Kansas City, Missouri. Lena became a cook at the county jail.[36]

On the surface, the life of the Conley sisters seemed typical of a settler family in Kansas City. Their schooling and jobs reflected colonial systems of education and capital economy. These systems, however, did not consume their lives. Kansas We^{n}dat/Wa^{n}dat, including the Conleys, continued to call upon their Indigenous cultural practices and knowledge as well. Eliza Sr had passed down key We^{n}dat/Wa^{n}dat teachings to her children. Medicine and healing practices were among some of the most significant teachings. The Conleys knew how to collect and use local plants with such sophisticated success that they gained a local reputation as healers. On more than one occasion, locals would visit the "Indian women" to cure themselves of persistent ailments.[37] The We^{n}dat/Wa^{n}dat also continued their ceremonies, practising the Green Corn Ceremony, for instance, every August.[38]

Thus, much like the Detroit River We^{n}dat/Wa^{n}dat and the Ohio We^{n}dat/Wa^{n}dat, despite the USA's attempts to ignore their existence through forced removals and enfranchisement, the Kansas We^{n}dat/Wa^{n}dat community continued to nurture their ancient Indigenous teachings and cultural practices. Federally recognized or not, they maintained their identity and fought against assimilation policies geared to erase their presence. As much as the Kansas We^{n}dat/Wa^{n}dat remained an active and vibrant Indigenous community among the Kansas City settler residents, they were constantly reminded that their choice to stay negated their rights as Indigenous people. Different from the Oklahoma We^{n}dat/Wa^{n}dat, the Kansas community were no longer federally recognized and therefore retained very little traction when it came to defending and protecting their sacred spaces. Nothing highlights this struggle more than the Huron Cemetery.

MOTHERWORK

Since its very inception, the fate of the Huron Cemetery has been precarious. Land speculators, politicians, and strategic businessmen tried to eliminate its presence from the landscape. We^{n}dat/Wa^{n}dat have always fought against these threats, acting to stop or slow down this process. Public protests prevailed, as We^{n}dat/Wa^{n}dat consistently called attention to the importance of protecting their ancestors and, as a result, their sacred connections to land and people. Lucy B. Armstrong remarked, "To remove the burying ground now would be to scatter the dust of the dead to the winds. What a sacrilege! I remember with reverence many of the good Wyandottes buried there, and my heart protests against such a desecration of that sacred ground. Such a sale is repugnant to every sentiment we cherish for our dead, as well as being offensive to the highest impulses of a Christian civilization."[39]

While activists like Armstrong were among the majority, the actions of Lyda B. Conley have had a unique and enduring impact on We^{n}dat/Wa^{n}dat society. The turn of the twentieth century saw a renewed interest in the cemetery grounds. This became particularly pressing when it was revealed that a provision had been hidden in a section of a sixty-five-page congressional appropriations bill in 1906, authorizing the secretary of the interior to sell a tract of land located in Kansas City, Kansas – the Huron Cemetery.[40] Congress passed the following on 21 June 1906:

> That the Secretary of the Interior is hereby authorized to sell and convey, under such rules and regulations as he may prescribe, the tract of land located in Kansas City, Kansas, reserved for a public burial ground under treaty made and concluded with the Wyandotte tribe of Indians on the thirty-first day of January, eighteen hundred and fifty-five. And authority is hereby conferred upon the Secretary of the Interior to provide for the removal of the remains of the persons interred in said burial ground and their reinterment in the Wyandotte Cemetery at Quindaro, Kansas, and to purchase and put in place appropriate monuments over the remains reinterred in the Quindaro Cemetery. And after the payment of the costs of such removal … and also after the payment to any of the Wyandotte people, or their legal heirs, of claims for losses sustained by reason of the purchase of the alleged rights of the Wyandotte tribe in a certain ferry named in said treaty, if, in the opinion of the Secretary of the Interior, such claims or any of them are just and equitable, without regard to the statutes of limitation, the residue of the money derived from said sale shall be paid per capita to the members of the Wyandotte tribe of Indians who were parties to said treaty, their heirs or legal representatives.[41]

It wasn't long after that the federal government began work on the cemetery in Kansas City, building a double wall and an ornamental entrance.[42] The secretary of the interior, James R. Garfield, selected a commission of three men to visit Kansas City, make the arrangements for the removal of bodies, and sell the cemetery. When they arrived, word spread quickly about the severity of the situation. Lyda Conley and her sisters took immediate action. On the morning of 23 July 1907, a group of We^{n}dat/Wa^{n}dat, supervised by the Conleys, brought a wagon filled with pine boards, shingles, nails, and hammers to the centre of the cemetery. By the end of the day, a small shack had been built, measuring approximately six by twelve feet. Signs were placed around the shelter and the cemetery warning "trespassers beware."[43] The women had a shotgun as a final means of defence for their sacred space.[44]

The sisters remained for months in what would become known as "Fort Conley." Federal troops considered intervening, but this never became a reality. Eventually the commissioners left to re-strategize. The Conleys stayed on, protecting the graves, providing continuity of care. As Lyda explained, "I personally, looked after and tended the graves of my parents and sister, for twenty years and over, – and the graves of my grandmother, relatives, and friends as well."[45] Further, Lyda described the severity of her defence in the following way: "I am part Indian, and I will not see my people so robbed of their rights and the bodies of their dead taken from the sacred burying ground of the tribe in defiance of the treaty because there is now no one to stand up for the rights of the Indians. I have tried to save the cemetery from being desecrated by law, and now I will take care of it myself, law or no law."[46]

For Conley the situation called for extreme measures. Beyond the federal commissioners, the Conleys took charge to guard the cemetery from any individuals who were deemed a potential threat. Lyda compared their actions to the way that someone might protect their home. She said, "In this cemetery are buried one-hundred of our ancestors … why should we not be proud of our ancestors and protect their graves? We shall do it, and woe be to the man that first attempts to steal a body. We are part owners of the ground and have the right under the law to keep off trespassers, the right a man has to shoot a burglar who enters his home."[47] As it happened, "trespassers" included notable Kansas City settlers such as George Cornell, the son of General Dudley E. Cornell, the former Mayor of Kansas City, Kansas. Cornell had entered the cemetery without indicating his intentions and was consequently escorted by Lyda Conley to the police station. Reports indicate that Cornell made no objections to the We^{n}dat/Wa^{n}dat women's claims of trespassing and promised that he "would offend no more" to avoid being jailed.[48]

Lyda did several media interviews about her occupation of Fort Conley. Through these published conversations, readers came to know the dedication and determination of her actions, which highlighted We^{n}dat/Wa^{n}dat obligations to honour ancestral contracts with the land. In 1909, she sat down with a journalist from *Kansas Magazine* to reflect on the experience. Fear was a major point of interest for the public. "Was I afraid in that cemetery? Afraid of the dead?" she said. "Afraid of what? Afraid of my mother – or of my grandmother – that their spirits would harm me, when I was enduring those hardships for the security of their last resting place? Why should I be afraid – of the dead? I builded the hut close to the grave of my mother and I felt secure every moment of my stay in the grounds that may appear to you, gloomy, but sacred to me for their memories." Still, the journalist pushed further. "Were you afraid of the troops from Leavenworth?" he asked. "Did you tremble when you thought that they might, perchance, march down upon you, and in the name of the government, demand that you surrender?" "No, I was not afraid of the troops," replied Conley. "I knew that was only a plan to scare me away from the place; I knew the constitution too well to be afraid of them." She added, "But if the troops had come, it would not have made one bit of difference; they would never turn over one of those graves, until they had first taken life from me."[49]

While the protest in the cemetery brought media attention and seemed to deflect the immediate threat of sale as a result of the 1906 act of Congress, the need to protect the cemetery in perpetuity remained unresolved. It was with this in mind that Lyda Conley decided to take the case to court, demanding that the American legal system acknowledge the rights of We^{n}dat/Wa^{n}dat people in Kansas through an injunction suit. Lyda explained the importance of her role by stating,

> You know one can plead his own case in any court, and this I intend to do. No lawyer could plead for the grave of my mother as I could, no lawyer could have the heart interest in the case that I have. Shall I win? … If I do not, then there is no cemetery in this land safe from sale, at the will of the government. The land was once deeded in perpetuity, by the government, as a burial place for the Wyandotte tribe; by common consent it has been used as such all these years, and congress overstepped its authority when it dared to pass a law to disturb those graves.[50]

Acting as both plaintiff and attorney, Conley submitted an injunction suit against the federal commission to prevent the execution of its orders by the Department of the Interior. She identified the defendants as James R. Garfield (secretary of the interior), Horace B. Durant, and Thomas G. Walker and William A. Simpson (the commissioners), claiming the sale of the burial ground and their attempts to desecrate the burial site as illegal.[51]

The first hearing was before Judge Pollock in the US District Court in Topeka, Kansas. The judge ruled against Conley because he believed it was outside of the court's jurisdiction. Conley appealed to the Supreme Court.[52] The significance of Lyda Conley's case cannot be emphasized enough. It was, in the history of the United States, the first time an Indigenous woman took a case before the US Supreme Court. Further, legal scholars believe this is likely the first time an attorney used the lineal descents of the tribal beneficiaries to a treaty as evidence in legal action against the federal government.[53]

Through this court case and Lyda Conley's arguments, we can see how this particular type of motherwork rested in both settler legal traditions as well as We^{n}dat/Wa^{n}dat belief systems. Conley's statement to the Supreme Court was as follows:

> As we shall attempt to speak to you, this afternoon, about Huron Cemetery, we are mindful of the fact that "In the sweat of thy face shalt thou eat bread till thou return unto the ground; for out of it wast thou taken: for dust thou art, and unto dust thou shalt return."
>
> History tells us that a superstitious reverence for and burial of the dead has been found a distinguishing trait of Indian character – to some extent we believe this to be true – as graves of the redmen were their only monuments so traditions were their only history. The Wyandots or Hurons, including the Eries or Erigas, Ahrendahronous, and the Attiwandorouk or "Neutral Nation" Canada, are one of the three divisions of the Wyandot-Iroquois Family – a distinct, and historically famous group, allied ethnically to the Algonquins, and linguistically, Morgan thinks, to the Dakotas.
>
> The Wyandots of Wyandot County, Ohio having been promised 148,000 acres of land in Kansas, in lieu of their annuity, which under the treaty of Jan. 29, 1817 was to have been paid annually

forever, were persuaded to sell their lands in the states of Michigan and Ohio, and came to what is now known as Wyandotte County Kansas, about the year 1842. The excuse for not keeping this agreement was that so large a tract of land could not then be found unclaimed. The Delawares, who in the year 1640 [*sic*] were compelled to purchase land from the Wyandots, feeling that they owed a moral obligation to the Wyandots sold them land in the fork of the Missouri and Kansas Rivers, consisting of 39 sections of land for which they paid approximately $48,000.

The Wyandots, we find adhered to the cause of the United States, during the war with Great Britain, and in consequence of such adherence their property was injured or destroyed, for which under the 12th article of the treaty of September 29, 1817, the United States engaged to pay in the course of the year 1818, damages to the amount of $4,319.39 at Upper Sandusky.

My grandfather Isaac Zane, whose Indian name was Mawcasharrow, was a scout, and also carried mail in the War of 1812. He was among the number of the head men of the tribe and chiefs who came to Kansas in the year 1843 to purchase the land of the Delaware Indians, which sale was commissioned July 25, 1848. This purchase included Huron Cemetery, which under the treaty of Jan. 31, 1855 was not ceded to the United States, being then in use as a public cemetery but on the other hand the 2nd article of said treaty provided: "The portion now enclosed and used as a public burying ground shall be permanently reserved and appropriated for that purpose", and the Supreme Court of the United States in 13 Peters 498,513 and 539, held that "whenever a tract of land has been legally severed from the mass of public lands, and no subsequent law, or proclamation, or sale will be construed to embrace it, or to operate upon it, although no reservation of it be made", and have held, also, that "It is well settled in the United States that Cemeteries are among the purposes for which land may be dedicated, and it is held that, upon such dedication, the owner is precluded from exercising his former rights over the land."

The first case of record three thousand seven hundred and eighty-three years ago states "and the field of Ephron which was in Machpelah, which was before Mamre, the field, and the cave which was therein, and all the trees that were in the field, that were in all the borders round about, were made sure, unto … his city. And after this, Abraham buried Sarah his wife in the cave of the field of Machpelah before Mamre: The same is Hebron in the land of Canaan. And the field and the cave that is therein, were made sure unto Abraham for a possession of a burying place by the sons of Heth." Gen.23:17–20, And that one hundred and eighty-three years later "Jacob called unto his sons, and, he charged them, and said unto them 'I am to be gathered unto my people: bury me with my fathers in the cave that is in Ephron the Hittite, in the cave that is in the field of Machpelah, which is before Mamre, in the land of Canaan, which Abraham bought with the field of Ephron the Hittite for a possession of a burying place. There they buried Abraham and Sarah his wife; there they buried Isaac and Rebekah his wife; and there I buried Leah.'"

"And his sons did unto him according as he commanded them. For his sons carried him into the land of Canaan, and buried him in the cave of the field of Machpelah, which Abraham bought with the field for a possession of a burying place of Ephron the Hittite before Mamre."

Like Jacob of old I too, when I shall be gathered unto my people, desire that they bury me with my fathers in Huron Cemetery, the most sacred and hallowed spot on earth to me, and I cannot believe that this is superstitious reverence any more than I can believe that the reverence every true American has for the grave of Washington at Mount Vernon is a superstitious reverence.

Huron Cemetery is known to be the oldest burial ground in the State of Kansas. Just when the first internment was made therein, we have not been able to ascertain. We find however, that … in the year 1844, Squeendechtee, another chief who was at that time 61 years of age, died and was buried therein. Other chiefs whose graves we find there are Rontondo [*sic*] or Warpole, Tauromee, Sommodowat, Hawdownwaugh or Matthews, Monocue or Thomas, Dawatout or John Hicks, Big Tree, Tall Charles, Sarahoss, Clark Armstrong and many others space will not permit us to mention.

> The wisest man the world has ever known admonishes "Remove not the ancient (landmark), which thy fathers have set." And that the hand of the desecrator "remove not the old landmark; and enter not unto the fields of the fatherless": "For their redeemer is mighty; he shall plead their cause with thee."
>
> Man goeth to his long home, and the mourners go about the street: or ever the silver cord be loose, or the golden bowl be broken, or the pitcher be broken at the fountain, or the wheel broken at the cistern.
>
> Then shall the dust return to the earth as it was: and the spirit shall return unto God who gave it.[54]

While this argument reflects a deep knowledge of American legal traditions and Christian value systems, it also highlights the lawyer's knowledge of the historical and cultural significance of burial grounds to Wendat/Wandat society. Using phrases such as "old landmark" and noting that cemeteries "were their only monuments," Lyda Conley aptly called attention to the Indigenous teachings of her ancestors. Deathways, and the ceremonies associated with them, represented a spiritual, cultural, and political relationship between the Wendat/Wandat and the land. The contracts between people and place were solidified through the burial of the dead. Therefore, the sale of the Kansas cemetery and the removal or destruction of the souls buried there would sever Kansas Wendat/Wandat from their homeland, the ultimate blow to their community rights and presence in the area.

Moreover, although Conley did not state it explicitly, her court case, in conjunction with the Fort Conley protests, provides evidence that Wendat/Wandat women continued to take on the task of preserving these traditions. The gendered circumstances of their protests provided additional opportunities for allyship for the Wendat/Wandat in the struggle. Connected by feminist solidarity at the very least, a number of settler women's organizations sympathized with the Conley sisters and the Wendat/Wandat fight for the cemetery. Male journalists took time to make note of women-run groups that voiced their support, like the Ladies' Reading Club of Kansas City. Their motivation, according to one journalist, was anti-"commercialism and twentieth-century progress," rather than any legitimate recognition of Indigenous rights and protection of sacred spaces.[55] Few reporters, and likely few allies, understood the deeper meaning behind what seemed to outside observers like a series of radical protests. In many ways, Conley's motherwork reflects the ancient roles and responsibilities of We^{n}dat/Wa^{n}dat faith keepers. Trained in a vast knowledge of ceremony, history, and culture, faith keepers acted as consultants to their communities for spiritual guidance. They organized feasts, buried the dead, healed the sick, and enforced codes of conduct. This position could be held by both men and women.[56] The Conley sisters, and in particular Lyda, fulfilled this role in a modern capacity as they became authorities on We^{n}dat/Wa^{n}dat deathways, healing, and traditions. This was most evident at the height of their popularity through the court case and public protests.

Despite the public attention and support for the Conley case, Lyda Conley did not win her legal battle. The Supreme Court denied her claim. The decision instilled anger among Conley supporters. Writing to the editor of the *Kansas City Star*, John McIntire Armstrong outlined his frustration and disappointment:

> I see by the *Star* the Supreme Court of the United States has rendered its decision, and Huron Cemetery is to be sold. The government has broken every treaty it has made with the Indians and they have been driven from place to place, until even the dead are not allowed to rest in peace. My father, who lies buried in the old cemetery, was the Chief of the Wyandotte Indians. He, with other prominent members of the tribe, made the treaty with the government, and Article No. 2. says "so long as grass grows, and water runs, this spot shall be used as a burial ground for the Wyandot Indians."
>
> I am not in accord with the method theretofore used to prevent the sale of this cemetery. I had hoped to see a movement on the part of the sale of this cemetery. I had hoped to see a movement on the part of the cultured people of this city to preserve this old cemetery, where lie many of the pioneers who came here and endured great hardship in developing this part of the country. Aside from my personal feelings in the matter, as a public spirited citizen I would suggest this matter be presented to Congress, asking it to rescind the bill. In that event, I would suggest that the

> park board be made custodians, and given power to beautify this sacred place. Then, this old historic spot will not only be a lasting ornament; but a pride to our city.[57]

Armstrong was not alone in his call for Congress to rescind the bill, despite the failure of Lyda's court case. It is perhaps in response to writings such as this editorial, and the subsequent public outcry, that Congress repealed the statute in 1913.[58] Further, Congress passed a bill in 1916 that guaranteed $10,000 for the "preservation and improvement of the Huron cemetery."[59] With this in mind, the immediate impact of Lyda Conley's motherwork was a success. She may not have won the battle, but her advocacy and public education about the cemetery won the war.

LEGACY

Lyda's life ended tragically on 28 May 1946.[60] After spending an evening at the Kansas City Public Library, located next to the cemetery, Conley was attacked. A man struck her on the head with a brick and stole her purse, which contained twenty cents. After suffering for twenty-four hours, Lyda Conley died at the age of seventy-seven.[61] One year later, the sale of the cemetery was again under review. At first it would seem that her protests had only gained immediate results, with little success in regards to lasting protection for the Kansas burial ground. Yet what becomes clear in the historical record is that her publicized battle reinforced and inspired future generations to honour We^{n}dat/Wa^{n}dat sacred spaces and deathways. Although Lyda would not witness the continued activism of other twentieth-century We^{n}dat/Wa^{n}dat, she had a leading role in the ways they countered continuous attempts to destroy the cemetery.

In 1956, US Congress terminated their 1916 agreement to care for the cemetery (effective 1 August 1959). The reaction from the Kansas We^{n}dat/Wa^{n}dat and their Kansas City allies was intense. A protest was organized and conversations about a march to Washington, DC, ensued. The protest garnered so much attention that the Kansas City mayor, Paul Mitchum, denounced the sale of the cemetery and pledged his support with the protestors.[62]

Protestors put pen to paper in order to make their position clear, signing a petition and sending letters outlining the significance of the cemetery. Recalling the words of their grandmother, Lucy B. Armstrong, E. Paul Armstrong, and Lucy M. Armstrong copied Lucy Sr's words in their personal letter, stating, "To remove the burying ground now would be to scatter the dust of the dead to the winds. Such a sale is repugnant to every sentiment we cherished for the dead as well as being offensive to the highest impulses of Christian Civilization." They concluded: "Her Grandchildren endorse her statement."[63] Many letters called for empathy and attention to protect the souls of their loved one. Paula Green from Kansas City wrote,

> I am a member of the Shawnee Mission Indian Historical Society. My great-grandmother was a member of the Shawnee Wyandotte Indian tribe, coming to Kansas from Amherstburgh, Canada West, at an early age, spending the most part of her life in Wyandotte and Johnson Counties. She, Harriet Brown, was the daughter of Adam Brown, a Wyandotte, and Theresa Brown, a Shawnee. Harriett Brown was married to Franklin Butler, who was adopted into the Shawnee Wyandotte Tribe. They were married in Johnson County, November 17th, 1858, and are both buried in Huron Cemetery, located in Kansas City, Kansas. I am sure you can appreciate my interest in this matter and I hope this letter will help in some way to defeat the destruction of this cemetery.[64]

Similar remarks were made by Nina G. Trantum, the We^{n}dat/Wa^{n}dat daughter of Walker Garrett: "I do not know how many of the Garretts are buried in this family lot; but among them is my Uncle, Charles B. Garrett, a veteran of the War of 1812. On May 16, 1924 … the Daughters of 1812 placed a gold star marker upon his grave. I am a member of that organization and was present and assisted in the ceremonies. As a descendant of both the Garrett and the Walker Families, I protest against the bill now in Congress calling for the desecration and destruction of historic Huron Cemetery."[65]

Others made more overt pleas to stop the sale, calling for empathy for the families and respect for the dead. "Please do not let them sell our cemetery," wrote Georgia Logan. "I have two dear ones buried there. My

Daddy and my sister, besides distant relatives. I am sure you would feel the same way if you were I."[66] John McAlpine wrote, "My grandparents and other members of the family are buried there, and I would not think of disturbing them."[67] Moreover, Kate Shipp made a list of her known relatives, explaining that, "I do not know how many Zanes are buried in Huron Cemetery; but among them are my grandmother, my father, mother, two sisters, three brothers, my husband and my son. I certainly will not allow these graves to be desecrated if there is any legal means that can be found to prevent it."[68]

Harry E. VanFossen chose to call attention to the important people buried in the cemetery and remind Congress of the significant role these individuals had had in the formation of Kansas City. He wrote,

> I am a great-grandson of Silas Armstrong, the man who brought the Wyandots to Kansas in 1843, who helped make the treaty of 1855 which extended the laws of Kansas over the Wyandotte County which, of course, included the Huron Cemetery which was dedicated to the public. Silas Armstrong is buried in Huron Cemetery with numerous of his descendants. He is buried with the Masonic Service and his grave is marked with a granite shaft which testifies to that fact. I voice the sentiment of every Wyandotte descendant here whom I know in opposition to the proposed sale of Huron Cemetery, and if we are forced to do so, we shall invoke the Kansas law against anyone who attempts to desecrate the graves of our forefathers and their descendants.[69]

Further, many We^{n}dat/Wa^{n}dat recalled Lyda Conley and her court case as evidence to support their protest. Edith Zane Yunghans, for instance, stated:

> The article in the (Kansas City) Kansan has just been received by me from a friend. Since leaving Kansas City, Kansas, I have not been too closely concerned about the burial place of my relatives including my father, mother, sisters and brother, also my own baby (Zane Yunghans). I had thought that this matter of selling the cemetery had been settled in court and I know my own grandfather died thinking his resting place was for always. We want the

> agreement made by the government with Miss Lyda Conley lived up to – I love our cemetery and am proud of it. Please do all you can to help us. If there is anything I can do, please let me know. I hope this will be settled this time for good. There are many of us who will need a place to be buried; but it won't be a pleasant thought, not knowing how long we will be able to stay.[70]

In her letter, Florence M. Schaub added:

> I am a descendant of the Wyandotte Indians, and having two brothers, grandparents and many close relatives buried in the Huron Cemetery, I am protesting any action as to the sale of it. The selling and abandonment of this cemetery has come up several times in the past, and ended in the U.S. Supreme Court which handed down the decision that this plot of ground was to be the burial place for the Wyandotte Indians as long as the sun shines and the river flows. Now when my loved ones were buried there, they and I, too, thought this was their last resting place and never to be disturbed. This is why I am appealing to you to do what you can to see that the decision which was handed down by the U.S. Supreme Court is not broken. I therefore oppose any action for the sale of the Huron Indian Cemetery.[71]

Writing from Camden, South Carolina, Celeste Mumford asked Congress to remember the efforts of Lyda Conley and to honour the cemetery she had fought so hard to protect. Mumford explained her connection to the cemetery in the following way:

> My grandfather, founder of Wyandotte, the latter named for the Wyandotte Indians, came with a few white people and Indians from Sandusky, Ohio in 1842 (and settled July 1843) on the banks of the Kaw opposite Kansas City, Missouri, on a site now called Kansas City, Kansas. Wyandotte soon became a town and my grandfather was President of the First town council. He was made Chief of the Wyandottes in order to handle all moneys from the government that was to be paid to the Indians. The latter were wards of the government then … My grandfather and his family are buried in

> the Indian cemetery, as are others who belong there. My mother was buried there. Besides being the resting place of our loved ones, it is a very historical and sacred place. Why destroy such a place, Mr. Scrivner when those who are buried there made your town a reality? Miss Conley, who fought so diligently to hold those cemetery grounds is gone; but should her efforts so soon be forgotten? It seems such a dreadful thing to desecrate such a spot.[72]

If the court case remained part of the We^{n}dat/Wa^{n}dat collective memory, so too did their respect for the ancestors, sacred spaces, and cultural landscapes. These themes were reiterated by many letter writers. Conley's motherwork of the early twentieth century influenced future generations of activists, giving them strength and historical grounds to further her motherwork. Chief Janith English of the Wyandot Nation of Kansas has reflected on the impact of Conley's activism in an unpublished manuscript entitled "Tears of My Grandmothers."[73] Her introduction explains: "Dozens of articles have been written about the Conley Sisters; but I have found few written records to support the sum of the oral traditions concerning my cousins. They were nieces of my Great-Great Grandfather, Ebenezer O. Zane Sr., and the daughters of his sister, Eliza Burton Conley Sr … Their courage and actions grew from the seeds of love for their families, Ancestors, and their Wyandot Heritage and Identity."[74] At the centre of English's writing is her unwavering desire to continue Conley's work. It was while visiting the Kansas cemetery as a young child with her grandmother that English realized her purpose. "It was on that day," she recalls, "that I began to internalize the oft told story of the daughters of my great-great aunt's Eliza Burton Conley, Sr., the three Conley sisters who referred to themselves as Ida, Lyda and Lena. Our family simply called them, 'The Sisters' or 'The Cousins.' Their lives were full of stories of heroism and heartache; respect and humiliating derision; inspiration for our people, and headaches for those who would intrude upon the rights of our People and, especially, to disrespect the bones and resting place of Our Ancestors."[75] For English, the battle to protect the cemetery was more than a local conflict. Rather than an isolated We^{n}dat/Wa^{n}dat issue, she connected the plight to patterns of destruction caused by settler colonial policies and their direct effect on Indigenous women. She writes,

> I later learned the stories that connected these women to our sisters whose courage and determination link them with Indigenous women throughout the world; for their stories contain the contemporary themes that today resonate among people who must engage in a struggle to preserve rights of justice and self-identity for themselves and their families. Within these stories is interwoven the thread of grief that arises from the tension created when a paradigm of fear, power and control is pitted against a journey toward interconnectedness and interdependence.[76]

It is not surprising, therefore, that almost a century after Lyda Conley's activism, Chief English was instrumental in a watershed legal agreement between the Wyandotte Nation (Oklahoma) and the Wyandot Nation of Kansas.[77] In July 1998, these two We^{n}dat/Wa^{n}dat nations signed a settlement that emphasized an alliance between the two parties and ensured cooperation for the future. Central to this agreement was that the Huron Cemetery in Kansas remain a sacred space, preserved for the purpose of We^{n}dat/Wa^{n}dat burials. Further, it stipulated that "the respective parties shall never permit construction, development, or business on, over, or under the site."[78]

In 2017, the cemetery became an American National Historic Landmark. Conley's motherwork, both legal and cultural, continued well beyond her years. Her fight to preserve the cemetery was a continuation of ancient We^{n}dat/Wa^{n}dat traditions that revolved around female leadership, and the critical need to protect We^{n}dat/Wa^{n}dat burial sites. Through Conley's motherwork as a modern faith keeper, the cemetery continued to allow We^{n}dat/Wa^{n}dat deathways to be "the oil of their ointments … the honey of their medicines, the preparations of their hardships, a star for their guidance … the spring of their activities … in short, the general instrument or condition without which nothing is done."[79] It is appropriate, therefore, that engraved on Lyda Conley's tombstone are the words "though I am dead the sun will glow, the stream will flow, the grass will grow," representing the bright and everlasting effects of her motherwork for generations to come.[80]

CHAPTER 6

Jane Zane Gordon (1871–1963)

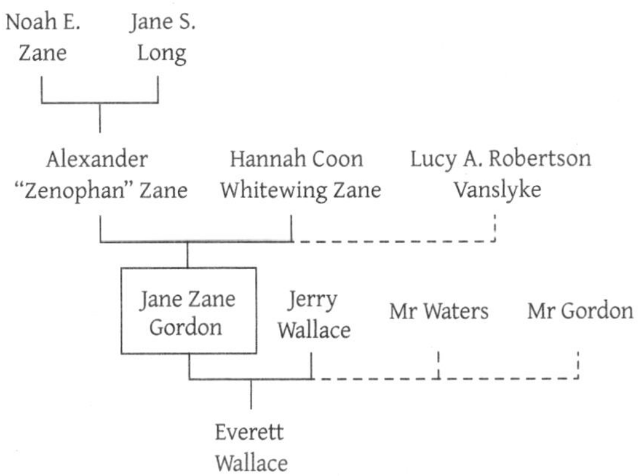

INTRODUCTION

In 1934, John Collier, the commissioner of Indian Affairs for the USA, explained the government's new strategy in the following way:

> We take the position that it is very necessary for Indians to be permitted to organize, to organize for many different purposes. It is necessary for Indians to be allowed to organize to do business in a modern business world in competition with the modern white world. In the world at large, the white world, the unorganized people are powerless. They are victims. Only organized groups have power in the white world … You can't govern yourselves, you can't do business, you can't protect yourself,

> unless you organize. That is true regarding everybody in the United States.[1]

This stance represented a new turn in American Indian policy. It addressed the numerous grievances brought about during the previous decades, in what would be become known as the Dawes Era (1887–1934).[2] Beginning with the General Allotment, or Dawes Act – after its sponsor Henry Dawes, senator and chair of the Indian Affairs committee – this period of history saw a progression of aggressive assimilationist strategies intended to complete the colonial conquest of Indigenous people living within the United States. This strategy rested on two principal notions: one, Indigenous nations were "vanishing," and two, Indigenous resources were part of the "public domain."[3] In general, the Act authorized the acquisition of millions of acres of treaty lands and sent Indigenous children to boarding schools to "civilize" them. Dawes justified the act by saying it was "the only way … to lead [the Indian] out into the sunshine, and tell him what the sunshine is for, and what the rain comes for, and when to put his seed in the ground … The idea is to make something of him, to make a man of him."[4]

The We^{n}dat/Wa^{n}dat were no exception to these policies, as their property was privatized and their children exposed to Western schooling. Those living in Kansas, such as the Conley family, continued to fight for federal recognition and preservation of sacred sights. Wyandottes living on the Oklahoma reservation, however, faced a harsh reality: their attempt to maintain sovereignty and treaty rights by relocating to Indian Territory in 1867 had failed. Under the Allotment Act, the US government surveyed reservation lands, divided them up, and assigned 160 acres to each head of family. Between 1889 and 1893, the US government purchased fifteen million acres of land in what would become the state of Oklahoma.[5] Unassigned lands were advertised to settlers for sale, resulting in a mass influx of eager homesteaders in what would become known as the "Oklahoma Run." In 1907, Indian Territory ceased to exist and was replaced with the state of Oklahoma.[6] In 1924, the US government imposed citizenship on Indigenous Americans (Indian Citizenship Act) and continued the process of allotment until 1934.[7]

John Collier's 1934 declaration of an "Indian New Deal," with an emphasis on supporting Indigenous organization and rights, therefore marks a change in strategy in Indian Affairs and a culmination of decades of activism on the part of both Indigenous and non-Indigenous people.[8] Settler groups, such as the Boston Indian Citizenship Association, the Women's National Indian Association, and the Indian Rights Association of the 1880s, for instance, urged the government to reject assimilation and allotment.[9] Later, in the 1920s, Collier himself established a Washington-based lobby group, known as the Indian Defense Association, to further these initiatives.

Similar activism grew from Indian Country. Ironically, one of the results of the Dawes Act was a generation of boarding school graduates who had mastered colonial systems of knowledge, including mainstream politics and activism. Simultaneously, boarding school students felt the personal attacks on their communities through land appropriation and cultural genocide. As a result, people like the acclaimed literary reformers Christine Quintasket (Okanagan) and Ella Cara Deloria (Yankton Dakota) drew on a combination of their schooling and traditional knowledge to promote Indigenous causes through their respective books *Cogewea* (1927) and *Waterlily* (written in the 1940s and published in 1988).[10] *Cogewea* was one of the first novels written by an Indigenous woman. It takes place on the Flathead Indian Reservation and explores the injustices caused by the Dawes Act.[11] Deloria's novel *Waterlily*, on the other hand, combines the author's vast collection of Indigenous oral histories to bring awareness to the vitality and importance of Dakota culture.[12] Together, the books contributed to a cohort of Indigenous women activist writers that included, among others, Lucy Hunter (Winnebago), Evelyn Pierce (Seneca), Elvira Pike (Uintah Ute), Angel DeCora (Winnebago), and Laura Cornelius Kellog (Oneida).

Scholars have taken note that the work of these early-nineteenth-century Indigenous women activists aimed to "keep in play a dialectic between integration and separatism, cultural adaptation and preservation" in order to change federal policies towards Indigenous people.[13] In addition, these writers had a particular interest in the lives of Indigenous women. Reflecting on the circumstances Indigenous women faced, Ella Deloria wrote,

> The Indian girl of today lives in a very different environment from that of her great-grandmother. Since the allotment of land

> in severalty the chances are that the girl lives with her parents on their allotment away from any other people. The rest of the tribe are also scattered, each family on its own allotment, missing the old environment and companionship of the community life and lacking the education and training for appreciating and using the new to advantage ... the girl of today is baffled and confused, and is struggling, consciously or unconsciously, to find her rightful place in the new scheme of things [ellipsis in original].[14]

We^{n}dat/Wa^{n}dat women experienced similar circumstances and made important contributions to this movement as well. Jane Zane Gordon (Wyandotte Nation), for instance, published *The Hollywood Story 7* (1948). The short novel traces the story of Eagle Feather, who visits Jane and describes his struggles since leaving Indian Country for the "white man's cities."[15] Although the character Eagle Feather is likely fictional, the content serves to highlight the very real plight of many Indigenous people. In the foreword, Jane writes, "Further, these secrets herein are old as time. Who first propounded them I do not know, hence I cannot give them the proper credit, I should like to. I hold that this book is worth $1.00 to some people, to another perhaps $25.00 and to others a fortune."[16] In other words, the information was invaluable depending on the audience. The book was sponsored by American Indian Unity, Inc., an entity that no longer exists but was likely another organization created to support Indigenous rights.

Current scholarship suggests that Jane was a minority voice in the Dawes Era critique, differentiating herself from Indigenous activists like Quintasket and Deloria who supported mainstream education, citizenship, and the dismantling of the reservation system. Instead, they argue, Jane opposed integration and citizenship altogether. This is mostly based off a 1924 article published in *Indian Tepee* in which Jane proclaimed that "the Federal Government assumes to control all that its citizens may eat, drink, or wear, where he shall go, and what he shall do. The Indian does not want the shell of a nut."[17] Yet, with further investigation, a more nuanced character comes to light.[18] Rather than calling for a complete rejection of American mainstream society, Jane situated herself as an American, with the same goals and aspirations as other Americans. She described her position in an interview with the *Boston*

Sunday Post in 1921, saying, "I know that some of my people have grown soft and lazy, but I think they are not the only ones. And I, too, am an American. The American doesn't stand by idly and theorize and complain when things go wrong. They've got to be changed. A lot of things have got to be clean forgotten and wiped off the slate to make way for the new happiness and the new understanding."[19]

Jane Zane Gordon's life story reflects her 1921 remarks. In addition to publishing *The Hollywood Story 7*, Jane maintained an impressive track record of motherwork connected by a consistent goal to unite Indigenous peoples and communities across the United States. This chapter outlines her national work through public talks and the creation of organizations like the Indian Memorial Film Company and the National Arts Foundation, as well as her momentous meeting with President Warren Harding in 1922. Together, Jane's actions historicize Collier's call to organize in 1934, situating it as an extension of earlier initiatives by people like Jane Zane Gordon.

FAMILY

Jane Zane Wallace Waters Gordon (Who-Shon-No/As the Deer Runs) was born on 14 May 1871. Her parents, Hannah Coon Whitewing Zane and Alexander (Zenophan) Zane, married in 1869.[20] Hannah and Alexander each had children from previous marriages: Mary Whitewing Kelly (Hannah's daughter) and Kate Zane (Alexander's daughter).[21] Hannah Coon came from a long line of We^{n}dat/Wa^{n}dat activists and was a member of the Deer Clan, making her daughters also Deer Clan. Sadly, Hannah and Jane's relationship was cut short, as Hannah passed away when Jane was around four years old.[22] Still, we see glimpses of this We^{n}dat/Wa^{n}dat woman in the historical records. In 1862, for instance, we find Hannah Coon's "mark" in a petition to the US Congress to honour the 1850 treaty with the We^{n}dat/Wa^{n}dat and make appropriate payments to them in compensation for the sale of their land and Indigenous status.[23] The petition concludes: "Your petitioners desire to say that their tribe has been, not only at peace, but in amity, with the United States … Your petitioners think that, in all human probability, this will be the last time they, as members of the late Wyandott nation, will address your honourable body as such … in asking for a final settlement and closing up of all business transactions – in short, a final balancing of the books."[24] Hannah's involvement in the petition highlights her engagement with Wyandotte community politics and her public support to hold the US government accountable for its historic neglect to honour Wyandotte treaties – an activist agenda that Jane would continue after her mother's death.

Jane's father, Alexander Zane, was also a member of the Wyandotte Nation. He had lived in Ohio, Kansas, and Oklahoma. Alexander Zane's parents were Noah E. Zane and Jane S. Long. The Zane family had a long history of prominence among the We^{n}dat/Wa^{n}dat; Alexander's ancestors included Isaac Zane and his wife Myreeh, the daughter of nineteenth-century Chief Tarhe, Grand Chief of the We^{n}dat/Wa^{n}dat.[25] The complicated circumstances of multiple marriages and orphaned children, as well as colonial policies that disadvantaged Indigenous people, shaped Alexander's relationship with his daughter Jane in important ways. They were never close, in part because Alexander coped poorly with his situation by self-medicating with alcohol, which led to violent outbursts and erratic behaviour.[26] The fragility of the relationship came to a head in 1895 on the Wyandotte Reservation. Jane and her first husband, Jerry C. Wallace, had a property neighbouring on Alexander's where they had lived for four years. Twenty-two acres of the allotment were under cultivation at the time, and although not of great monetary value, the area had historical and political significance as one of the 241 allotments guaranteed to the Wyandottes after the removal to Oklahoma.[27]

Over the years, father and daughter had argued about the boundary line between the two properties. On 7 March 1895, with no resolution in sight, Alexander decided to take action, entering Jane's property while Jerry was ploughing the field. What followed was a disastrous encounter with lethal consequences, summarized in a subsequent US Supreme Court case: "While W. [Jerry] was ploughing his land, Z. [Alexander], being then under the influence of liquor, entered upon the disputed tract and brought a quantity of posts there, for the purpose of erecting a fence on the line which he claimed. W. ordered him off, and continued his ploughing … and W. … unhitched his horses and put them in the barn. In about half an hour he returned with a gun, and an altercation ensued, in the course of which W. was stabbed by a son of Z. and Z. was killed by a shot from W.'s gun."[28] Jerry was charged with murder, but appealed successfully on the grounds of self-defence. Jane witnessed the events and tried to intervene on Jerry's behalf, asking her father to leave the property and warning Jerry of the impending attack. Jerry testified that Alexander Zane had grabbed him and yelled, "Damn you, I will kill you." This was followed by Jane yelling, "Look out, Jerry." He then admitted, "I fired this gun."[29]

While the court deemed Jerry Wallace innocent, the trauma of the ordeal left Jane unable to cope with her marriage. Jerry and Jane had a son, Everett, who was only two at the time of Alexander's death and Jerry's trial. Perhaps it was Everett's future, along with her own need to escape, that led Jane to divorce Jerry. She subsequently rented her controversial property, and left the Wyandotte Reservation.[30]

There is little else known about Jane's relationship to her immediate family. Not long after her departure from the reservation, Jane was asked if she supported her "family in as good shape as [her] neighbor?" She replied, "Yes, and lots better."[31] Yet, in later years, she referred minimally to her relatives, choosing to focus more on her connections to wider Indigenous networks and broader historical kinship ties among the We^{n}dat/Wa^{n}dat diaspora. Although the reasons behind her dissociation cannot be known for certain, the death of her mother at an early age and the violent nature of her relationship with her father help contextualize this reality to some extent. Jane's definition of family extended beyond reservations and bloodlines, incorporating Indigenous relatives across the United States instead.

COMMUNITY

Although the altercation between her father and husband in 1895 prompted Jane to move away from the Wyandotte Reservation, it was not the first time she had left home; in fact, her connections to people and places outside her home community had begun early in life. Jane was born on the Wyandotte Reservation, located near Wyandotte, Oklahoma. The We^{n}dat/Wa^{n}dat moved to the area in 1867.[32] There, they acquired a reservation of 20,000 acres. By 1893, there were 241 land allotments associated with the Wyandotte tribe. By 1911, the population was approximately 250 individuals.[33] Although the Wyandotte Nation and Oklahoma territory remained close to Jane's heart, she spent most of her life living elsewhere. Her formative years, for instance, were spent living in boarding schools. In light of her mother's early death, as well as Dawes Era policies that forced Indigenous children to attend Western-style schools, Jane attended both the Seneca Indian School and Haskell Institute.[34] Despite the intention of the schools to "civilize" their students by separating them from their home communities and families, they ironically and simultaneously fostered deep bonds among the children that served to cultivate a community of Indigenous activists familiar with colonial systems and ways to confront them.

Jane first attended the Seneca Indian School at the age of four, after her mother's death. The school was established in 1872 by Quakers near the Wyandotte Reservation for the purpose of delivering Western education to Wyandotte, Seneca, and Shawnee children.[35] Jane's circumstances as an orphaned student were not unique to the Seneca School, as many students found themselves in similar situations. School records indicate that by 1910, 70 out of 132 students were orphans.[36] Typical days included five hours of academic study. In addition, four hours were spent doing gender-specific tasks as defined by the school. Boys worked the gardens and fields and girls completed domestic tasks such as laundry, cooking, and sewing.[37] The academic success of the Seneca Indian School remains unclear, but an 1886 annual report from the Bureau of Indian Affairs documented that the graduating class of 1885 had a number of students continue their studies at institutes for higher learning, including five who went to the Haskell Institute.[38]

The Haskell Institute, located near Lawrence, Kansas and in close proximity to the Wyandot Nation of Kansas, opened in 1884 under the name the "United States Indian Industrial Training School."[39] Its student body consisted of predominantly Shawnee children, but included We^{n}dat/Wa^{n}dat and other Indigenous students as well. The first enrollment was twenty-two students, but the number increased to 400 within one year.[40] Much like the Seneca Indian School, boys spent time dedicated to activities such as tailoring, wagon-making, blacksmithing, harness-making, painting, shoemaking, and farming. Girls studied cooking, sewing, and homemaking.[41] In 1894, the school expanded beyond elementary students in response to growing demands for the training of Indigenous teachers who could return to their communities and educate from within. At the same time, Haskell acquired five typewriters, and initiated the first "touch-typing" class in Kansas.[42]

Life within the schoolhouse was a series of varied experiences for the students. Indeed, the circumstances within Seneca and Haskell reflect what one scholar describes as falling "somewhere between the depiction of boarding schools as irredeemably destructive institutions and [the] sentiment that [the boarding school] 'really was a marvelous school.'"[43] This seemingly contradictory situation, where lives were "severely regimented in many ways, astonishingly free in others" is reinforced by Jane's story.[44]

In 1874, the Wyandotte Nation established a committee to inspect the Seneca School. Reports demonstrated considerable levels of neglect. The committee blamed the teachers for keeping the children dirty and unkempt. As a result, many Seneca and Shawnee parents refused to send their children back to the school.[45] In addition, sickness was a chronic problem. In 1884, for instance, measles claimed the lives of three students.[46] Similar circumstances existed at Haskell. Records indicate numerous cases of sickness, compounded by long days of manual labour and malnutrition. In some cases, students died due to the extreme circumstances.[47] This said, the Western-style education provided a means for Indigenous students to learn colonial traditions and familiarize themselves with writing, reading, and European knowledge systems. This may explain the persistent requests by students and their families to attend. Haskell, for example, required applications that were rigorously reviewed and only a select number were admitted.[48]

Community was a vital source of survival for boarding school students like Jane. Students from various Indigenous Nations gathered together through their common experience of Western schooling, while often retaining Indigenous perspectives. Records indicate that Jane embraced the teachings, yet she did not hesitate to resist and reform the environment in which they were delivered. As an adult, Jane recalled her experience, stating that they "were a bunch of little abused and annoyed Indian girls."[49] Jane's dislike for the boarding schools was so strong that at the age of seven she led a revolt, heading a group of younger girls to burn down the schoolhouse. In an interview with the *Boston Sunday Post*, Jane disclosed details of the events. She remembered that they began planning the resistance when they "held a regular old-fashioned council of war." She turned to the girls and said, "'Look here. I've got a plan. We won't have to go to school any more. We'll burn up the school house.'" She told the reporter, "And we did. And we danced a regular war-dance about the fire."[50]

This kind of collective behaviour created a bond between students. A universal experience forged in response to a common enemy allowed for the students to form unique strategies of resistance, based on like-minded goals that related to their status as Indigenous people living within the US colonial state. The Dawes Era evoked a need to unify despite differences between homelands and Indigenous nations. It is this sense of national community that would inform Jane's future motherwork.

MOTHERWORK

As a graduate from the Seneca Indian School and Haskell, Jane possessed a keen knowledge of colonial society – a skill that she put to good use in a number of different ways in order to improve the situation for Indigenous peoples across the Unites States. She did this through numerous public talks and interviews, the creation of organizations like the Indian Memorial Film Company and the National Arts Foundation, and her momentous meeting with President Warren Harding in 1923.

Jane had a talent for public oratory and the written word. She used this to her advantage as a means of spreading her message to mainstream audiences. Throughout the 1920s, Jane spent energy educating the public on the history of the We^{n}dat/Wa^{n}dat, as well as the cultural and political assault on Indigenous peoples across the USA. She gave talks in a number of different forums, including the Los Angeles District Conservation Federated Club, the Annual Convention for the Society of American Indians, and a synagogue in California. She also wrote editorials in the *New York Times* and conducted numerous interviews with local and national newspapers like the *Daily Reporter* (Indiana), the *Los Angeles Times*, the *St. Louis Star*, the *Boston Sunday Post*, and the *Dearborn Independent*. Consistent in these public forums are three key messages. First, Indigenous people have sophisticated societies that are connected by universal attachments to Turtle Island. Second, Indigenous people can be proud Americans while also preserving their Indigenous heritage and culture. Finally, many Indigenous people, including the We^{n}dat/

Wa^{n}dat, supported women's rights through matricentric system of governance and social order before European contact.

Jane's advocacy included a call for increased employment of her Indigenous kin, as well as a return to Indigenous relationships with the land. In one talk, she outlined a plan to address the inequalities resulting from colonial administrations, providing the following solution:

> The government of the United States appropriate $15,000,000 per year for the reforestation of the denuded hills and mountains of the country … and that Indians be employed and paid from the appropriation. Tremendous results would be immediately apparent … he would be put at a task which would meet with a deep response in his heart. The Indian is the natural-born child of forests. He loves forests naturally. He is happy in a forest. And nothing would so gladden him as to re-create forests – make a new forest grow in a place where an ancient forest had been destroyed.[51]

Jane furthered her proposed project a year later during an interview with the *Daily Reporter*. She explained that "the encroachments of agriculture, the consumption of lumber and ravages of fire have reduced this area [the United States] to, approximately 137,000,000 acres of timber … A natural willing agent in the task of preserving the forests may be found in the Indian, who might be employed by the nation, the state and the private owner of the land in the great work of reforestation."[52]

While Jane's universal "pan-Indianism" of Indigenous people might seem problematic, the fight for Indigenous rights and survival was widespread as a result of the implementation of federally regulated policies. This call by Jane – one that drew on ancient Indigenous connections to the land, as well as a romanticized view of Indigenous conservation – can be seen as a strategic move, reinforcing the popular romanticized view of Indigenous conservation, while countering other myths that perpetuated notions of laziness and dependency.

Issues concerning Indigenous women continued to be a main focus for Jane. She made a point in her *New York Times* editorial to discuss the exploitation of Osage women by white men in their quest for oil resources and money.[53] Further, she explained in an interview with the *St. Louis Star* that among the We^{n}dat/Wa^{n}dat and other Iroquoian tribes, "the officers of the council were nominated by women, who were believed to be better informed and best fitted to determine who should govern the tribes … Indians granted suffrage to their women because they believed the women were entitled to equal rights."[54] It was, as she later stated as a delegate to the annual meeting of the Society of American Indians, "Indians, long before the advent of the white men to America, [who] had a league of nations and allowed suffrage to women."[55]

Beyond talks and interviews, Jane Zane Gordon's growing notoriety allowed for alternative forms of disseminating and educating the public about Indigenous people and their struggles within the United States. She applied her skill and popularity as an artist to establish the Indian Memorial Film Company (IMFC), of which she was the director and treasurer. In addition, she wrote and intended to produce *The First American*, a film that explained the ancient traditions of Indigenous people. Jane described the film in the following way: "I wrote out my story. Don't think it's a story of an ancient grudge or foolish pretence that every Indian is an angel and every white man a devil. Far from it. That wouldn't be the truth."[56] Significantly, the cast was going to be strictly Indigenous actors – a goal never yet achieved on the silver screen at that time.[57]

The context in which the idea behind the film was formed was as important as the film itself. Jane explained that

> one day we passed a moving picture theatre in which one of the regular Wild West cowboy and Indian pictures were on display, and outside the door … was a white man in a ridiculous costume which no real Indian who ever lived would put on his back, jumping about and yelling imitation war whoops and so on to attract attention to the show. When I saw that, my blood simply boiled. I said to myself, "I'm going to do all the Great Spirit will let me to stop this. And I'm doing it. Don't forget I'm a Huron, and we've been outnumbered, but never beaten."[58]

The main goals of the film aligned with her other motherwork. She said, "What I'm trying to do is to show the real spirit of the Indian, the nobility of his ideals, before they were sullied by Western civilization, and to recall to the Indians, themselves, their spiritual birthright and their duty in the nation of which they are now to become citizens."[59]

Her message was both to the mainstream public as well as Indigenous communities. "The idea is this," she said. "You, survivors of a vanishing race, are in the melting pot of this great nation. Hold fast to your ancestral greatness, to honor, to generosity, bury resentment and fear. Know that the truer you are to yourselves, the more certain you will be to retain your birthright and add to the strength and the purity of the metal that shall come from the fire."[60]

The American Indian Arts and Crafts Foundation (AIACF) was another of Jane's initiatives. This Washington-based national organization was established in 1921 as a way "to help Indians help themselves."[61] The foundation set a goal of establishing small centres on, or near, reservations in order to preserve traditional artistic practices among Indigenous Nations, as well as support modern forms of commercialization.[62] The centres were Jane's true "dream." It was there that Indigenous people could "learn how to do any kind of art work they wish, while contributing to the community to earn their keep."[63] In addition, the foundation had plans to create a larger "central arts center." This building, according to Jane, would "be the storehouse for all our designs" where, she continued, "we shall have examples of all work being done on the other reservations. It will be a storehouse for goods … it will be our clearing house … it will be a 'Friendly Tipi' or meeting place for Indians and will be used for obtaining employment for Indians, both men and women, and to encourage Indians to preserve their own arts and crafts."[64]

Speaking about the impetus for the foundation, Jane explained that "the Indian has not had much of a chance here in his own native land. While we are calling for justice on behalf of all peoples of the ends of the earth, may we not stop to think about justice at home?"[65] Bureau of Indian Affairs commissioner and foundation chairman Charles H. Burke congratulated Jane's involvement in this "movement" and the establishment of the AIACF. He described her as a "capable and bright Indian woman" with "scientific and businesslike plans … all directed toward helping Indians become self-supporting."[66] The foundation gained administrative and financial support from the country's "big people," including senators, activists, writers, professors, ethnographers, and financiers.[67] Jane estimated that there had been a total of five million dollars raised from "friends of the Indians" in order to support the foundation.[68]

Jane gained an audience with President Warren Harding in 1922 as a result of her widespread popularity and in direct recognition of her work with the IMFC and AIACF and her proposed film, *The First American*.[69] Pictured in newspapers across the country, Jane and President Harding posed for journalists as they descended the White House staircase.[70] The discussions that ensued are left to the imagination, but it is likely that Jane took the opportunity to further her advocacy for the preservation of Indigenous culture by educating Harding in the same consistent way she had educated the public and other politicians for decades. This would be the first and last meeting of the two, as President Harding died the following year.[71]

Overall, Jane's motherwork attempted to meet her goal of seeing "the Indians taken out of politics, their freedom protected, property rights given to them, and an opportunity afforded them to go into business as the white man does and learn to take care of themselves. What other races have done, the Indians can do."[72] Jane tried to gain support from the general public by calling attention to the fact that she was not only an "Indian," but also an American: "And now I'll appeal to you, if I can," she said, "I'll talk to you, not as an Indian, but as an American whose very creed is personal liberty and freedom."[73] Still, she remained rooted in her We^{n}dat/Wa^{n}dat heritage. "I feel I'm Indian. I am Huron." she explained in an interview. "We're outnumbered, but never beaten. The Great Spirit still cares for us. He understands. I cannot fail in what I am doing, for he is always helping me. Nothing can get in my way."[74]

At the heart of Jane's motherwork was her desire to help Indigenous women as a way to sustain Indigenous culture. "I want to see something done for the Indian women … They are the mothers of future generations," she said, "and it is in them that the traditions of the race, the artistic ability, the memory of things that are great and gone, are preserved."[75]

LEGACY

In 1923, one year after Jane's meeting with President Harding and before his death, the Harding administration formed the "Committee of One Hundred," an organization where "concerned and influential citizens" informed the president on "Indian matters" and made recommendations to Indian Affairs. The group comprised "activists and celebrities."[76]

A decade later, in 1934, Congress passed the Indian Reorganization Act to address the status of Native Americans in the United States. Often referred to as the "Indian New Deal," the main purpose was to reverse the previous attempts at assimilation that had been the focus of the Dawes Era. In addition, the act looked to support and strengthen Indigenous communities, along with their culture and traditions.[77] In 1935, in accordance with this legislation, the Department of the Interior created a new agency, the Indian Arts and Crafts Board (IACB), to "promote the economic development of federally recognized American Indians and Alaska Natives through the expansion of the Indian arts and crafts market." In addition, the IACB provides "business advice, information on the [Indian Arts and Crafts] Act and … promotional opportunities to Native American artists, craftspeople, and cultural organizations of federally recognized tribes."[78]

Although historical records leave little evidence of a direct connection between the activism of Jane Zane Gordon and the establishment of the Committee of One Hundred or the IACB, the shift in policy and the creation of these nationally focused organizations provide proof that the lobbying by Jane and other "activists and celebrities" made a difference. In particular, the motivations behind the IACB and its goals align to address the main concerns highlighted by Jane's writings, film, and organizations. Further, the national, pan-Indigenous nature of the IACB would have resonated with Jane, as she advocated for solidarity across the United States and among the various Indigenous nations.[79]

Similar developments came decades later in Wyandotte Country. In 2016, the Wyandotte Nation (Oklahoma) opened its very own cultural centre. The building consists of 7,625 square feet and includes a museum, classrooms, a multipurpose room, a gift shop, and tribal heritage department offices. The centre also features an eternal flame, a symbolic reminder of the role Wyandottes played as the keepers of the Council Fire. Programming for the centre includes a variety of activities including language and art classes. The centre also hosts the annual Gathering, where Wyandottes meet to "connect and learn more about their culture, traditions, language and history."[80] Speaking about the significance of the centre, Chief Billy Friend said:

> We know this is something that is not only going to benefit our generation, but generations to come … We as Wyandotte people,

> because of our forced removal … like many other tribes we lost a lot of our culture, our traditions and our ceremonies. They were not dead, but had laid dormant for many years. Many of us grew up not knowing what it meant to be Wyandotte. So many of us did not have the benefit that our children and our grandchildren are going to have today – learning what it is to be Wyandotte and knowing what that actually means, knowing their identity, knowing where they came from, knowing their family, and knowing their ancestors … This was something we always wanted … We wanted a place that we could bring our children, we could bring our grandchildren, and teach them our traditions, our customs, teach them our language, so that in seven generations to come these things will still be taught. These things will still be carried forward.[81]

The centre also houses tribal artifacts. Of particular note within their collection is a buckskin dress that belonged to Jane Zane Gordon. Jane wore the dress when she met President Harding in 1922. The dress was passed down to Wyandotte member Mary Jane Gallaspy for safekeeping after Jane's death. Gallaspy preserved the dress and used it occasionally when she visited local schools to instruct the children about her We^{n}dat/Wa^{n}dat heritage. Gallaspy passed away in 2005 and her family donated the dress to the Wyandotte Nation.

Sallie Cotter Andrews, a member of the Wyandotte Cultural Committee, explained the importance of artifacts such as the buckskin dress during the Wyandotte Culture Days. A team of Wyandottes spent years compiling the histories behind the museum acquisitions and before allowing the public to view the exhibit, Andrews took a few minutes to explain the process:

> I want to emphasize that these stories were not "gone" – they were all out there – in files, books, newspaper articles, at people's homes, in memories and on the internet. We just had to find them. The artifacts were not "gone" – we knew where they were, which was more than we knew about the stories. Yet – to me – this project was like a brand new big jig-saw puzzle with lots of pieces inside the box. As we found the stories and put them

> together with the artifacts, like puzzle pieces – we found little notches and indentations that connected to other pieces and groups of pieces. Soon, we had complete photographs of individuals and a sense of their personalities – and as we put them all together – we built a picture of our people and nations at a moment in time. There were some things that our "completed" puzzle told us – we went through years when there were many orphaned children, we had many very young single mothers, alcoholism and health issues were prevalent – but there was also a love of beauty, artistry, innovation in objects of utility, and we were a people of good reputation and hard work.[82]

Although her words were meant to be a general overview of the Wyandotte experience, it is also reflective of Jane Zane Gordon's life. Despite her mother's death, difficult boarding school experiences, an abusive father, and distance from her home community, Jane maintained a dedicated quest to protect and preserve Indigenous culture. Certainly, she retained a We^{n}dat/Wa^{n}dat "love of beauty, artistry, [and] innovation in objects of utility," drawing from "a people of good reputation and hard work." Her motherwork reflected this dedication, and her public talks and interviews, and the IMFC and AIACF, are testaments to this.

CHAPTER 7

Dr Éléonore Sioui (1924–2006)

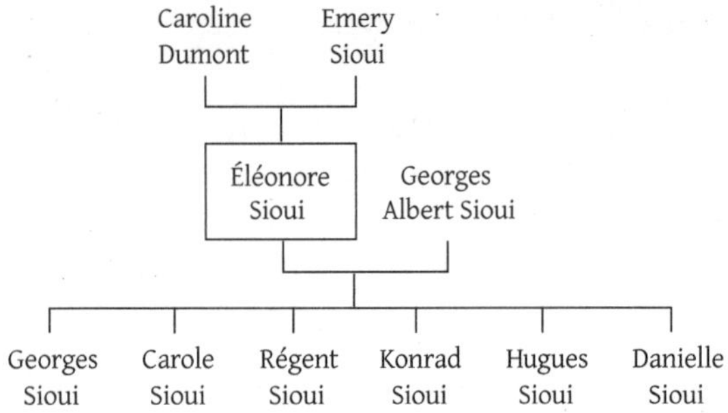

INTRODUCTION

"If only she were a boy," the future We^{n}dat/Wa^{n}dat Chief Emery Sioui proclaimed as he held his firstborn, a baby girl.[1] The year was 1924 and the eastern We^{n}dat/Wa^{n}dat world was in flux. Éléonore Sioui was delivered into a complex settler society infused with centuries of conflicting colonial policies. Indeed, it was only four years earlier that the deputy superintendent general of Indian Affairs, Duncan Campbell Scott, had infamously proclaimed, "Our object is to continue until there is not a single Indian in Canada that has not been absorbed into the body politic, and there is no Indian question and no Indian Department."[2] The major piece of legislation guiding Canadian federal relations with First Nations, the Indian Act (1876), reinforced Scott's declaration, promoting an imperial patriarchal system that disregarded We^{n}dat/Wa^{n}dat traditions of matriarchy and matrilineality. This policy swept across the

Canadian nation-state, transcending provincial borders and informing mainstream society's attitudes toward Indigenous peoples.

Although the 1920s, with Scott's declaration, seemed to suggest a new wave of racist and sexist objectives, the national policies remained consistent with the historical process of colonization and imperial rule in North America that Sioui's We^{n}dat/Wa^{n}dat sisters (the other case studies in this book) experienced before her. Sioui's life is a reflection of this long history and provides a window into twentieth-century Indigenous social movements, such as the political activism of the 1970s, the quest for higher education in the 1980s, and the efforts to harmonize Indigenous international rights in the 1990s. Similar to Jane Zane Gordon's *national* initiatives, Éléonore's participation in these *international* movements demonstrates an example of motherwork that went beyond We^{n}dat/Wa^{n}dat local communities, extending into greater global initiatives.

Since World War II and the 1960s, there has been a growing movement toward a globalization for social justice of Indigenous people. This so-called "indigenous peoples' project" has framed the movement with "a new agenda for Indigenous activity … that goes beyond the decolonization aspirations of a particular indigenous community towards the development of global indigenous strategic alliances."[3] This new wave of activism connects Indigenous people who "developed a shared international language or discourse which enables indigenous activists to talk to each other across their cultural differences while maintaining and taking their directions from their own communities or nations."[4]

Éléonore Sioui witnessed the ongoing marginalization of Indigenous Peoples at home and abroad, motivating her toward a lifetime dedicated to combating these policies and empowering Indigenous women like herself. Scholars have paid particular attention to the ways in which Indigenous women, like Sioui, have differentiated themselves from mainstream feminist movements, drawing first from pre-colonial mother-centred notions of responsibilities and then focusing on regaining their status and rights within colonial society.[5] Historically, this kind of Indigenous feminist activism relied heavily on Indigenous notions of womanhood rather than settler-defined ones.[6] This chapter uses Sioui's life story to deliver important insights into these trends, revealing ways in which Indigenous women used colonial systems of education in collaboration with traditional knowledge to successfully navigate the colonial world and engage in transnational movements of decolonization, thus empowering themselves. Put another way, motherwork, when studied in relationship to so-called "global indigenism,"[7] is focused on the restoration of mother-centred values to local, national, and international families and communities.

FAMILY

Éléonore Sioui was born into a historically significant and well-known eastern We^{n}dat/Wa^{n}dat family, the first daughter of Caroline Dumont and Emery Sioui. The Sioui people (aka Seawi or Tseawi) first appear in the written record in the 1690s, amidst geopolitical negotiations between the We^{n}dat/Wa^{n}dat, the Haudenausaunee, and the French over the seventeenth-century North American landscape. Perhaps most famous is the belief that the We^{n}dat/Wa^{n}dat leader and architect of the Great Peace of Montreal of 1701, Kondioronk, was a "seawi:aga."[8] Other important figures came from the Sioui family as well, including Jules Sioui, founder of the twentieth-century North American Indian Nation Government.[9] The Dumont family had similar fame attached to their name. In particular was their connection to Gabriel Dumont, the Métis leader and comrade-in-arms of Louis Riel.[10]

Éléonore's parents were both We^{n}dat/Wa^{n}dat and followed the traditional teachings of their ancestors. Emery Sioui was the son of a long line of We^{n}dat/Wa^{n}dat leaders and was the last hereditary Chief of the We^{n}dat/Wa^{n}dat of the Forty Arpents.[11] Emery Sioui was given a seat at the Lorette Council from 1935 to 1938, making him one of a number of Council Chiefs. Throughout his brief life, Chief Sioui strove to support his growing family. He established himself as a well-respected hunter and guide and built a successful fur-ranching business, which only failed after World War II and the rapid decline in luxury markets. Caroline also contributed to the household and held a respected reputation of her own. She was not only Emery's business associate, but also a celebrated artisan. In addition, Caroline was the daughter of Éléonore Rosalie Gros-Louis, a famous medicine woman. Queen Victoria called her "Butterfly," a token of admiration for her fine moose-hair embroidery.[12] These teachings were passed down to Caroline, who became a skilful healer and midwife in the community. Finally, spiritual life had an important role to play in the Sioui family and dominated much of Éléonore's childhood. Caroline and Emery were devoted Catholics and brought their children to the local parish of Saint-Gérard Majella. Recalling her parents' devotion to the Christian community, Éléonore described her family as very "religious and Catholic," never missing a single church service.[13]

Education was another aspect of central importance to the Sioui household. Although the Sioui family spoke French at home, Caroline learned English at an early age as her family spent considerable time in Ontario during the winter months, returning to the reserve in the summer.[14] Emery, on the other hand, took it upon himself later in life to learn the language for trade and tourism. It wasn't until he was in his forties that he successfully taught himself to read and write in English. Education was seen as a skill set that could lead to social and economic mobility, a message that was passed down to their children.[15] From the territorial boundaries of the reserves, to francophone Catholic Québécois settler society, to the Canadian nation-state and Anglophone markets, Caroline and Emery exposed their children, including the young Éléonore, to a transnational and transcultural existence.

In 1946, Éléonore expanded her kinship network by marrying Georges Albert Sioui. Georges lived most of his life at Jeune Lorette and was recognized as a "good Reserve Indian," abiding by the laws and boundaries contrived by the church and state.[16] Éléonore's decision to marry within the community did not go without criticism; some considered her marriage a risky engagement that could lead to economic and social suicide. Certainly, things were not easy for Éléonore's young family, as they struggled to make ends meet from Georges's traditional trapping and guiding career. This became even harder as their family grew to include seven children. Many years later, their eldest son would remember overhearing his mother's friends commenting on her situation, "You should have done like us and married a White guy. Now look how you are!"[17]

The influence of oppressive and often ruthless racist policies had lasting effects on many Indigenous peoples. Georges felt these implications, as many We^{n}dat/Wa^{n}dat did, eventually turning to alcohol to soothe the wounds of his personal and communal historic trauma. The struggle was too much for Éléonore and eventually pushed her to leave Georges, taking the children with her.[18] Georges died in 1984, two decades before Éléonore in 2006. Éléonore was survived by her seven children and twenty-one grandchildren, a kinship network that "[ordered] the peace of mind" and served as the source of "real happiness."[19]

Family undoubtedly shaped Éléonore Sioui's activism and motherwork. She stated, "I learned very early that we would only get what we fought for … I learned this more from attitudes of my family and my People than from any systematic analysis."[20] Her parents and children, in particular, inspired her. Emery's leadership within the community informed his daughter's sense of traditional We^{n}dat/Wa^{n}dat responsibilities and activism, while the recognition her mother earned for her in-depth knowledge of healing practices and ceremonies served as a model for spiritual leadership. Reflecting on her experiences, Sioui stated, "I am proud to say that my main educational background was acquired through my constant contact with my family. Since I was very young I was following my father and mother, aunts and grandparents speaking of their experiences."[21] Beginning with her grandmother (Éléonore Sr) and her mother (Caroline), Éléonore received extensive training in We^{n}dat/Wa^{n}dat healing practices. This included knowledge about medicinal plants and ceremonies – information that was passed down through the oral traditions of her ancestors.[22]

In addition to these familial forms of inspiration, Éléonore located her activism beyond individuals she knew and looked to a broader Indigenous family of notable historical figures to inform her motherwork. Perhaps the most influential role model for Sioui was the late-seventeenth-century Shawnee leader Tecumseh. Originally drawn to Tecumseh because of his efforts to unite Indigenous peoples and fight the North American colonial regimes, Sioui's affection grew further when she discovered his overt respect for women.[23] Highlighting his support for mothercentred societies, Éléonore published an excerpt from a nineteenth-century play about the Shawnee leader, entitled *Tecumseh and the Prophet of the West*.[24] The passage reads:

> O! love of Country! Passion of the Soul!
> Inherent in the human mind and heart, –
> Implanted by our Mother's sacred tones,
> As points she to the hearth of love and hope!

It does not claim the city only, or the wild;
It emanates from love Maternal here,
And rises from that Parent to our God![25]

The speaker's emphasis on maternal love and respect attracted Sioui the most. In her editorial comments, she explains the significance further. "The affection of Tecumseh for the memory of his maternal parent amounted to the filial adoration: what other proof is required of the noble heart of Tecumseh? The memory of a mother. I have ever hesitated to form even an acquaintance with a man who should speak harshly of women," she writes, "but I have with alacrity endeavored to secure the friendship of that man who should view a mother with faithful affection for I have felt convinced that that friendship should be lasting and I have never been deceived."[26] For Éléonore, the credibility of Tecumseh, as well as his quest to unite the western tribes against the Americans in the War of 1812 and negotiate with the British colonies, was rooted in his acknowledgment of the central role of the mother in Indigenous societies. This served as "proof" of his "noble heart." The role of "mother" transcended tribal affiliations and connected the Indigenous community in a "cultural countering" to the oppressive patriarchy of the British and the settler North Americans. Further, Éléonore's 1976 editorial suggests that she was part of a group of activists that supported international alliances and global Indigenism decades before the global Indigenous movement became formalized. Indeed, Sioui would have found striking similarities in Tecumseh's discourse of sovereignty, rights, and pan-Indian identity with the global Indigenous movement's focus on "strengthening an emerging indigenous identity based on common experiences of historical and ongoing colonialism."[27] It seems likely, therefore, that Sioui's regard for Tecumseh's vision of international alliance-making and respect for women in the 1970s remained strong as she continued to look for, and engage in, modern movements that connected Indigenous peoples across the world.

With Indigenous leaders like Tecumseh, as well as the teachings of her family, Éléonore received the training and guidance needed to develop a successful strategy to promote the rights of and opportunities for Indigenous women. Through these role models, she came to understand the importance of uniting Indigenous peoples and the central role that women must have in this process.

COMMUNITY

Despite generations of separation between the lives of eastern We^{n}dat/Wa^{n}dat Cécile Gannendâris and Éléonore Sioui, the community of We^{n}dat/Wa^{n}dat living near Quebec City remained similar in many ways. Over the years, they maintained close connections with the French, while also preserving Traditional cultural practices and belief systems.[28] In 1742, after re-settling the area for nearly a century, We^{n}dat/Wa^{n}dat gained title to 1600 arpents of land originally held by the Jesuits.[29] This included the Seigneurie de Sillery, the Seigneurie St Gabriel, a 9,600-acre hunting territory known as Rocquemont, and additional land identified as lot 270 of the parish of Saint Ambroise de la Jeune Lorette.[30] "Forty Arpents," as lot 270 came to be known, developed somewhat autonomously from the associated We^{n}dat/Wa^{n}dat villages, and it was there that Éléonore's parents were born and raised. In 1904, Forty Arpents was sold along with several other portions of We^{n}dat/Wa^{n}dat land to the Canadian government. The so-called land surrender indicated that "the Hurons cede to the Government of Canada the Quarante Arpents Reserve for sale purposes."[31] Eventually, the entire We^{n}dat/Wa^{n}dat community amalgamated on approximately 143 hectares of land in what is now the Wendake reserve.[32]

It is this community that Éléonore Sioui called home. The reserve is situated on the east bank of the Lada8anna River, near Kabir Kouba falls and eight kilometres north of Quebec City. By the time of Éléonore's birth, the village had a population of approximately 450 people.[33] Compared to other Canadian reserves, Wendake has achieved relative success. Historians have explained these results as a reflection of their "flexible culture that integrated past practices with new ways of relating to space and neighbors."[34] Further, historians have identified four specific strategies:

> First, they acquired legal title to nearby censives in order to ensure access to agricultural land and forest resources. Second, they maintained and strengthened ties with neighboring Indigenous peoples, such as the Wendats at Detroit and the Abenakis and Mohawks in the Saint Lawrence valley … Third, they embraced … manufacturing of equipment, including canoes, sleighs, and

> snowshoes, as well as deploying schooling and alphabetic literacy to better understand the legal workings of French, and later British, colonial regimes. Taken together, these three strategic approaches helped maintain a distinct Wendat identity.[35]

Combined, these strategies allowed for favourable reputations and considerable success well into the twentieth century. While hunting and guiding continued for some, many We^{n}dat/Wa^{n}dat were able to engage in the manufacturing of high quality "artisanal" items.[36] The transition allowed We^{n}dat/Wa^{n}dat to enter into wider markets. According to Indian Affairs, "had it not been for the introduction into the village of a new work, the making of canvas canoes, many families would have found themselves in discouraging want."[37] As a result, We^{n}dat/Wa^{n}dat families such as the Siouis, the Picards, the Bastiens, and the Gros-Louis established factories to meet the high demand. While this departed drastically from previous trade customs, it remained in line with We^{n}dat/Wa^{n}dat traditions of socio-economic strategies and adaptation.[38] Canoes, moccasins, and snowshoes were not new to the We^{n}dat/Wa^{n}dat, but the level and method of production were.

Christian traditions continued to intertwine with We^{n}dat/Wa^{n}dat customs on the Wendake reserve. The Jesuits remained integral to the Christian mission there. In 1696, they received a plenary indulgence from the Vatican for the festival of the annunciation. This made the eastern We^{n}dat/Wa^{n}dat mission villages an important pilgrimage site for Catholics, as they could visit the chapel of Notre-Dame de la Jeune-Lorette to receive remission of temporal punishment due to sin. The Vatican renewed the plenary indulgence in 1699 and again in 1711.[39] In light of this status, the We^{n}dat/Wa^{n}dat received visits from many notable colonial officials, including Michel Bégon de la Picardière, the intendant of New France, in 1721. Bégon was met with a military reception, a feast, and public speeches.[40] In 1730, the community built the Notre-Dame de Lorette chapel in the centre of the reserve.[41] It remains a key historical marker for the We^{n}dat/Wa^{n}dat and its cemetery is where Éléonore is buried.

A focus on education and colonial styles of schooling remained strong throughout the centuries. In the eighteenth century, most students attended the seminaries run by the Catholic Ursulines and Jesuits.[42] Later on, however, after 1763 and the British victory over the French in North America, many We^{n}dat/Wa^{n}dat sought to strengthen their ties with the new imperial power and pursued an English-Protestant education at schools like Moor's Indian Charity School and Dartmouth College. The son of Grand Chief Nicolas Vincent Tsawenhohi, Louis Vincent Sawantanan, was one such student. Sawantanan graduated in 1781 as a trained teacher and interpreter. He spoke French, We^{n}dat/Wa^{n}dat, English, and Mohawk fluently and was the first Indigenous person in what would become Canada to receive a Bachelor of Arts.[43] With these accomplishments complete, Sawantanan returned to Wendake, setting up a school in 1794 that would serve the community. The We^{n}dat/Wa^{n}dat teacher encouraged his students to learn their history and culture at the same time as he acknowledged the benefits of mastering colonial subjects. This curriculum, he believed, would provide the We^{n}dat/Wa^{n}dat with the tools necessary to address settler discrimination and make headway in treaty rights.[44] Sawantanan's education initiatives reflect the persistent We^{n}dat/Wa^{n}dat interest and engagement with colonial systems of schooling. Two hundred years later, his influence continued to be felt as Éléonore Sioui sought out a similar path with similar goals.

MOTHERWORK

Sioui realized early in life that to conduct motherwork effectively, she needed to use the same "vocabulary that the Government officials used so well."[45] This strategy pushed her to learn "to understand the dominant culture, by accepting some of its elements, by twisting and turning them to create a new integration of the cultural and the social."[46] This process led Sioui to create and articulate a critique of colonialism that is understandable to the larger public, and specifically those colonial regimes she was evaluating.

In order to achieve this goal, Éléonore added to her Indigenous We^{n}dat/Wa^{n}dat knowledge base by incorporating Western schooling. She attended a French-language convent school until the age of fourteen, graduating with "grande distinction." Despite this promising start, her parents faced debilitating hardships and made the difficult decision to keep her at home for the rest of her teenage years. The reasons behind the choice are unclear, but as the oldest of her siblings, it is likely that Éléonore was needed at home to help care for the younger children and act as support for her parents' business. Still, Caroline and Emery tried to continue with the convent school lessons and Caroline taught Éléonore English.[47]

Sioui's Western training was typical for We^{n}dat/Wa^{n}dat women and girls in Canada. Since the seventeenth century and the days of Cécile Gannendâris and the Ursuline seminary, We^{n}dat/Wa^{n}dat girls had attended Catholic schools in Quebec. Western schooling enforced European languages (French and English), culture, and notions of womanhood. Curriculum in the twentieth century reflected assimilationist policies, forbidding Indigenous languages and knowledge systems, while teaching girls skills that would prepare them to be subordinate wives, household mothers, or domestic servants. These lessons reminded Sioui and other young Indigenous women that Canadian society privileged European culture and patriarchy – messages that persisted beyond the classroom.[48]

Despite the ongoing marginalization of Indigenous women throughout Éléonore's Western schooling, she did not abandon it. Sioui joined a growing number of Indigenous intellectuals who sought to obtain university degrees as a means to use institutional education to combat colonialism. This was not an easy task in Canada. In the 1880s, the federal government deemed "university-educated Indians and those who had entered one of the professions" to be enfranchised; thus, they lost Indian status. One hundred years later, the Canadian government "capped" financial support for post-secondary education and cut adult education programs.[49] Still, Éléonore enrolled in courses, attained degrees, and attended seminars. She justified her schooling as a means to demonstrate to her children the importance of education. She was accepted at Université Laval, and took courses in French literature, philosophy, and Spanish.[50] In addition, Sioui earned a diploma in international cooperation from the University of Ottawa in 1981.[51]

In 1982, Indigenous education rights were entrenched in the Canadian constitution. Yet, as scholars have pointed out, this did not eradicate the "cognitive imperialism" that pervaded the system and institutions.[52] The pattern of Canadian exclusionary and restrictive measures towards higher education continued, pushing Sioui to consider alternatives. Universities in the United States offered a solution. As early as 1972, the US government began to implement policies that supported higher education for Indigenous people, culminating in the reauthorization of the Indian Education Act (1988) and a call for a White House conference on Indian education that same year.[53] It was during this time that Éléonore applied to the University of Miami's Master of International Studies program, which included courses in Latin American and Caribbean social and economic development.[54] Upon completion of her MA, Éléonore decided to remain in the United States to pursue her PhD at the Union for Experimenting Colleges and Universities (UECU), renamed the Union Institute and University in 2001. Established in 1964, this "university without walls" was based in Cincinnati, Ohio. Its PhD program sought to address concerns about the length of time and increasing expense involved in completing doctoral work. Most importantly, the programs were designed to be accessible to adults often restricted by "educational background, personal circumstances, or social status," offering a curriculum geared towards interdisciplinary research and social justice.[55] This type of education gave Sioui the flexibility to integrate both her Indigenous ways of knowing and learning with Western traditions of classroom schooling. Éléonore completed her degree in Native American Philosophy in 1988, becoming the first Indigenous woman in Canada to earn a doctorate. She was sixty-eight.

Combined, Éléonore's Indigenous training and Western schooling allowed her to effectively navigate between Indigenous and non-Indigenous societies. Her ability to communicate in French, English, and Spanish, along with her knowledge of Indigenous worldviews and European value systems, made her a desirable candidate for jobs with transnational and intercultural agendas. These positions proved powerful as they facilitated opportunities for Sioui to critique colonial policies from within. In Canada, for instance, she took a job as a switchboard operator for the federal government. Although an entry-level job, Sioui took advantage of the situation, and before long she had gained a reputation as a formidable candidate for jobs that related more closely to her motherwork. The 1970s were particularly formative for Éléonore. Set within the context of the Red Power movement and the formation of political organizations like the National Indian Brotherhood (1972), Sioui worked as a consultant for the federal ministry of Indian Affairs, an economic developer and teacher for the Quebec branch of Indian

Affairs, and a French-language teacher for military officers at the Shilo Military Base in Manitoba and the Royal Military College in Saint-Jean-sur-Richelieu, Quebec.[56]

These paid positions empowered Sioui. Through her vocations, she was able to learn from, influence, and engage with settler society. None of these positions would have been possible without the education that she received. For Sioui, the connection between her Indigenous training, her Western schooling, and her work outside the We^{n}dat/Wa^{n}dat community could not be separated. Still, although she often took jobs that brought her within the jurisdictions of provincial, national, and international borders, her focus remained at home. According to Sioui, education was a "must," and the number one factor in the decolonizing process. This would lead to paid positions with agencies that would further her ultimate goal "to re-establish credibility to my people."[57] They would also serve as support and inspiration for her motherwork.

The global Indigenous movement is based on the premise that the agendas of the extra-national organizations must promote the needs of the local communities. Sioui's activism reflected this ideology, as her initial projects focused on targeting the socio-economic struggles of the We^{n}dat/Wa^{n}dat people living in Quebec. Sioui attended band council meetings to get a sense of the status of leadership and governance within the community. Her attendance soon developed into participation, as she refused to remain silent during the council meetings. Often, she was found questioning the representatives and the system as a whole. Specifically, she wanted to know, "Why were the Huron kept in ignorance? Why had the Huron no possibility to speak or be listened to? Why were the Huron kept in poverty? Why did women have no chance to study?" She justified her questions by saying that she "wanted [her] children to develop and have a better life."[58] As years progressed, she began to look beyond the band council for answers and forums for activism. Every experience and encounter she had "increased her appetite for more" and pushed her toward connecting her motherwork with the larger global Indigenous community.[59]

Éléonore Sioui was a prolific author who used the written word to express her beliefs, propose solutions, and disseminate an anti-colonial critique of contemporary oppressive regimes. Her publications transcended borders and were distributed worldwide. Historian Kim

Anderson argues that "writing offers both a means to resist and an opportunity to reinvent" at the same time as it gives Indigenous women "a means of surviving oppression and a way to engage in a healing process."[60] In Sioui's case, this theory holds true. She equated her writing to "herbs and other healing substances" that, in her view, should be used in a similar manner to address the wounds and diseases brought about by colonialism.[61]

Sioui was the creator and editor of *Kanatha*, a bilingual magazine dedicated to exploring and promoting the "balance between spiritual and materialistic values." The magazine ran for six years, beginning in 1973.[62] According to Éléonore, this was the first magazine written and published by Indigenous people in Canada. The original intent was to connect First Nations throughout the province of Quebec, complementing the work of the Indians of Quebec Association. This, Sioui hoped, would be a unifying factor and a means to negotiate land settlements and other legal battles. She believed that "the reservation needed a broader representation."[63] *Kanatha* gained a reputation not only among Quebec's Indigenous communities, but also throughout Canada and, in a very short time, the world. Sioui recalled receiving an overwhelming amount of requests outside Canada for copies. Even more significant perhaps, in terms of Sioui's progress as an activist, she identifies the founding of *Kanatha* as the moment where she developed her "writing voice."[64]

Poetry became Sioui's favourite form of written expression. She published hundreds of beautifully crafted reflections on numerous topics in her magazine and in book form. Her books, *Andatha* (1985), *Femme de l'île* (1990), and *Corps à coeur éperdu* (1992), were circulated outside the reserve and to the wider Canadian Indigenous community.[65] Indian Affairs, for instance, distributed 300 copies of *Andatha* to reserve schools in order to promote Indigenous authors and writing in general.[66] Her poem "To Be" explains the significance of the title of her book:

> I am able to impart
> Health, Truth, Happiness.
> This is my reason for existing.
> Kindness, love, patience, encouragement.
> I am a healing convenor.
> I am Andatha*

*Wyandot word: the Soul, the heart, convergence[67]

Indian Affairs explained their support for her poetry in a letter to Léonard Paul, school principal at École Indienne de Betsiamites in northern Quebec, writing, "This collection of poems represents the Amerindian World as perceived by Mme. Sioui … This book can also be presented to students to encourage them to write about their thoughts, their ideas, and their experiences. This is a way to incite them to write so that one day we will have an Amerindian literary tradition."[68]

Sioui made efforts of her own to disseminate her work. Highlighting this fact is a letter from US President Bill Clinton to Éléonore, acknowledging receipt of her work with an added personal note: "Thank you so much for sending the book. I look forward to reviewing it … I appreciate your thoughtfulness."[69] The letter is dated 19 January 1993, the day before Clinton's inaugural speech. At the time, Sioui lived in Miami, Florida, and would have taken a special interest in the new president's platform. Clinton ran a campaign on the importance of a "global vision," which he then articulated in his January speech, emphasizing that "there is no longer a clear division between what is foreign and what is domestic. The world economy, the world environment, the world AIDS crisis, the world arms race: they affect us all."[70] By gifting the president with one of her books, Sioui was most likely demonstrating her support for his global vision (which reflected her own), while also directing Clinton to keep in mind the worldwide struggle of Indigenous people for rights and recognition (including those in the United States and Canada).

Unpublished petitions created a similar vehicle for Sioui to express her desires in written form. She used these letters to critique governments and promote an Indigenous feminist agenda. Within her personal papers are numerous correspondences with government officials discussing a variety of issues concerning Indigenous people within and outside Canada. Repeatedly, her focus was on Native women and girls. In 1986, for example, she wrote a three-page typed letter to the minister of Indian Affairs, Frank Vieni. In it, she requested that he take special care to protect "unfavoured and forgotten" Indigenous women. She expanded on this particular aspect, arguing that the poor treatment of Canada's Aboriginal women is even more intolerable because Canada is a country that believes itself to be a defender of human rights.[71] Whether through published magazines, editorials, and poems or in unpublished petitions and letters, there is no doubt that Éléonore used writing as not only a form of resistance, but also a means of action and a vehicle to offer solutions. This strategy was an expression of her motherwork and her dedication to bettering the lives of Indigenous women and peoples.

One of the most defining moments for Éléonore's activism was her experience in the country of Dominica. In 1981, the minister of foreign affairs offered her a position as a consultant to the Indigenous peoples of Dominica, the Caribs. Sioui was an ideal candidate given that the position required someone who had first-hand knowledge of and experience with the problems facing the Indigenous peoples of Canada.[72] Specifically, it asked for a person "sensitive to the needs of an isolated Amerindian culture for a three-month period to evaluate a project" that would create a viable economic and cultural future for the Carib Reserve in North Dominica.[73]

Although excited by the challenge, Sioui was terrified during her initial first few days in the foreign country. Unaware of the domestic politics or the cultural demographics, she questioned her safety and security. These fears were soon dispelled, however, and she quickly grew to appreciate her host society. Over the course of her three-month stay, she successfully developed what she called "An American Indian to American Indian Project." Sioui's work did not go unnoticed, as one observer recalled her reputation as a "very forceful negotiator."[74] Much like a mother defending her children, Sioui advocated for the Caribs so that they might one day become self-governing and improve their quality of life. Her diplomacy was an extension of her motherwork, as she tried to nurture and protect the community's culture, health, and history for generations to come. By the time her position ended, letters of recommendation were sent to request an additional two years of support for Sioui to continue her work.[75] Throughout her time in Dominica, Sioui connected with Caribs over issues concerning many Indigenous people. Discussions of sovereignty, human rights, and education, infused with a common experience of colonial oppression, allowed Sioui to connect with international Indigenous communities and conduct motherwork on the ground.

Sioui's motherwork led her to international forums focused on intercultural understanding. At the World Women's Conference held in East Berlin in 1976, Sioui's reputation as a community mother supported her position as the representative for American Indian women. This widely popular and highly public conference required Sioui to speak to approximately 2,700 women from over 146 countries about the problems facing Indigenous women living in Canada.[76] Once the conference finished, Sioui submitted a report to the Canadian government describing her observations and reflections on the topics covered in Berlin. She included a proposal to create a project aimed at addressing the specific economic circumstances of Aboriginal women in Canada.[77]

This kind of international engagement continued throughout Sioui's life. In 1992, she was the invited guest of honour to the Collectifs Grenoblois 1492–1992 conference in Grenoble, France. This international gathering was a commemoration that marked the 500-year anniversary of Christopher Columbus's "discovery" of the "New World." The major theme throughout the presentations was "500 years of resistance."[78] Sioui delivered information sessions on medicinal plants, Indigenous philosophy, American and Canadian Aboriginal culture, and Indigenous rights. In addition, she gave several public poetry readings to offer a glimpse into the "Amerindian World."[79] Encapsulating her overall message was to keep an eye on the future, a future "where Indigenous people reclaim their place in the world as keepers of Mother Earth."[80]

Three years later, at the Conference of Languages, Culture and Values in Canada, Sioui found herself delivering speeches concerning the conflicting relationship between the nation-state, Indigenous feminism, and Indigenous notions of nationhood. After a day of listening to many different perspectives on the topic from a wide range of experts, including scholars and politicians, Sioui was given the opportunity to make the closing remarks. Similar to her role in Berlin, she was asked to represent the women of the "undeveloped" world, an interest group predicated on so-called Fourth-World conditions of internationally unrecognized nations.[81] Standing before the conference participants, Sioui first explained her role and responsibilities to Indigenous women. "I am here to speak for the fourth-world woman," she said, "whom you never hear about because they are too poor and way back in the reserves and we don't even know that you are talking about organizations of women."[82] She then began to address the larger issue of Indigenous nationhood: "In 1763," she said,

> England, and some of our headmen, have been signing a treaty and it has been recognized by the government of Canada,

unanimously, by nine judges at the supreme court of Canada, as something real and something that they accept like a treaty. And those men, who were one part Huron, who are our ancestors … were recognized as a nation … I don't know what has been happening since then because right now the term Amerindian, Indian, tribes, bands, Aboriginal, it looks like it tries to wipe out the name of the nation, calling us autochton tries to wipe out the concept of nation.[83]

Sioui then discussed her vision and solutions for the future:

The world is turning, the world is a necessity to get ways to solve our children, to solve our nations of the world from disappearing as nations, as societies, as humans. We are speaking about developing the world, the richnesses of the world, the wealth, but they never speak about developing the human resources. If we want to develop the wealth, you have to develop the human resources. Our Indian human resources, eh, sixty percent of the prisons of Canada, so where is our human resources? Where can be the role? Where can our place, our nation, I was speaking about, that they say it doesn't exist anymore, it is so proud that it doesn't exist … And when you came, you could see that the man, as man, had rights to be what he wanted to be. And children had the right to be respected and the woman had the right to choose their men and put them at the head and if they didn't work good for the nations they would be pushed away. So the women were the confirmers. I don't mean women have to be the head, I mean the women have to develop the full potential and bring – as being fifty-one percent of the population of the world – their own wealth, superior intellectual or whatever, but bring it and develop it for the well-being of the world.[84]

She concluded with "I thank you for listening to me."[85] Sioui's talk pushed the conference participants to think critically about the relationship between the colonial nation-states and the Fourth World. She encouraged them to consider the important role that Indigenous women had in healing communities impacted by colonial policies regarding specific issues concerning sexism, racism, poverty, lack of education, and patriarchal dominance. Despite the seemingly constant desire for discussion throughout the day leading up to Sioui's speech, the room remained silent after her presentation. As a result, the chair closed the session, referencing Éléonore's eloquent words and call to action as an important perspective that deserved reflection.[86]

LEGACY

Sioui's motherwork did not go unnoticed. Recognition came in many forms, but all pointed to an acknowledgment of her initiatives to better Indigenous communities at home and abroad. Throughout her many initiatives, this commitment never wavered – whether she was writing, speaking, or working on the ground with communities. When asked point-blank by a federal politician what the Indigenous people wanted and what he could do for them, Sioui did not hesitate to answer that, above all else, "equal accessibility to education and higher learning for girls and women as for men."[87] It was this kind of focused vision and action that led one participant at a conference about Indigenous children and social services to present Sioui with a brooch, explaining that it was in recognition of her "courage to speak out," and suggest that a parental organization be established to give voice to Indigenous communities seeking to protect their children from wrongful government intervention.[88]

Courage marked many of the comments about Éléonore's motherwork. Georges Erasmus, the former national chief of the Assembly of First Nations, identified this as a major attribute of her character. In a letter to Sioui, he declared that her "courageous example shines on all of our First Nations."[89] For Erasmus, Sioui's activism not only served Canada's Indigenous people, but would continue to serve as inspiration for future generations and initiatives across the globe. In his words, her "success will give an impetus to, and reinvigorate, our efforts."[90] More public forms of recognition have also taken place. In 2001, Sioui received the Order of Canada from Governor General Adrienne Clarkson for her work "to raise general awareness of the condition of Aboriginals and to promote the Huron-Wendat culture."[91] A private letter from the Prime Minister of Canada, Jean Chrétien, further reinforced this public honour, contending that Sioui's motherwork and actions "are an inspiration for many Canadians."[92]

Finally, the public legacy of Sioui's work extends beyond her lifetime. Six years after her death, the University of Ottawa dedicated their 2012 Matrilineal Societies: Redefinitions, Survival and Worldviews conference to the late Éléonore Sioui. Inspired by the work of Sioui and others like her, this two-day workshop questioned "the contemporary fate of matrilineal societies in the face of globalization" – a topic grounded in themes of Indigeneity and feminism. Participants came from around the world to attend.[93]

These points of reference and acknowledgment are important indications of the success and reach of Sioui's motherwork. Her influence was not only felt within her local community of Jeune Lorette at band council meetings, or in reserve schools throughout Quebec, but also nationally and internationally. Her sense of community expanded as she became part of a global Indigenous network. As a result, her sense of motherwork evolved from her family, to her reserve, to Quebec, to Canada, to North America, and then to the world at large. Despite this expansive conceptual framework of community, her responsibilities as "mother" did not change. Her focus on improving the lives of Indigenous peoples, through education and public advocacy, remained at the heart of every experience.

Sioui's focus on "mothering" the greater Indigenous family was, however, often done at the expense of her biological children. Even Éléonore herself admits that her work in school and education was "at great expense of personal time which I might have spent with my family."[94] Frequently her time abroad relied heavily on the support of her extended family, who looked after her children at home.

In addition, her outspoken criticism of governing bodies and people threatened the stability of her family, as there remained a constant chance that they would report her to social services as an unfit mother in order to limit her activism. In this case, the definition of "unfit" is a colonial construct enforced through the pervasiveness of dominant ideologies concerning non-Indigenous mothering.[95] Social workers and Indian agents evaluated mothers on Eurocentric standards that privileged a hetero-patriarchal household with biological parents as sole caregivers. The scrutiny Sioui received from *outside* the community, therefore, although very real (the government agents had the ability to take her children and place them in foster care), did not necessarily reflect definitions of "fit" and "unfit" from *inside* the community. A network of extended "parents" (aunties and grandparents) was, and remains, a customary approach to parenting within many Indigenous nations.[96] Historically, women who deviate from this norm – usually Indigenous women, lesbian women, poor women, single women, and immigrant women, among others – are considered "bad mothers" or "unfit" and have therefore been regulated socially and legally.[97]

Georges Sioui Jr, Éléonore's eldest son, remembers the stigma attached to his mother. He recalled, "My mother endured being looked at basically as an insane woman because she talked about women's right to education, because she challenged the authority of these three men [the priest, the Indian Agent, and the Chief], and the validity of their system."[98] Knowing that people judged and criticized his mother must have been difficult, yet as Georges and his siblings grew, so too did their understanding of the importance of their mother's initiatives. Despite her absence, Sioui believed that her work helped her sons and daughters as they, too, became part of the larger Indigenous community. In some cases, she may have even served as a role model and inspiration for their initiatives. Konrad Sioui, for instance, having just returned from a meeting in Nicaragua with President Daniel Ortega, explained that he walked in his "mother's path" when he delivered a speech requesting recognition of human rights for the country's Indigenous population.[99] Konrad later became the Grand Chief of the Huron-Wendat Nation in 2008.

Georges Sioui, a noted activist, author, and professor of Indigenous studies, also believes that his mother instilled important teachings that drove his scholarship and understanding of the world.[100] Most significantly, he remembers the importance she placed on women. "Our mother and leader Éléonore," Georges explained at a presentation for the Native American and Indigenous Studies Association in 2013,

> ingrained in all of us that women have the power to create societies: they know the price and the value of life because they conceive and give birth to us; they are the ones who teach us the reasons why we have to have compassion, care and solicitude for others and for all other-than-human beings. Therefore, allowing

> women to have and take their place at the Centre of our communities and societies is much more than an act of justice: it is an irreplaceable strategy for our global survival. That is certainly something which I learned from my mother.[101]

Thus, despite her extended responsibilities to a global Indigenous family, Sioui maintained a connection with her children. She encouraged her children to follow in her footsteps, as educator, activist, and feminist, and to continue her agenda, just as she had continued the work of her parents.

Éléonore Sioui was born into a settler-colonial world. Her ancestors suffered centuries of racism and cultural attacks under patriarchal regimes that privileged European traditions of male-centred societies, ultimately doubly subjugating Indigenous women. It was in this context that Chief Emery took his first-born child and spoke the words "if only she were a boy." Being a man of insight and experience, Emery imagined the road ahead for his little daughter. A road blocked by lack of education, poverty, and oppression. It was not that he desired a boy over a girl; rather, he knew that life for a twentieth-century We^{n}dat/Wa^{n}dat boy might present fewer challenges.

The experiences of Éléonore's life suggest that, in many ways, Emery's foresight was justified. Sioui was subject to discrimination and injustice as she struggled to be a supportive wife and raise her seven children. Her family felt the effects of an alcoholic father, the imposition of hetero-patriarchal parenting policies, the lack of federal support for Indigenous education, and the corruption of colonial politics. Yet, her experience was not unique. Éléonore became a member of a much larger community of Indigenous women who battled similar episodes of colonialism. As a result, her vision grew and her strategy internationalized, as did her projects. "I feel that my vision is global," Sioui stated, and rooted in a "passion for social justice, for equity, for human dignity."[102] Consequently, she recognized that her activism was directed toward the "well-being of humanity and its advancement."[103] In brief, her vision encompassed a global community of Indigenous peoples.

Éléonore's motherwork reflects this international and intercultural vision. Inspired by family members and notable historic figures such as Tecumseh, Sioui strove to unite and educate Indigenous people. By educating herself and promoting the education of other Indigenous women, Sioui empowered Indigenous communities to engage with settler society and contest oppressive policies. Although her activism took many forms, her writing served and still serves as a material mechanism to promote her agenda. Of course, by becoming a global mother and figure, her own family received less attention than she would have liked. Still, her message was heard at home, as her children and grandchildren continue to "walk in [their] mother's path."

In the end, her strategy remains a success. She was recognized throughout her lifetime and afterward as a powerful advocate for Indigenous peoples and a successful defender of women's rights. Her message has been heard across the world, from the local reserve school, to meeting rooms in Dominica, to conference halls in Europe. Underscoring this message, Georges Jr delivered a presentation on his mother's activism for the Native American and Indigenous Studies Association annual conference. His words, touched with emotion and admiration, serve as an appropriate summary of Éléonore's life, her motherwork, and this chapter. "Like her parents and her Ancestors before her," Georges said,

> my mother's prime purpose was ... to use the vision and the spiritual medicine of her people in order to heal a world already sick and getting sicker as time goes by. For that purpose, she saw the need to enlist the help, strength and power of all people, the whole human family, while affirming and acknowledging the primary role that has to be played by the First Nations people. This is where I touch on the most central tenet in her philosophy: that in order for any healing to be possible, the woman has to be permitted to return to the central place she once occupied in our Nations.[104]

EPILOGUE

The We^{n}dat/Wa^{n}dat Women's Advisory Council

There is no evidence to suggest that the women of the case studies in this book knew each other – separated by generations and various homelands. Yet, they remain connected. They are kin, Sisters, and the descendants of Aataentsic. Similar ties bind the We^{n}dat/Wa^{n}dat Women's Advisory Council. While living across the extensive territory of Turtle Island and what we now call Canada and the USA, they maintain both a collective and individual dedication to carrying on the motherwork of their Ancestors. They, too, are Daughters of Aataentsic.

What, then, does it mean to be a Daughter of Aataentsic? The previous chapters give some indication as we have explored the ways in which We^{n}dat/Wa^{n}dat women have consistently attempted to preserve and protect their culture for future generations. This motherwork is deeply embedded in a We^{n}dat/Wa^{n}dat identity connected to matricentric traditions and social order. But how do their descendants view this kind of legacy? More specifically, how do the We^{n}dat/Wa^{n}dat Women's Advisory Council members situate themselves within this history?

What follows are the answers to these questions. Rather than trying to relay *my* interpretation of their opinions, this epilogue includes *their* own voices – voices that have shaped every aspect of the writing of this book, but have yet to find a real presence within these pages. Their reflections are as unique as they are common. Based in personal experiences, as well as historical processes, they explain their place in the world through stories, poems, and free verse. As you read their replies, consider the power behind their perspectives. They are the past, present and future. Tizameh/Tiawenhk/Merci/Thank you.

MANON SIOUI (NATION HURONNE-WENDAT)

My name is Manon Sioui. I am from the Bear Clan and I am a Wendat woman and artist from Wendake, Quebec. I was born in the big city of Montreal in 1962 and moved into the village of Wendake when I was six years old. For me, to be a Wendat woman is to be born with a cultural identity belonging to your own people.

It is to be a little girl and to be able to see people that are not from this world. It is to be able to play whenever I please. It is to visit my grandmother and watch her do beadwork on moccasin tops. It is to pick up wild berries and eat more than I will bring back home. It is to play in the bush and admire the beauty of wildflowers. It is to feel the sun's heat on my little cheeks. It is to sense the raindrops dripping on my face. It is to go trapping and fishing with my dad and watch my mom cook the fish. It is to feel the morning dew on my small bare feet. It is to go canoeing with my dad at dawn while the mist is still there. It is to watch my mom making all kinds of native crafts and beadwork.

It is to grow up and still see those people that are not from this world. It is to bead my own moccasin tops. It is to discover a deep interest of my people and for my culture. It is becoming a young woman who finds out about the rich history of her family and her Ancestors. It is at that moment that my passion for art emerges and my desire to create take place.

It is to become a grown-up woman and create links with other First Nations people. It is to take care of Mother Earth and fight for her rights. It is to support other communities and want the well-being of her own village.

It is to give birth to my two masterpieces, my little boys, and become a loving mother. It is to discover how big is something so small, how strong is something that seems so fragile, and how deep the love of a mother can be.

It is to get older and find peace, love, and harmony. It is to still see those people that are not from this world. It is to be called on a spiritual path, the path of the medicine masks. It is to preach humility, joy and laughter and compassion.

It is to assist at my ancestor's reburial and discover deep in my soul that I was one of them. This following is a poem I wrote to commemorate the deep and historical relationship between mother and daughter and the Homeland.

Letter from a mother to her daughter

Village of St-Ignace
Huronia
Year 1649

My dear daughter,

At the moment of the massacre that took place in the village of St-Ignace, I was in the long house.
I heard screaming outside.
I looked at you tenderly while you were sleeping.
I left you for a short moment to see what was going on outside.

It was at that moment that I realised the magnitude of what was happening.
The entire village was in flames.
People, terrified, were running in all directions … But why?

We were under attack by the Iroquois, burning all the houses on their passage.
Among them, I recognised some of our people.
Some traditionalists that lost all senses of loyalty rank at their sides.

I was looking at my people dying under the Iroquois and trader's knifes and war clubs.
The sight was unbearable and the fear took over me.
I suddenly saw my beloved husband collapse at my feet.
He had just been stabbed under my eyes.

All this took place in a few minutes only.

I was suddenly invaded by a deep sadness and knelt down, putting down my arms around him and lengthening my body over his.
Emptiness built up inside me.

All of a sudden, my love for you vividly emerged.
I had to go get you to protect you.
But at the moment I was about to get up, I saw a war club above my head quickly ending its race in my back.
All of a sudden the pain invaded me.
I wanted to get up but I couldn't, looking towards the screams and cries of a child who was beckoning me.
For a brief moment our eyes met, and time stood still.
It was you my daughter, my dearest girl.
You were only four years old and you had seen your father and your mother get slaughtered in front of you and your village be reduced to ashes.

The heat was intense, but the pain of a mother who could not protect her child and not knowing what would happen to you was even more.

Unable to move, unable to speak, staring at you with the background of our longhouse in this inferno, I died little by little having in mind the desire to see you again, you my little girl.
I miss you so much already.

I left this world with the guilt of failing to my duty, one to protect you, hoping that you will forgive me one day and with the fear that you think I abandoned you.

But know that I never abandoned you.
I loved you and at the moment I decided to leave you in your child's dreams when you were asleep so deeply, my intention was to come back and get you.

I have been looking for you since this death and I have finally
found you.

I love you with all my heart.

What happened to them belongs to me and
What belongs to them belongs also to me

This is my history
This is my story

The story of a Wendat woman

SALLIE COTTER ANDREWS (WYANDOTTE NATION)

My name is Sallie Cotter Andrews, Tewatronyahkwa (Lifting the Sky) – Deer Clan, citizen of Wyandotte Nation. I am a seated faithkeeper of the Wandat Yanohsetsih in Wyandotte, Oklahoma. Faithkeeper means "worker" for the Creator and it represents my commitment to serve my people for the remainder of my life. I am also very humbled and excited to be a Daughter of Aataentsic. That honour has two meanings for me.

First, being a Daughter of Aataentsic represents being associated with a group of Wendat Women from across the USA and Canada who have come together at the hand of the Creator and our lovely friend and mentor, Dr Kathryn Magee Labelle, to further the understanding of our cultural heritage and history. We women are citizens of our Nation's four different bands and we live hundreds of miles apart, but we are true sisters in our hearts, and our connection to each other is powerful and binding. I believe there is also a DNA connection present in our bodies today, and its strands extend back into history and reach far into the future. It is an eternal connection. Each of us Daughters of Aataentsic brings very different experiences and talents to the table, but these experiences and talents blend together like a fine culinary dish with exquisite flavor. To meet and work together as Daughters of Aataentsic on projects such as this book is a true gift from the Creator.

Second, being a Daughter of Aataentsic represents who I am as a Wyandotte woman. I think that all Wendat people are sons or daughters of Aataentsic, the woman who fell from the sky. Some of us have a responsibility to learn all we can, to share our knowledge and to serve others. I take my responsibility seriously to build a bridge for the next generation of seekers of our history and heritage. I am grateful to all who came before me and lived as traditional people. I am thankful for those who remembered our history or gathered information from many sources and wrote it down and helped me on my path of learning. I want to continue that kind of legacy.

As I reflect on the women presented in this book, I am amazed and inspired by their accomplishments, fortitude, resilience, activism, and commitment. It is vital to preserve and share their stories so we can follow the path that these women forged through time and be strengthened by them. They lived with purpose. Preserving and sharing their stories builds a bridge for future generations.

In closing I would like to share a personal reflection. Our road is not always smooth; sometimes doors close and we can be hurt. But, the Creator knows our hearts and knows us – and guess what, he really does open a window when a door closes! The window that he opened for me to be a Daughter of Aataentsic has been a wonderful, loving, healing, educational experience, and more than I could have ever dreamed! I am so grateful to be a Daughter of Aataentsic. We are the keepers of our traditional ways – the Keepers of the Council Fire – the Wyandotte, Wyandot, Wyandott, Wendat women that we are.

LINDA SIOUI (NATION HURONNE-WENDAT)

My name is Linda Sioui and I was born in Montreal, Canada, in 1960. Of Huron-Wendat origin, I have pursued an interest in the culture and heritage of my people. I am the holder of a bachelor's degree in sociology from the University of Ottawa and a master's degree in anthropology from Université Laval (Quebec City). In 1983 I worked on indexing the field notes of the Quebec anthropologist Charles Marius Barbeau, and the following summer I visited the Wyandottes of Oklahoma on behalf of the Canadian Museum of Civilization. This initial contact was followed by other visits. Questions of identity, in relation to material culture and the revitalization of the ancestral language, have been a continual source of curiosity and concern for me. I am the author of

"La réaffirmation de l'identité wendate/Wyandotte *à* l'heure de la mondialisation" (The Reaffirmation of Wendat/Wyandotte Identity at a Time of Globalization). I am a member of the Huron-Wendat First Nation and live in the community of Wendake, just outside of Quebec City, Canada.

For me, being a daughter of Aataentsic means continuity of my people. Moreover, it is strengthening of our bond, and ultimately, of our Confederacy. It is the ultimate statement of surviving formidable odds for the Wendat people, and it insures hope for tomorrow. It also means healing, as each and every one of us accepts the others for whom they are. Comfort for just "being." Daughters of Aataentsic have a responsibility to the rest of the Confederacy, as we gain a deeper understanding of the need for our unity. We are the materialization of our Ancestors' hopes for a better tomorrow.

JUDITH PIDGEON-KUKOWSKI (WYANDOT OF ANDERDON NATION)

My name is Judith Pidgeon-Kukowski. I am a Wyandot of the Deer Clan. Being a Daughter of Aataentsic means that I have dedicated myself to the people of my community with special emphasis on the women who have gone before me. Those were the women who blazed the trail and passed down the knowledge of our Ancestors.

My method for passing on the knowledge of our Ancestors has always been genealogy and history. I started with those from my closest known family and have worked back to the late fourteenth and early fifteenth centuries one family at a time. I have started and torn up many family trees. But they all interconnect to become the Huron/Wendat, Wyandot of Kansas, Wyandot of Anderdon, and Wyandotte Nation. I have found that we are all related.

The first contact was by Samuel Champlain. He was impressed by the loving and peaceful nature of our people. Those early family stories set the stage. My father's mother was Stella Chene. The Chesne/Chene family figures prominently in early French Detroit. It was grandma Bertha Pidgeon who told me that we were not really French as much as Wyandot.

It started with Pierre Chesne dit St Onge who came from France in 1676 and married Louise Jeanne Bailly dite LaFleur. I have been able to document eight children. Charles Chesne (1694–1755) and his younger brother Pierre Chesne dit LaButte (1698–1774) married Indian women. Charles is my grandfather. He married Catherine Sauvage on 18 January 1722 at Detroit, L'Assomption de Sandwich de Windsor. She is the daughter of Catherine Jean dite Vien and Jacques Sauvage. Other women figure prominently in the Wyandot(te) Nations. That family tree that I started so long ago has turned into a monumental work of over 17,000 souls. They include the women of all four of the Confederacy Nations.

JUDITH MANTHE (WYANDOT NATION OF KANSAS)

I am Tronniaęnk, a Wyandot woman.

I have always known I was the granddaughter of Chief Tarhe, the only surviving Chief of the Battle of Greenfield. My grandmother Edith Zane Yunghans would show me the books from Ohio and tell me about my grandparents, and that I should never forget the history in my family tree. I have much gratitude to Dr Kathryn Labelle for selecting me to serve on the advisory council. If I had not been selected, I would not have gone to Ontario for the reburial in 2013. This event shook me to the core. The honour to be the one able to carry my Ancestors' bones to their final resting place is something I will hold dear to my heart and never be able to forget. I met so many of my brothers and sisters from Wendake. Each one I met, I felt pieces of my self being more complete. I didn't realize there was an emptiness, but now I know there are many more I need to meet for my being to become whole.

During this trip, I was able to visit Eckerondi, Midland, Ste Marie Among the Hurons, and I was impacted by all but mostly by the village site of Crawford Lake. While walking alone to the lake after visiting the Longhouse, I had a feeling of being surrounded by spirits. I just had to drop to the ground and absorb the welcome I felt from the Ancestors welcoming me home, and home is exactly what I felt. Each time I return I feel a stronger connection. I embrace my past and future, helping and teaching other tribal members to learn more of their history. I am Tronniaęnk which means She Is In The Sky, Is Happy.

CATHERINE TÀMMARO (WYANDOT OF ANDERDON NATION)

My name is Taǫmęˀšreˀ
date:žátǫ ^{n}gyaˀwiš hatiyerunǫˀ

I was born in Toronto, Canada, and raised in Toronto and the US. I received my associate's degree in general studies from the Ontario College of Art in 1982. I have a fifty-year history of art making, including fine art and award-winning design, assemblage, soundscape/installation, photographic/written journalism, extensive photo-based digital illustration, and graphic design. My multimedia works have been exhibited in both traditional and alternative gallery spaces and my written works have been published in various journals both online and in print. My solo music project is called subductionCurrent and I have been involved in many musical collaborations as a co-composer and vocalist with my late husband Phil Ogison, the Moon Dandies with Phil and Jeff Howard, and others. Over the years, I have been involved in a wide array of interdisciplinary collaborations, ongoing special projects, and themed exhibitions as originator, curator, coordinator, performer, and exhibitor. I am Akin Collective's premiere Indigenous Elder Artist in Residence and I work across Toronto in various capacities as Elder, Teacher, Mentor, Painter, Ceremonial conductor, Collaborator and FaithKeeper. In the summer of 2017 I was seated as a FaithKeeper for the Anderdon people in Detroit, Michigan, the first in well over 130 years. I reside in Toronto as I have for fifty-five of my sixty-five years.

What follows is a reflection piece entitled "Dreaming Creation" that serves as my understanding of myself as a woman of the Spotted Turtle Clan, "The Keepers of the Heavens – the Carriers of the Fire." It reflects my acceptance and understanding of Ancestral memory and my becoming; the acknowledgment of my Wyandot blood and identity.

Dreaming Creation ~ Winter Solstice 2014. Toronto, Canada

Darkness surrounds me, like layers of fine indigo-coloured linen, speckled and splendid with stars, as I go about my tasks fashioning the sun and moon, for the Young Woman Fallen From Above. She has fallen through a tear in the celestial ceiling and descends, cradled lovingly by beautiful geese. I hold up the night sky, as a huge canopy. Arched forward, I pull the heavens about my carapace and as a remembrance of the first light of the first evening star – my spotted back reflects the cosmos. I am small and slow moving as I go about my tasks fashioning the sun, moon, stars, and galaxies for the Young Woman Fallen From Above. She has fallen through a tear in the celestial ceiling – she has fallen onto the back of a great turtle, the Moss Back, my cousin.

My sister and brother animals readily swim to assist her as they attempt to bring the mud and foundation of earth up from the depths, the foundation for the the sister seeds which will sprout the corn, beans, and squash which will nourish the Peoples – the tobacco for ceremony, the heart shaped berry … her feet move in ancient skyworld patterns, pressing the earth about the back of the Great Turtle floating in the vast waves of sky and ocean. The depths of waters and the movement of waves cradle the great Moss Back; the blue green island in the night of creation – lighted, white caps and at this turning point of the year, the stars are reflected on my back – I have made the Sun and for this moment, the Sun, our Elder Brother, stands still.

Through the darkness I move, through the vast cosmic ocean of stars and waves. Sparking as I go … out of the abyss I emerge, out of the dark night, out of the dark womb into the most profound realisation of my own existence. The cosmos is reflected upon my back and I leave a trail of comets and meteors as I move through the Heavens. I am the Keeper of the Heavens, the Speckled One. The stars are reflected upon my back and as I move through the vast cosmic streams of space and time, now aware of my own existence, and I see before me the faces of those yet to be born; generation upon generation ~ along the great trail of turtle time … I have planted Elder Brother Sun and Grandmother Moon in the great night sky ~ and we are of one mind.

I am spotted as the night sky ~ it is reflected upon my back. I am aware of my own existence in the great and vast celestial ocean and like the stars and sun, I am the Coming Day. I am the pressure of illumination against darkness … I, Small Turtle, in creating the light, hold myself up to it for all to envisage. No longer swimming through vast emptiness, I, Keeper of the Heavens, Carrier of the Fire, am held within creation. I bring the Coming Day, the promise of hope. I am the carrier of the fire, striking bolts of lightning together; maker of stars. I hold myself up to the light and have become light, embodied. The Ancestors know who I am. Our Ancestors know my name – I hold myself up to their light and I am filled with love.

CHIEF JANITH ENGLISH (WYANDOT NATION OF KANSAS)

I was fortunate to have spent most of my life in or near Wyandotte County, Kansas City, Kansas. Home was across the river from the old Wyandot Reserve at the confluence of the Kaw (Kansas) and Missouri Rivers. I earned an associate's degree at Kansas City Kansas Community College School of Nursing, and received bachelor's and master's degrees from Ottawa University. My work in a clinical setting included that of a primary nurse and nurse supervisor. One of my most rewarding experiences of my nursing career paths was that of serving my patients and their families as a Hospice RN Case Manager. These experiences resulted in a focus on identifying constructive ways to effectively address the age-old and contemporary effects of multigenerational grief, trauma, and depression; and assisting others to identify pathways toward renewed strength and resiliency. I have been honoured to serve the People of the Wyandot Nation of Kansas as both Second and, subsequently, Principal Chief.

I grew up in an era of great civil unrest when it was unpopular or even dangerous to embrace one's Indigenous heritage. However, I was privileged to have strong Wyandot women to relate the stories and encourage me to honour the vision and examples of my Ancestors. I learned that my fifth-great-grandfather was Chief Tarhe, who sought to bring peace to Ohio in 1795 by being the first to sign the Treaty of Greenville. My great-great-grandparents, Ebenezer O. and Rebecca Zane, were abolitionist Wyandot who participated in the founding of Quindaro, the first Freeport in the state of Kansas. They built a hotel with a tunnel in the basement that led to the Missouri River that offered protection for Freedom Seekers fleeing slavery. I learned about my cousins Sallie, Helena, Ida, and Lyda Conley. Lyda (Eliza Burton Conley Jr) was the first Indigenous woman attorney to argue a case before the United States Supreme Court, presenting her case to preserve and protect Huron Indian Cemetery (a.k.a. Wyandott National Burying Ground) in Kansas City, Kansas from destruction and desecration.

In June of 1999, 350 years after our removal and dispersal from our beautiful homeland on Georgian Bay, we joined leaders of the Wendat Confederacy and representatives of the Anishinabe, Six Nations, Canadian, and Ontario governments, the French, Dutch, Roman Catholic, Anglican, and Evangelical churches, and the archeological community in Midland, Ontario in a private weekend of reconciliation. In August of that year, leaders and Wyandots from our four Nations met together to formally reaffirm the Wendat Confederacy on the Papal Field of Martyrs Shrine in Midland, Ontario. The next day, through cooperation between the Royal Ontario Museum and the Huron-Wendat of Lorette, People of the Confederacy and their old friends, enemies, and allies met to rebury the remains of over 500 of their Ancestors in their original resting place at Ossassane.

In 2012, members of the Wyandot Nation of Kansas gratefully joined their Wendat brothers, sisters, and friends and representatives from the Government of Ontario to participate in the largest reburial in North American history, laying to final rest the remains of over 1,750 of the Ancestors who had been stored in boxes in various museums. I am now working with the Wyandot Nation of Kansas to expand the National Archives of the Wyandot Nation of Kansas through its Historical Archives program designed to assemble, organize, and share our history and culture in a way that is easily accessible and freely available. My methodology is simple and was emphasized in the practice of nursing: Be kind to and respect one another; and see one, do one, and teach one.

The stories in this book connect these women to our sisters whose courage and determination link them with Indigenous women throughout the world; their stories contain the contemporary themes that today resonate among people who must engage in a struggle to preserve rights of justice and self-identity for themselves and their families. Within these stories is interwoven the thread of grief that arises from the tension created when a paradigm of fear, power, and control is pitted against a journey toward interconnectedness and interdependence.

I have internalized the oft-told story of the daughters of my great-great-aunt Eliza Burton Conley Sr, the four Conley sisters who are mentioned in this book and referred to themselves as Sallie, Ida, Lyda, and Lena. Our family simply called them "The Sisters" or "The Cousins." Their lives were full of stories of heroism and heartache; respect and humiliating division; inspiration for our people and headaches for those who would intrude upon the rights of our People and, especially, would disrespect the bones and resting place of our Ancestors.

Our people have been encouraged and inspired by the assertive advocacy of the women and men of our Nation. Throughout our history in Kansas they have joined together not only when the cemetery's sanctity was threatened but also for matters of justice and equity in the lives of our people. Today, women of the four Nations of the international Wendat Confederacy – the Huronne-Wendat of Lorette (Quebec, Canada), the Wendat of Anderdon Nation (Michigan, USA), the Wyandot Nation of Kansas (USA), and the Wyandott Nation of Oklahoma (USA) – communicate as "Women of the Longhouse" and work together to address justice and quality of life issues for the People. These same issues also challenge our Indigenous sisters of today's world; and we support their struggles to maintain their identities, heritage, and cultures.

BEVERLEE PETTIT (WYANDOTTE NATION)

Born of the Wyandotte Nation of Oklahoma, I spent my early years just outside of Tahlequah, Oklahoma, along the winding Illinois River. Because I was born in autumn, my earliest memories are of colourful leaves fluttering in the breeze with sunlight twinkling and glittering. Nicknamed Becky because I could not pronounce Beverlee, the name perfectly described the little girl who loved to sing. My first years of school were at the Bagley Primary School in Tahlequah while my mother attended college at Northeastern State University. I graduated at the oldest Indian college in the United States, Bacone, which is located in Muskogee, Oklahoma. I am now an employee of the Indian Health Service, Alaska Area Native Health Service as a Human Resource Specialist and live in Anchorage, Alaska. My thirty years of government service also includes work with the Department of the Interior, Bureau of Indian Affairs. In addition, I have worked almost ten years in tribal government positions as an employment and human resources specialist. I am also a published poet.

I have been asked to speak a word to the future women of my tribe. There are many thoughts, memories, faces, and places flowing through my brain. Like rivers and oceans flooding my eyes, rolling around and around, running, flowing down, cascading over my cheeks, dripping from my chin, a waterfall crashing down on my breast. Too many to speak, too many to share. Not even a book can contain. My head hangs down as I ponder and frown. Lifting my chin … I say, be true, be honest, be you.

NOTES

INTRODUCTION

1 Origin stories are generated from ancestral knowledge and typically depict the creation of the world and those who inhabit it.

2 The words *Huron*, *Wendat*, *Wyandot*, and *Wyandotte* describe the same People who have ancestral ties to the seventeenth-century Wendat Confederacy. The spelling used in this book – *We^{n}dat/Wa^{n}dat* – represents two pronunciations of the name the People called themselves before European contact: WHEN-dot and WAHN-dot. There is a significant amount of work being done to build our knowledge of the We^{n}dat/Wa^{n}dat language and contribute to the revitalization movement. For examples of work being done by the Huron-Wendat, see *Langue Wendat* (http://languewendat.com/en); for work being done by the Wyandotte of Oklahoma, see the entry for "Wendat (Wandat)" at *Omniglot.com* (https://www.omniglot.com/writing/wyandot.htm). Other Iroquoian Peoples include the Haudenosaunee, Cherokee, Neutral, Erie, Wenrohronon, and Susquehannock.

3 "The Wendat Confederacy," original copy accessed with permission of Chief Janith English; digital copy accessed at http://www.wyandotofanderdon.com/wp/wp-content/uploads/2013/11/1999ConfederacyAgreement.jpg.

4 Reuben Gold Thwaites, ed., *The Jesuit Relations and Allied Documents: Travels and Explorations of the Jesuit Missionaries in New France, 1610–1791: The Original French, Latin, and Italian Texts, with English Translations and Notes*, 52 vols (Cleveland: Burrows, 1897), 10:125; 9:223.

5 Charles Marius Barbeau, *Huron-Wyandot Traditional Narratives: In Translations and Native Texts* (Ottawa: Canada Department of Northern Affairs and National Resources, 1960), 25, 158–69.

6 Matricentric cultures place the woman at the centre of society. In the case of We^{n}dat/Wa^{n}dat society, the women also were the heads of households, had political authority, and were responsible for the land.

7 Karen L. Anderson, *Chain Her by One Foot: The Subjugation of Women in Seventeenth-Century New France* (London and New York: Routledge, 1991); Theda Perdue, *Cherokee Women: Gender and Culture Change, 1700–1835* (Lincoln: University of Nebraska Press, 1998); Peter C. Mancall and James Hart Merrell, eds., *American*

Encounters: Natives and Newcomers from European Contact to Indian Removal, 1500–1850 (New York: Routledge, 2000).

8 Anderson, *Chain Her by One Foot.*

9 Kathryn Magee Labelle, *Dispersed but Not Destroyed: A History of the Seventeenth-Century Wendat People* (Vancouver: University of British Columbia Press, 2013), 159–75.

10 Paula Gunn Allen, *The Sacred Hoop: Recovering the Feminine in American Indian Traditions* (Boston: Beacon Press, 1986); Kim Anderson, *A Recognition of Being: Reconstructing Native Womanhood* (Toronto: Sumach Press, 2000); Brenda Child, *Holding Our World Together: Ojibwe Women and the Survival of Community* (New York: Viking Books, 2012); Carol Devens, *Countering Colonization: Native American Women and Great Lakes Missions, 1630–1900* (Berkeley: University of California Press, 1992); Joyce Green, ed., *Making Space for Indigenous Feminism* (Black Point, NS: Fernwood Publishing, 2007); Kathryn Magee Labelle, "'For Home and Country': Agency, Activism and Education of Alberta's Native Women's Clubs, 1942–1970," *Native Studies Review* 18, no. 2 (2009): 27–49; Barbara Alice Mann, ed., *Make a Beautiful Way: The Wisdom of Native American Women* (Lincoln: University of Nebraska Press, 2008); Devon Abbott Mihesuah, *Indigenous American Women: Decolonizing, Empowerment, Activism* (Lincoln: University of Nebraska Press, 2003); Lucy Eldersveld Murphy, "Public Mothers: Native American and Métis Women as Creole Mediators in the Nineteenth-Century Midwest," *Journal of Women's History* 14, no. 4 (2003): 142–66; Nancy Shoemaker, ed., *Negotiators of Change: Historical Perspectives on Native American Women* (New York: Routledge, 1995); Susan Sleeper-Smith, *Indian Women and French Men: Rethinking Cultural Encounter in the Western Great Lakes* (Amherst: University of Massachusetts Press, 2001); Lina Sunseri, *Being Again of One Mind: Oneida Women and the Struggle for Decolonization* (Vancouver: University of British Columbia Press, 2011).

11 Lisa Udel, "Revision and Resistance: The Politics of Native Women's Motherwork," *Frontiers: A Journal of Women Studies* 22, no. 2 (2001): 43.

12 Jo-Anne Fiske, "Pocahontas's Granddaughters: Spiritual Transition and Tradition of Carrier Women of British Columbia," *Ethnohistory* 43, no. 4 (1996): 663–81; Patricia Hill Collins, "Shifting the Center: Race, Class, and Feminist Theorizing about Motherhood," in *American Families: A Multicultural Reader*, ed. Stephanie Coontz, Maya Person, and Gabrielle Raley (New York: Routledge 1999), 197–217; Udel, "Revision and Resistance," 43–62; Sunseri, *Being Again of One Mind.*

13 Originally the council consisted of seven women, to represent the sacred number seven. Upon further reflection, we changed the composition so that there was equal representation from each First Nation. As a result, Manon Sioui graciously agreed to join the council in 2015.

14 For works that deal specifically with the importance of community-based research as an ethnohistorical approach, see Keith Carlson, John Lutz, and David

Schaepe, "Turning the Page: Ethnohistory from a New Generation," *The University of the Fraser Valley Research Review* 2, no. 2 (2014): 1–8; Keith Thor Carlson, Albert Jules McHalsie, David M. Schaepe, and John S. Lutz, *Towards a New Ethnohistory: Community-Engaged Scholarship among the People of the River* (Winnipeg: University of Manitoba Press, 2018); Sean Kidd and Michael Kral, "Practicing Participatory Action Research," *Journal of Counseling Psychology* 52, no. 2 (2005): 187–95.

15 Nick Salvatore, "Biography and Social History: An Intimate Relationship," *Labour History* 87 (2004): 187–92; Jean Barman, "Writing Women Into the History of North American Wests, One Woman at a Time," in *One Step Over the Line: Toward a History of Women in the North American Wests*, ed. Elizabeth Jameson and Sheila McManus (Edmonton: University of Alberta Press; Athabasca, AB: Athabasca University Press, 2008), 100.

16 Doris Jeanne MacKinnon, *Métis Pioneers: Marie Rose Smith and Isabella Clark Hardisty Lougheed* (Edmonton: University of Alberta Press 2018), xxiv.

17 Kim Anderson and Bonita Lawrence, eds., *Strong Women Stories: Native Vision and Community Survival* (Toronto: Sumach Press, 2003); Child, *Holding Our World Together*; Renya K. Ramirez, *Native Hubs: Culture, Community, and Belonging in Silicon Valley and Beyond* (Durham, NC: Duke University Press, 2007); Sunseri, *Being Again of One Mind*.

18 Ramirez, *Native Hubs*.

19 The phrase "time immemorial" is used to explain time extending beyond the reach of memory, record, or tradition.

CHAPTER ONE

1 Established in 1616 and also referred to as the "Parish of Quebec."

2 Both of these public displays went above and beyond normal funeral rights. According to the Jesuit missionaries, the Bishop's initiative was "a thing which is not usually done on the death of a Savage." Reuben Gold Thwaites, ed., *The Jesuit Relations and Allied Documents: Travels and Explorations of the Jesuit Missionaries in New France, 1610–1791: The Original French, Latin, and Italian Texts, with English Translations and Notes* [hereafter *JR*], 52 vols (Cleveland: Burrows, 1897), 52:257.

3 Françoise Juchereau de Saint Ignace, *Histoire de l'Hôtel-Dieu de Québec* (Paris: 1751), 201.

4 *JR* 52:247–51.

5 Marie de l'Incarnation, *Words from New France: Selected Letters of Marie de l'Incarnation*, ed. and trans. Joyce Marshall (Toronto: Oxford University Press, 1967), 81–2; Saint Ignace, *Histoire de l'Hôtel-Dieu de Québec*, 198–201.

6 Narcisse-Eutrope Dionne, *Serviteurs et servantes de Dieu en Canada: Quarante biographies* (London: Forgotten Books, 1918), 287–8.

7 Kathryn Magee Labelle, *Dispersed but Not Destroyed: A History of the Seventeenth-Century Wendat People* (Vancouver: University of British Columbia Press, 2013), 171–3.

8 Natalie Zemon Davis, "Iroquois Women, European Women," in *Feminist Post-Colonial Theory: A Reader*, ed. Reina Lewis and Sara Mills (New York: Routledge, 2003), 146–7.

9 For examples see Cecile Garenhatsi, *JR* 45:51; Cecile Arenhatsi, *JR* 36:21; Algonquin Cecile Kouekoueaté, *JR* 45:47.

10 Carol Blackburn, *Harvest of Souls: The Jesuit Missions and Colonialism, 1632–1650* (Montreal: McGill-Queen's University Press, 2000).

11 *JR* 41:155.

12 John Steckley, personal correspondence with author, 12 October 2015.

13 John Steckley, *Words of the Huron* (Waterloo: Wilfrid Laurier Press, 2007), 125.

14 Labelle, *Dispersed but Not Destroyed.*

15 *JR* 52:247.

16 Ibid.

17 *JR* 52:251.

18 Dionne, *Serviteurs et servantes*, 287.

19 *JR* 52:249.

20 Ibid.

21 Gary Warrick, *A Population History of the Huron-Petun, A.D. 500–1650* (Cambridge: Cambridge University Press, 2008), 145, 399.

22 Kathryn Magee Labelle, "'They Only Spoke in Sighs': The Loss of Leaders and Life in Wendake, 1633–1639," *Journal of Historical Biography* 6 (Autumn 2009): 1–33.

23 Labelle, *Dispersed but Not Destroyed*; Bruce G. Trigger, *The Children of Aataentsic: A History of the Huron People to 1660* (Montreal & Kingston: McGill-Queen's University Press, 1987).

24 *JR* 19:209.

25 "Ratification par le roi de la concession de Sillery, par la compagnie de nouvelle France, en faveur des sauvages, sous la direction des Pères Jesuits" (July 1651), Wendake Archives [WA], Collection François Vincent [CFV], cartable:1-b; *JR* 24:19–43.

26 Trigger, *The Children of Aataentsic*, 49–50.

27 Marie-Florine Bruneau, *Women Mystics Confront the Modern World: Marie de L'Incarnation (1599-1672) and Madame Guyon (1648-1717)* (New York: SUNY Press, 1998), 96–7.

28 *JR* 24:45.

29 Ibid.

30 Ibid.

31 *JR* 52:249.

32 Saint Ignace, *Histoire de l'Hôtel-Dieu de Québec*, 200; *JR* 52:249.

33 De l'Incarnation, *Words from New France*, 81–2.

34 *Régistre des entrées et sorties de petites filles françoises et sauvage de 1641* (Quebec: Les Archives de Monastère de Québec), 22–30.

35 *JR* 36:215–219.

36 Seventeenth-century wampum was a series of shelled beads or belts that served as a material record of events, agreements, and alliances.

37 *JR* 36:215–19.

38 Mairi Cowan, "Education, *Francisation*, and Shifting Colonial Priorities at the Ursuline Convent in Seventeenth-Century Québec," *Canadian Historical Review* 99, no. 1 (2018): 1–29.

39 "Francisation" was a French policy that used conversion to Catholicism and adoption of French cultural practices as a means to colonize North America. Cowan, "Education, *Francisation*, and Shifting Colonial Priorities," 7.

40 Ibid., 6–8.

41 *JR* 41:229.

42 Saint Ignace, *Histoire de l'Hôtel-Dieu de Québec*, 161–3; François de Laval, *La Solide dévotion à la très-sainte famille, de Jesus, Marie & Joseph* (Montreal: Chez F. Mesplet, Imprimeur & Librairie, 1787), 6–9.

43 Marie-Aimée Cliche, "La confrérie de la Sainte-Famille à Québec sous le régime français, 1663–1760," *Sessions d'étude - Société canadienne d'histoire de l'Église catholique* 43 (1976): 79.

44 Mary Dunn, ed., *From Mother to Son: The Selected Letters of Marie de L'Incarnation to Claude Martin* (New York: Oxford University Press, 2018): Letter 220 (29 October 1665), 193.

45 Cliche, "La confrérie de la Sainte-Famille," 80.

46 Ibid., 82.

47 Gilles Havard, "'Les forcer à devenir Ctoyens': État, Sauvages et citoyenneté en Nouvelle-France (XVIIe–XVIIIe siècle)," *Annales, Histoire, Sciences Sociales* 64, no. 5 (2009): 989–1000.

48 *JR* 36:205.

49 *JR* 52:249.

50 Translation is my own. Laval, *La Solide*, 19–21.

51 Ibid., 28–9.

52 Translation is my own. Ibid., 29.

53 Ibid., 31–3.

54 Ibid., 34.

55 *JR* 52:249.

56 Richard White, *Middle Ground: Indians, Empires, and Republics in the Great Lakes Region, 1650–1815* (New York: Cambridge University Press, 1991), 62.

57 Trigger, *Children of Aataentsic*, 80–1.

58 *JR* 57:255–7; Labelle, *Dispersed but Not Destroyed*, 94.

59 *JR* 52:25.

60 *JR* 52:251.

61 Dionne, *Serviteurs et servantes*, 274.

62 André Vachon, "Laval, François de," in *Dictionary of Canadian Biography* 2 (University of Toronto/Université Laval, 2003), accessed 17 February 2019, http://www.biographi.ca/en/bio/laval_francois_de_2E.html.

63 Victoria Jackson, "Silent Diplomacy: Wendat Boys' 'Adoptions' at the Jesuit Seminary, 1636–1642," *Journal of the Canadian Historical Association* 27, no. 1 (2016): 139–68.

64 Dionne, *Serviteurs et servantes*, 274–5.

65 Saint Ignace, *Histoire de l'Hôtel-Dieu de Québec*, 189, 195, 198.

66 Labelle, *Dispersed but Not Destroyed*, 166–7.

67 Saint Ignace, *Histoire de l'Hôtel-Dieu de Québec*, 154.

68 Translation is my own. Laval, *La Solide*, 25–6.

69 *JR* 52:243.

70 *JR* 52:251–3.

71 *JR* 52:251.

72 Ibid.

73 *JR* 52:245.

74 Muriel Clair, "Notre-Dame de Foy en Nouvelle-France (1669–1675): Histoire des statuettes de Foy et des *wampum* des Hurons chrétiens," *Annales de la Société archéologique de Namur* 83 (2009): 170.

75 *JR* 52:233–5; *JR* 53:111; Jonathan Lainey, "Le prétendu wampum offert à Champlain et l'interprétation des objets muséifiés," *Revue d'histoire de l'Amérique française* 61, nos 3–4 (2008): 404n19. Jonathan Lainey explains that a wampum belt of 1,000 wampum beads would have been considered "large." The headman's gift of 4,000 would therefore have been of considerable value.

76 *JR* 52:257.

CHAPTER TWO

1 Saliha Belmessous, "Assimilation and Racialism in Seventeenth and Eighteenth-Century French Colonial Policy," in *The American Historical Review* 110, no. 2 (2005): 322–49.

2 Belmessous, "Assimilation and Racialism," 347.

3 Ibid., 341.

4 Ibid., 324. See also Mairi Cowan, "Education, *Francisation*, and Shifting Colonial Priorities at the Ursuline Convent in Seventeenth-Century Québec," *Canadian Historical Review* 99, no. 1 (2018): 1–29.

5 Kathryn Magee Labelle, "'They Are the Life of the Nation': Women and War in Traditional Nadouek Society," *Canadian Journal of Native Studies* 28, no. 1 (2008): 119–38.

6 Jacques Légaré, Bertrand Desjardins, and Hubert Charbonneau, "Repertory of vital events (baptisms, marriages, burials) 1621–1849 Quebec and French Canada," Université de Montréal, *Programme de recherche en démographie historique de l'Université de Montréal*, http://www.genealogie.umontreal.ca, #59418, Catherine Jean, Baptism, 31 August 1676, Québec (Notre-Dame-de-Québec). Charlesbourg is a suburb of Quebec City and only a few kilometres from the Wendat Reserve of Lorette/Wendake.

7 Suzanne Boivin Sommerville, "'But I Read It…': Is Catherine Jean *dite* Vien the Same Woman as the Huron Named *La Vielle* Catherine and *Sk8ateenre* (*Achi8taa*) Recorded in Father Pierre Potier's 1747 Census of *Village Huron de L'Ile aux Bois Blancs*?" *Michigan's Habitant Heritage* 34, no. 2 (2013): 69–74.

8 Baptismal Record (Collection Drouin) Actes d'état civil et registres d'église du Québec 1621–1967. Accessed via Judith Kukowski's *Ancestry.ca* account.

9 *Programme de recherche en démographie historique*, #7361, Catherine Vien (Gateau), Burial (21 April 1726).

10 Sommerville, "'But I Read It,'" 70; *Programme de recherche en démographie historique*, #7009, marriage of Jacques Sauvage and Catherine Jean (10 January 1690).

11 Sommerville, "'But I Read It,'" 73; Judith Kukowski's *Ancestry.ca* account.

12 Sommerville, "'But I Read It,'" 71.

13 Ibid., 74; Gail Moreau-DesHarnais, "People Buried from Ste. Anne de Detroit (1766–1776): Part III," *Michigan's Habitant Heritage* 31, no. 4 (2010): 208.

14 Clarence M. Burton, *"Cadillac's Village," or "Detroit Under Cadillac." With List of Property Owners and a History of the Settlement 1701 to 1710* (Detroit: Clarence M. Burton, 1896), 41–3.

15 Victoria Jackson, "Silent Diplomacy: Wendat Boys' 'Adoptions' at the Jesuit Seminary, 1636–1642," *Journal of the Canadian Historical Association* 27, no. 1 (2016): 143; Roger Magnuson, *Education in New France* (Montreal & Kingston: McGill-Queen's University Press, 1992), 47; Carole Blackburn, *Harvest of Souls: The Jesuit Missions and Colonialism in North America, 1632-1650* (Montreal & Kingston: McGill-Queen's University Press, 2000), 13.

16 Bruce G. Trigger, "Champlain Judged by His Indian Policy: A Different View of Early Canadian History," *Anthropologica* 13, nos 1–2 (1971): 85–114.

17 Reuben Gold Thwaites, ed., *The Jesuit Relations and Allied Documents: Travels and Explorations of the Jesuit Missionaries in New France, 1610--1791: The Original French, Latin, and Italian Texts, with English Translations and Notes*, 52 vols (Cleveland: Burrows, 1897) [hereafter *JR*] 5:225; 9:223.

18 *JR* 6:85.

19 *JR* 4:225.

20 Most recently Darryl Leroux has used Pillard as a case study of misidentification, supporting her French identity. This argument is refuted adamantly by Catherine Pillard's Wyandot descendants. See: Maura Forrest, "Indigenous or a French Colonist? How the Fight over This 17th-Century Woman's Identity Could

Affect Tens of Thousands of Her Descendants," *National Post*, 30 January 2018, https://nationalpost.com/news/canada/a-new-world-mystery-how-a-17th-century-french-woman-became-indigenous-then-became-white-again; Darryl Leroux, *Distorted Descent: White Claims to Indigenous Identity* (University of Manitoba Press, 2019), 86–93, 97–101.

21 Gail Moreau-DesHarnais, Suzette Leclair, and Johan Robitaille, "Catherine Pillard, Native of La Rochelle: In Search of the Truth," *Michigan's Habitant Heritage* 30, no. 2 (2009): 1–9; Gail Moreau–DesHarnais, Suzette Leclair, and Johan Robitaille, "Catherine Pillard, Native de La Rochelle: À la recherche de la vérité," *Le Chaînon* 27, no. 1 (2009): 53–62.

22 For instance, Father Pierre Potier interred the Mohawk man Pierre Sauvage from St Regis, Canada on 15 June 1784. See Robert Toupin and Pierrette L. Lagarde, eds., *Les écrits de Pierre Potier* (Ottawa: Presses de l'Université d'Ottawa, 1996), 932.

23 John Askin, *The John Askin Papers*, ed. Milo Milton Quaife (Detroit: Detroit Library Commission, 1928–1931), 410; Cyprien Tanguay, *Dictionnaire généalogique des familles canadiennes depuis la fondation de la colonie jusqu'à nos jours, Vol. I* (Montreal: E. Senécal, Imprimeurs-éditeurs, 1887), 540; Friend Palmer, *Early Days in Detroit* (Detroit: Hunt & June, 1906), 640.

24 Toupin and Lagarde, eds., *Les écrits de Pierre Potier*, 576.

25 Judith Kukowski, personal correspondence with author, 23 July 2014.

26 D.A. Mihesuah, "American Indian Identities: Issues of Individual Choices and Development," *American Indian Culture and Research Journal* 22, no. 2 (1998): 193–226; Hilary N. Weaver, "Indigenous Identity: What Is It, and Who *Really* Has It?" *American Indian Quarterly* 25, no. 2 (2001): 240.

27 Weaver, "Indigenous Identity," 243.

28 Ibid., 245.

29 Bruce G. Trigger, *The Children of Aataentsic: A History of the Huron People to 1660* (Montreal & Kingston: McGill-Queen's University Press, 1976), 214–28; Roland Tremblay, *The St. Lawrence Iroquoians: Corn People* (Montreal: Pointe-à-Callière, Montréal Museum of Archaeology and History, 2006).

30 Jeune Lorette became a reserve now known as "Wendake" and is located a few kilometres north of Quebec City. Kathryn Magee Labelle, *Dispersed but Not Destroyed: A History of the Seventeenth-Century Wendat People* (Vancouver: University of British Columbia Press, 2013), 107.

31 Gilles Havard, *The Great Peace of Montreal of 1701: French-Native Diplomacy in the Seventeenth Century* (Montreal & Kingston: McGill-Queen's University Press, 2001); Labelle, *Dispersed but Not Destroyed.*

32 The founding of a post at Detroit was only possible once the Great Peace of Montreal of 1701 had officially ended large-scale warfare between the Haudenosaunee Confederacy, the Indigenous Peoples of the Great Lakes, and New France.

All treaty signatories agreed to recognize the territory around the southern Great Lakes as a "common bowl," a shared hunting territory for Iroquoian and Algonquian peoples. Havard, *The Great Peace of Montreal of 1701*, 145, 148–9; Karen Marrero, "On the Edge of the West: The Roots and Routes of Detroit's Urban Eighteenth Century," in *Frontier Cities: Encounters at the Crossroads of Empire*, ed. Jay Gitlin, Barbara Berglund, and Adam Arenson (Philadelphia: University of Pennsylvania Press, 2013), 67–8.

33 Marrero, "On the Edge of the West," 76; Catherine Cangany, *Frontier Seaport: Detroit's Transformation into an Atlantic Entrepôt* (Chicago: University of Chicago Press, 2014), 21.

34 Detroit was an important stronghold in a series of posts that guaranteed French access to the heart of North America, the western Great Lakes, Illinois Country, and the Lower Mississippi Valley (Louisiana). Claiborne A. Skinner, *The Upper Country: French Enterprise in the Colonial Great Lakes* (Baltimore: Johns Hopkins University Press, 2008), 93–4; Richard Weyhing, "'Gascon Exaggerations': The Rise of Antoine Laumet dit de Lamothe, Sieur de Cadillac, the Foundation of Colonial Detroit, and the Origins of the Fox Wars," in *French and Indians in the Heart of North America, 1630–1815*, ed. Robert Englebert and Guillaume Teasdale (East Lansing: Michigan State University Press, 2013), 95–6.

35 David Edmunds and Joseph L. Peyser, *The Fox Wars: The Mesquakie Challenge to New France* (Norman: University of Oklahoma Press, 1993), 53–8; Marrero, "On the Edge of the West," 67, 69–70; Cangany, *Frontier Seaport*, 9–10.

36 For more on the establishment of Detroit in 1701 see Dale Miquelon, *New France 1701–1744 "A Supplement to Europe"* (Toronto: McClelland and Stewart, 1989), 33–40; Peter Moogk, *La Nouvelle France: The Making of French Canada - A Cultural History* (East Lansing: Michigan State University Press, 2000), 9–15; Susan Sleeper-Smith, *Indian Women and French Men: Rethinking Cultural Encounter in the Western Great Lakes* (Amherst: University of Massachusetts Press, 2001), 54–72; Lina Gouger, "Le peuplement colonisateur de Détroit, 1701–1765" (PhD diss., Université Laval, 2002), 53, 87–93; Andrew Sturtevant, "Jealous Neighbors: Rivalry and Alliance among the Native Communities of Detroit, 1701–1766" (PhD diss., College of William and Mary, 2011), 22–32.

37 Richard White, *The Middle Ground: Indians, Empires and Republics in the Great Lakes Region, 1650–1815*, 2nd ed. (New York: Cambridge University Press, 2001), 146, 149–50; Cangany, *Frontier Seaport*, 9–10, 22.

38 Marrero, "On the Edge of the West," 74–6, 83–4; Weyhing, "'Gascon Exaggerations,'" 82.

39 Sommerville, "'But I Read It,'" 73.

40 Ibid., 71; *Programme de recherche en démographie historique*, #14788.

41 Cangany, *Frontier Seaport*, 18–20; Karen Marrero, "Women at the Crossroads: Trade, Mobility, and Power in Early French America and Detroit," in *Women in*

Early America: Transnational Histories, Rethinking Master Narratives, ed. Thomas Foster (New York: New York University Press, 2015), 159–85.

42 Godefroy died on 2 May 1744 at the age of sixty-five. Sommerville, "'But I Read It,'" 7.

43 Sommerville, "'But I Read It,'" 71n13.

44 John Steckley, *The Eighteenth-Century Wyandot: A Clan-Based Study* (Waterloo: Wilfrid Laurier University Press, 2013), 1–2.

45 Although this is speculation, there is good chance it is true. Catherine is not found on the 1747 census of the We^{n}dat/Wa^{n}dat settlement, but neither is her daughter Catherine Chesne (née Sauvage) as she, too, married a French Canadian.

46 Andrew Sturtevant, "'Inseparable Companions' and Irreconcilable Enemies: The Hurons and Odawas of French Détroit, 1701–38," *Ethnohistory* 60, no. 2 (2013): 219–43; Andrew Sturtevant, "'Over the Lake': The Western Wendake in the American Revolution," in *From Huronia to Wendakes: Adversity, Migrations, and Resilience, 1650–1900*, ed. Thomas Peace and Kathryn Magee Labelle (Norman: University of Oklahoma Press, 2016), 35–73; Andrew Sturtevant, "'The Rest of their Nation': Wyandot Politics in Pontiac's War, 1763–1765," American Society for Ethnohistory 2018 Meeting, October 2018, Oaxaca, Mexico, unpublished conference paper.

47 We^{n}dat/Wa^{n}dat women have a long history of choosing the headmen or Chiefs of their village, nation, and confederacy. Labelle, "They Are the Life of the Nation," 119–38.

48 Sommerville, "'But I Read It,'" 73; Judith Kukowski's *Ancestry.ca* account.

49 The last name is also spelled Chene and Chen in the historical records.

50 Steckley, *The Eighteenth-Century Wyandot*, 179.

51 Ibid., 40–8.

52 Ibid., 188.

53 Ibid., 189; *JR* 41:104–5.

54 Labelle, "They Are the Life of the Nation"; Steckley, *The Eighteenth-Century Wyandot*, 174–200.

55 Steckley, *The Eighteenth-Century Wyandot*, 173; Pierre François-Xavier de Charlevoix, *Journal of a Voyage to North America, Volume 1*, ed. and trans. Louise Phelps Kellogg (Chicago: The Caxton Club, 1923), 25.

56 Pierre François-Xavier de Charlevoix, quoted in Steckley, *The Eighteenth-Century Wyandot*, 174.

57 Labelle, "They Are the Life of the Nation"; Joseph-François Lafitau, *Customs of the American Indians Compared with the Customs of Primitive Times*, ed. and trans. William N. Fenton and Elizabeth L. Moore (Toronto: Champlain Society, 1974), 69.

58 Judith Kukowski, "The Effects of Settler Culture on Wyandot Women at the Time of the War of 1812," unpublished manuscript, public presentation: River Raisin Battlefield, Munroe, Michigan, 14 March 2015.
59 Steckley, *The Eighteenth-Century Wyandot*, 189; *JR* 41:104–5.
60 Drouin Records, Detroit L'Assomption de Sandwich Church, Volume 1710–1801, Page 2, image 3 (18 January 1722), US French Catholic Church Records.
61 Father Pierre Potier mentions Chesne in his 1747 census. Sommerville, "'But I Read It,'" 74; Toupin and Lagarde, *Les écrits de Pierre Potier*, 261.
62 Toupin and Lagarde, *Les écrits de Pierre Potier*, 824, 1240.
63 Catherine Jean is not listed in Potier's register of 1747 and neither is her daughter Sondakwa, although we know that they are both living in the Detroit area. In 1743, for instance, records indicate that Catherine Jean attends the baptism of her granddaughter Catherine dit Beaubien. See Sommerville, "'But I Read It,'" 73.
64 C.W. Butterfield, *An Historical Account of the Expedition Against Sandusky Under Col. William Crawford in 1782* (Cincinnati: Robert Clarke & Co, 1873), 164–5.
65 Genealogical Research Library, Ontario, Canada, *Canadian Genealogy Index, 1600s–1900s* [database online]; Provo, UT: *Ancestry.com* Operations Inc, 2005; Tanguay, *Dictionnaire généalogique des familles canadiennes*, 53. See also the accounts of the burial in Joseph Moore, "Journal of a Tour to Detroit, In Order to Attend a Treaty, Proposed to Be Held with the Indians at Sandusky," in *Historical Collections: Collections and Researches Made by the Michigan Pioneer and Historical Society including Reports of Officers and Papers Read at the Annual Meeting of 1890, Vol. XVII*, ed. M. Agnes Burton (Lansing: Wynkoop Hallenbeck Crawford, State Printers, 1910), 645.
66 "Extract of a Declaration Made to Caesar Cormic to the Therein Named Witness, at Detroit, 11 June, 1761," in *Historical Collections: Collections and Researches Made by the Michigan Pioneer and Historical Society, Vol. 27*, ed. Michigan Pioneer and Historical Society (Lansing: Robert Smith Printing State Printers and Binders, 1897), 632–3.
67 Chesne is listed as a captain during the American Revolutionary War. He is also listed as an officer on 24 October 1779. Charles Irish Walker, *The North-west During the Revolution. Annual Address before the State Historical Society of Wisconsin, Tuesday Evening, January 31, 1871* (Madison: Atwood & Culver, State Printers, 1871), 41–2.
68 Ernest J. Lajeunesse, *The Windsor Border Region, Canada's Southernmost Frontier: A Collection of Documents* (Toronto: Champlain Society, 1960), 160–1.
69 Sturtevant, "Over the Lake," 35–73.
70 Catholic Records (Drouin Collection), 1802–1967, Luniere 4, Reducation 19 (Amherstbourg Paroisse St Jean Essex Ontario, 1802–1829), 118–19; 126.

71 White, *The Middle Ground*, 516; Stickney to Hull (25 May 1812) Esarey, *Harrison Messages*, 54.

72 Katie Chinn, "Isadore Chene," Wyandotte Nation, https://www.wyandotte-nation.org/traditions/biographical-panels/isadore-chene/.

73 John H. Gwathmey, *Historical Register of Virginians in the Revolution: Soldiers, Sailors, Marines, 1775–1783* (Richmond: Dietz Press, 1938), 401.

74 French Catholic Church Records (Drouin Collection), 1695–1954, 1811–1824, "Sandwhich, Paroisse Assumption, Essex County, Ontario," 1625; Alexander Scott Withers, *Chronicles of Border Warfare, or A History of the Settlement by the Whites, of North-Western Virginia, and of the Indian Wars and Massacres in that Section of the State*, ed. Reuben Gold Thwaites (Cincinnati: Stewart & Kidd Company, 1912), 72–3.

75 "Adam Brown," Wyandotte Nation, https://www.wyandotte-nation.org/culture/history/biographies/adam-brown/. Excerpted from *The Provisional Government of Nebraska Territory and the Journals of William Walker, Provisional Governor of Nebraska Territory*, ed. William E. Connelley (Lincoln: State Journal Company, Printers, 1899).

76 Brownstown Historical Society, *Celebrating 187 Years: 1827–2014* (Brownstown: Brownstown Historical Society, 2014), 2; Charles Garrad, *Petun to Wyandot: The Ontario Petun from the Sixteenth Century* (Ottawa: University of Ottawa Press, 2014), 133.

77 Steve Gronda quoted in Sallie Cotter Andrews, "Walk-In-The-Water: A Wyandot Chief," Wyandotte Nation, www.wyandotte-nation.org/culture/history/biographies/walk-in-the-water.

78 Kukowski, "The Effects of Settler Culture on Wyandot Women."

79 Kukowski states: "I spend a lot of time reading the Drouin Records of the Catholic Church. They are the baptism, marriages and burials of the people. I began noticing a pattern. Our main ceremony is the Naming Ceremony (Komaskwema'a) always held in the summer at the Green Corn Feast. The Wyandots were bringing their children to be baptized in Assumption Church in Windsor. Baptism and the Naming Ceremony would be mutually synergetic. But why back to Canada? There were other Catholic Churches along the way from Ohio and past Monroe. I firmly believe they were coming together to celebrate the Green Corn Feast as family. Marius Barbeau who spent much time studying the Wyandots talks about the Green Corn Feast. This was a time for renewing friendship and making alliances. Young men and women could meet and perhaps find spouses. This also meant the women could hold council and discuss strategies for survival and lend each other the support they needed." Kukowski, "The Effects of Settler Culture on Wyandot Women."

80 Chief Billy Friend, "Busy Summer at Nation," *The Turtle Speaks: Gyah'-Wish Atak-ia* 21, no. 3 (2017): 2.

81 Wyandotte Nation Cultural Committee, "Gathering of Little Turtles Seeing Continual Growth," *The Turtle Speaks: Gyah'-Wish Atak-ia* 21, no. 3 (2017): 6.

82 William Swaim, "The Princess Diaries," *The Turtle Speaks: Gyah'-Wish Atakiia* 21, no. 3 (2017): 10.

83 Chief Billy Friend, "A Letter from the Chief: September 10, 2012," Wyandotte Nation, https://www.wyandotte-nation.org/from-our-chief/letter-from-the-chief/.

84 Sallie Cotter Andrews, personal correspondence with author, 8 July 2019.

85 Media News Group, "DAR Chapter Replaces Historical Marker," *News-Herald*, 19 August 2012, http://www.thenewsherald.com/downriver_life/life/dar-chapter-replaces-historical-marker/article_56d7d248-8a9e-5f49-b18e-2673418dfc8e.html.

86 Trenton Trib, "River Current: Tribe members display heritage at refuge," *Trenton Trib*, 15 July 2013, https://trentontrib.com/trenton-mi-tribe-members-display-heritage-at-refuge.html.

87 Judith Kukowski, personal correspondence with author, 23 July 2014.

88 Author's personal observation when attending the Women's Sharing Circle in 2017.

CHAPTER THREE

1 Andrew Sturtevant, "'Inseparable Companions' and Irreconcilable Enemies: The Hurons and Odawas of French Détroit, 1701–38," *Ethnohistory* 60, no. 2 (2013): 219–43.

2 United States of America, Record of the Committee on the Interior and Insular Affairs and Its Predecessors, *Chapter 13: Public Lands (1805–1951)*, section 13.8, Petitions and Memorials, http://www.archives.gov/legislative/guide/house/chapter-13-public-lands.html

3 Ibid.

4 Francis Paul Prucha, *The Great Father: The United States Government and the American Indians* 1 (Lincoln: University of Nebraska Press, 1984), 206.

5 Prucha, *The Great Father*, 241n58; Russell Thornton, "The Demography of the Trail of Tears Period: A New Estimate of Cherokee Population Losses," in *Cherokee Removal: Before and After*, ed. William L. Anderson (Athens, GA: University of Georgia Press, 1991), 75–93; John Ehle, *Trail of Tears: The Rise and Fall of the Cherokee Nation* (Knopf Doubleday Publishing Group, 2011), 390–2.

6 Debbi Snook, "Ohio's Trail of Tears," Wyandotte Nation, https://www.wyandotte-nation.org/culture/history/published/trail-of-tears/; Larry K. Hancks, *The Emigrant Tribes: Wyandot, Delaware & Shawnee: A Chronology* (Kansas City, 1998).

7 Thelma R. Marsh, *Daughter of Grey Eyes: The Story of Mother Solomon* (T.R. Marsh, 1984), 33, 34. The original speech was made in Wyandot, but was translated into English by John McIntire Armstrong and is transcribed in Marsh.

8 Lucy Eldersveld Murphy, "Public Mothers: Native American and Métis Women as Creole Mediators in the Nineteenth-Century Midwest," *Journal of Women's History* 14, no. 4 (2003): 143, 151.

9 Murphy, "Public Mothers," 142–66. See also Barbara Welter, "The Cult of True Womanhood: 1820–1860," *American Quarterly* 18, no. 2 (1966): 151–74; Jacqueline Louise Peterson, "The People In Between: Indian-White Marriage and the Genesis of a Metis Society and Culture in the Great Lakes Region, 1680–1830" (PhD diss., University of Illinois, 1981); Mary P. Ryan, *Cradle of the Middle Class: The Family in Oneida County, New York, 1790–1865* (New York: Cambridge University Press, 1981), 210–18; Laurel Thatcher Ulrich, *Good Wives: Image and Reality in the Lives of Women in Northern New England, 1650–1750* (New York: Vintage Books, 1991), 59–65; and Lucy Eldersveld Murphy, *A Gathering of Rivers: Indians, Métis, and Mining in the Western Great Lakes, 1737–1832* (Lincoln & London: University of Nebraska Press, 2005), 45–76.

10 Hancks, *The Emigrant Tribes*; Mary Stockwell, *The Other Trail of Tears: The Removal of the Ohio Indians* (Yardley: Westholme Publishing, 2014); Ronald I. Marvin Jr, *A Brief History of Wyandot County Ohio* (Charleston: History Press, 2015).

11 James Joseph Buss, *Winning the West with Words: Language and Conquest in the Lower Great Lakes* (Norman: University of Oklahoma Press, 2011), 250n12.

12 Marsh, *Daughter of Grey Eyes.*

13 Ashley Simmons and Sallie Cotter Andrews, "Mary Greyeyes," https://www.wyandotte-nation.org/traditions/biographical-panels/mary-GreyEyes/; Marsh, *Daughter of Grey Eyes*, 11.

14 Hancks, *The Emigrant Tribes*, 255; Marsh, *Daughter of Grey Eyes*, 11.

15 Hancks, *The Emigrant Tribes*, 495.

16 Michael Cox, "The Ohio Wyandots: Religion and Society on the Sandusky River, 1795–1843" (PhD diss., UC Riverside, 2016), 113, 145; *Wyandotte County and Kansas City, Kansas. Historical and Biographical. Comprising a condensed history of the state, a careful history of Wyandotte County, and a comprehensive history of the growth of the cities, towns and villages* (Chicago: Goodspeed, 1890), 168.

17 Hancks, *The Emigrant Tribes*, 255.

18 Marsh, *Daughter of Grey Eyes*, 11; Hancks, *The Emigrant Tribes*, 486.

19 Hancks, *The Emigrant Tribes*, 375.

20 Marsh, *Daughter of Grey Eyes*, 11.

21 Hancks, *The Emigrant Tribes*, 156.

22 Simmons and Cotter Andrews, "Mary Greyeyes."

23 Ibid.; Hancks, *The Emigrant Tribes*, 468.

24 Hancks, *The Emigrant Tribes*, 489.

25 Ibid., 156.

26 Carol Swihart, "The Soul of Mother Solomon Took Its Flight: A Noted Character Gone," *The Wyandot County Republican Newspaper*, 21 August 1890. Transcribed in Marsh, *Daughter of Grey Eyes*, 50.

27 Swihart, "The Soul of Mother Solomon Took Its Flight" in Marsh, *Daughter of Grey Eyes*, 50.

28 Stockwell, *The Other Trail of Tears*, 314.

29 Marvin, *A Brief History of Wyandot County Ohio*, 38; Marsh, *Daughter of Grey Eyes*, 41.

30 Hancks, *The Emigrant Tribes*, 420.

31 Andrew Sturtevant, "'Over the Lake': The Western Wendake in the American Revolution," in *From Huronia to Wendakes: Adversity, Migrations, and Resilience, 1650–1900*, ed. Thomas Peace and Kathryn Magee Labelle (Norman: University of Oklahoma Press, 2016), 35–73.

32 James B. Finley, *History of the Wyandott Mission, at Upper Sandusky, Ohio, Under the Direction of the Methodist Episcopal Church* (Cincinnati: R.P. Thompson, 1840), 45.

33 Marsh, *Daughter of Grey Eyes*, 1.

34 Ibid., 5.

35 Ibid., 7.

36 Ibid., 15; Hancks, *The Emigrant Tribes*, 89.

37 The Green Corn Feast was still celebrated during this period, for instance. Andrew Sturtevant, "'Over the Lake,'" 50; Marsh, *Daughter of Grey Eyes*, 2.

38 Michael Leonard Cox, "Wendats, Presbyterians, and the Origins of Protestant Christianity on the Sandusky River," in *From Huronia to Wendakes: Adversity, Migrations, and Resilience, 1650–1900*, ed. Thomas Peace and Kathryn Magee Labelle (Norman: University of Oklahoma Press, 2016), 111–43.

39 Cox, "Wendats, Presbyterians, and the Origins of Protestant Christianity," 111–43.

40 Finley, *History of The Wyandott Mission*, 110.

41 Ibid., 115.

42 "Treaty with the Wyandots, etc., 1817," in "Foot of the Rapids (Fort Meigs), 1817," Clarke Historical Library, CMich.edu, https://www.cmich.edu/library/clarke/ResearchResources/Native_American_Material/Treaty_Rights/Text_of_Michigan_Related_Treaties/Pages/Foot-of-the-Rapids-(Fort-Meigs),-1817.aspx.

43 Charles Elliott, *Indian Missionary Reminiscences, Principally of the Wyandot Nation. In Which Is Exhibited the Efficacy of the Gospel in Elevant Ignorant and Savage Men* (New York: T. Mason and G. Lane for the Sunday School Union of the Methodist Episcopal Church, 1837), 70.

44 Ibid., 78–9.

45 Ibid., 88; Marsh, *Daughter of Grey Eyes*, 20.

46 Elliott, *Indian Missionary Reminiscences*, 80.

47 Ibid., 80–107.
48 Marsh, *Daughter of Grey Eyes*, 57.
49 Ibid., 56.
50 Hancks, *The Emigrant Tribes*, 93.
51 Elliott, *Indian Missionary Reminiscences*, 93.
52 Finley, *History of The Wyandott Mission*, 17.
53 Elliott, *Indian Missionary Reminiscences*, 82–3.
54 Ibid., 90, 108.
55 Ibid., 82–3.
56 Stockwell, *The Other Trail of Tears*, 300–1; James Joseph Buss, "The Politics of Indian Removal on the Wyandot Reserve, 1817–1843," in *Contested Territories: Native Americans and Non-Natives in the Lower Great Lakes, 1750–1850*, ed. Charles Beatty-Medina and Melissa Rinehart (Michigan State University Press, 2012), 167–93.
57 *The History of Wyandot County, Ohio: Containing a History of the Country; its Townships, Towns, Churches, Schools, etc.; General and Local Statistics; Military Record; Portraits of Early Settlers and Prominent Men; History of the Northwest Territory; History of Ohio; Miscellaneous Matters* (Chicago: Leggett, Conaway, 1884), 295–6.
58 Henry Howe, *Historical Collections of Ohio: An Encyclopedia of the State: History Both General and Local, Geography with Descriptions of Its Countries, Cities and Villages, Its Agricultural, Manufacturing, Mining and Business Development, Sketches of Eminent and Interesting Character, Etc., with Notes of a Tour Over it in 1886* (Norwalk: Laning Printing, 1896), 2:900.
59 *The History of Wyandot County*, 296–7.
60 David Young is listed on page one and his household includes two adults and three children. See "Muster Roll of the Wyandott Indians Who Departed Upper Sandusky, Ohio," transcribed in Marsh, *Daughter of Grey Eyes*, 59–60.
61 Stockwell, *The Other Trail of Tears*, 300.
62 Marsh, *Daughter of Grey Eyes*, 34.
63 *The History of Wyandot County*, 296–7.
64 Ibid., 297.
65 John P. Bowes, *Land Too Good for Indians: Northern Indian Removal* (Norman: University of Oklahoma Press, 2016), 146.
66 Rev. James Wheeler, "Kansas," Wyandotte Nation, https://www.wyandotte-nation.org/culture/history/wheeler-memoirs/arrival-in-kansas/.
67 Snook, "Ohio's Trail of Tears."
68 Marsh, *Daughter of Grey Eyes*, 39.
69 Wheeler, "Kansas."
70 Stockwell, *The Other Trail of Tears*, 300–1.
71 Snook, "Ohio's Trail of Tears."

72 *Wyandotte County and Kansas City, Kansas. Historical and Biographical. Comprising a Condensed History of the State, a Careful History of Wyandotte County, and a Comprehensive History of the Growth of the Cities, Towns and Villages* (Chicago: Goodspeed, 1890), 170.
73 Stockwell, *The Other Trail of Tears*, 300–1.
74 Marvin, *A Brief History of Wyandot County*.
75 Hancks, *The Emigrant Tribes*, 190.
76 Ibid., 208, 477; Marvin, *A Brief History of Wyandot County*.
77 Marvin, *A Brief History of Wyandot County*, 38.
78 Ibid., 41–4.
79 Marsh, *Daughter of Grey Eyes*, 44.
80 Marvin, *A Brief History of Wyandot County*.
81 Marsh, *Daughter of Grey Eyes*, 13.
82 Elliott, *Indian Missionary Reminiscences*, 64.
83 Ibid., 62.
84 Ibid.
85 Marsh, *Daughter of Grey Eyes*, 8.
86 Marvin, *A Brief History of Wyandot County*.
87 Marie Battiste, "Maintaining Aboriginal Identity, Language, and Culture in Modern Society," in *Reclaiming Indigenous Voice and Vision* (Vancouver: University of British Columbia Press, 2000), 192–208.
88 Howe, *Historical Collections of Ohio*, 2:900–2.
89 *Ohio Archaeological and Historical Publications* (Columbus: Ohio Archaeological and Historical Publications, 1902), 10:203.
90 Marvin, *A Brief History of Wyandot County*, 38–9.
91 Ibid.
92 The hymn "Come Thou Fount of Every Blessing" was written by John Robinson (1735–1790).
93 Marsh, *Daughter of Grey Eyes*, 51.
94 Snook, "Ohio's Trail of Tears."
95 Stockwell, *The Other Trail of Tears*, 314.
96 Marvin, *A Brief History of Wyandot County*, 39.
97 Swihart, "The Soul of Mother Solomon Took Its Flight" in Marsh, *Daughter of Grey Eyes*, 50.
98 Ibid.
99 *Magazine of Western History* (New York: Magazine of Western History Publishing, 1890), 699; *Ohio Archaeological and Historical Publications*, 12:203.
100 "The Last of the Wyandots: Death of Margaret Solomon Near Upper Sandusky, Ohio," *The Daily Herald*, 18 August 1890.
101 Roxanne Dunbar-Ortiz and Dina Gilio-Whitaker, *"All the Real Indians Died Off": And 20 Other Myths About Native Americans* (Boston: Beacon Press, 2016).

102 Betsy Bowen, "June Report" (Upper Sandusky, Ohio: John Stewart United Methodist Church Records [JSUMC] and History Committee, 2018), 1.

103 Marvin, *A Brief History of Wyandot County*, 143; Bowen, "June Report," 1.

104 Betsy Bowen, "December Report" (Upper Sandusky, Ohio: John Stewart United Methodist Church Records [JSUMC] and History Committee, 2016), 8–9.

105 Bowen, "June Report," 1.

106 Ibid.

107 United States of America, Record of the Committee on the Interior and Insular Affairs and Its Predecessors, *Chapter 13: Public Lands (1805–1951)*, section 13.8, Petitions and Memorials, http://www.archives.gov/legislative/guide/house/chapter-13-public-lands.html

108 Bowen, "June Report," 1.

CHAPTER FOUR

1 Col. McKee to Sir John Johnson, 5 May 1790, in *Collections and Researches made by the Pioneer and Historical Society of the State of Michigan* (Lansing: Thorp & Godfrey, 1888), 12:24; "District of Hesse, Land Board, 14 May 1790" in *Third Report of the Bureau of Archives for the Province of Ontario*, ed. Alexander Fraser (Toronto: L.K. Cameron, 1906), 8.

2 Alan Taylor, *The Divided Ground: Indians, Settlers, and the Northern Borderland of the American Revolution* (New York: Vintage Books, 2007).

3 Helen Hornbeck Tanner, ed., *Atlas of Great Lakes Indian History* (Norman: University of Oklahoma Press, 1987), 61.

4 "District of Hesse, Land Board, 14 May 1790," 8.

5 Russel L. Barsh, "Grounded Visions: Native American Conceptions of Landscapes and Ceremony," *St. Thomas Law Review* 13 (2000): 127–34; Winona LaDuke, *All Our Relations: Native Struggles for Land and Life* (Chicago: Maymark Books, 1999); Elizabeth Berton-Reilly, "Our Corn Is Still Standing: Indigenous Foodways and Identity in New England," *Digest: A Journal of Foodways and Culture* 5, no. 1 (2016): 1–16; Taiaiake Alfred, "The Akwesasne Cultural Restoration Program: A Mohawk Approach to Land-Based Education," *Decolonization: Indigeneity, Education & Society* 3, no. 3 (2014): 134–44.

6 Barsh, "Grounded Visions," 130.

7 Nathalie Kermoal and Isabel Altamirano-Jiménez, eds. *Living on the Land: Indigenous Women's Understanding of Place* (Edmonton: AU Press, 2016); Stephanie Fitzgerald, *Native Women and Land: Narratives of Dispossession and Resurgence* (Albuquerque: University of New Mexico Press, 2015); Kim Anderson, *A Recognition of Being: Reconstructing Native Womanhood* (Toronto: Sumach Press, 2000).

8 Bruce G. Trigger, *The Huron: Farmers of the North* (New York: Holt, Rinehart and Winston, 1969); Kathryn Magee Labelle, "Women: Unity, Spirituality, and Social

Mobility," in *Dispersed but Not Destroyed: A History of the Seventeenth-Century Wendat People* (Vancouver: University of British Columbia Press, 2014), 159–75.

9 Charles Marius Barbeau, *Huron and Wyandot Mythology* (Ottawa: Geological Survey of Canada, 1915); Charles Marius Barbeau, *How the Huron-Wyandot Language Was Saved From Oblivion* (Philadelphia: American Philosophical Society, 1949); Charles Marius Barbeau, *Huron-Wyandot Traditional Narratives: In Translations and Native Texts* (Ottawa: Canada Department of Northern Affairs and National Resources, 1960).

10 John Steckley, *Beyond Their Years: Five Native Women's Stories* (Toronto: Canadian Scholars' Press, 1999); Charles Garrad, "Mary McKee (1838–1922)," *Petun Research Institute Bulletin* 41 (North York, Ontario: Petun Research Institute, 2013); Charles Garrad, *Petun to Wyandot: The Ontario Petun from the Sixteenth Century* (Ottawa: University of Ottawa Press, 2014); Sallie Cotter Andrews, "Mary McKee," Wyandotte Nation, https://www.wyandotte-nation.org/traditions/biographical-panels/mary-mckee/.

11 Frederick Wulff, *Alexander McKee the Great White Elk: British Indian Agent on the Colonial Frontier* (Parker, CO: Outskirts, 2013), 6.

12 Wulff, *Alexander McKee*, 6.

13 McKee's home was destroyed by the Americans during the war.

14 Daniel Palmer, "The McKee Treaty of 1790: British Aboriginal Diplomacy in the Great Lakes" (master's thesis, University of Saskatchewan, 2017); Reginald Horsman, "McKee, Alexander," in *Dictionary of Canadian Biography* 4 (University of Toronto/Université Laval, 2003), accessed 12 July 2019, http://www.biographi.ca/en/bio/mckee_alexander_4E.html.

15 Charles Garrad, "Mary McKee" (unpublished manuscript, Charles Garrad Private Collection), 1.

16 "School Report to Governor Cass from John L. Lieb, October 1st, 1825," transcribed in Thelma R. Marsh, *Daughter of Grey Eyes: The Story of Mother Solomon* (T.R. Marsh, 1984), 56.

17 Garrad, "Mary McKee," 2.

18 "Death of an Aged Indian Woman: December 22, 1876," Reprinted in *Essex County Scrap Book* Essex, ON: 1986 in Charles Garrad Private Collection (Document #005.1).

19 Garrad, "Mary McKee," 2.

20 "Katie is the 'Belle of Bowery Dances,'" Michigan newspaper clipping, 16 August 1896, in Charles Garrad Private Collection.

21 "Death of an Aged Indian Woman," page unknown.

22 Ibid.; "Died – CLARK – In Anderdon on Tuesday, March 26th, James Clark, aged 91 Years," *Amherstburg Echo*, 29 March 1895; "Death of Alex Clark, Sr.," *Amherstburg Echo*, 14 April 1876, 15.

23 Garrad, "Mary McKee," 3.

24 Adele E. Rahn, "Notes on Wyandot Families Associated with Brownstown and the Huron Reserve (Anderdon Township)," 8, in Charles Garrad Private Collection.

25 "Birth Record," Document #009, in Charles Garrad Private Collection; Photograph, a slide by the Huron-Clinton Metropolitan Authority, shared by Charles Garrad. The caption reads, "Chief Quo Qua's cabin in later years, modified with an addition by subsequent owner Home Norton, section 27, Huron Township, Wayne County, Michigan (Now Willow MetroPark)."

26 Steckley, *Beyond Their Years*, 203.

27 Garrad, "Mary McKee," 1.

28 Ibid., 6. Charles Garrad interviewed Wyandot elder and Mary McKee's cousin Cecile Wallace Shun-diah-wah in September 1976.

29 Peter Dooyentate Clarke, *Origin and Traditional History of the Wyandotts, and Sketches of Other Indian Tribes of North America, True Traditional Stories of Tecumseh and His League, in the Years 1811 and 1812* (Toronto: Hunter, Rose, 1870).

30 James Clarke's father was dismissed by Colonel Elliott during the war for some "trivial offense." Peter D. Clarke to Lyman C. Draper of the Cabin Creek Cherokee Nation, 30 May 1873, Lyman C. Draper Manuscript Collection, Madison, Wisconsin.

31 "Death of an Aged Indian Woman," page unknown; "Died – CLARK – In Anderdon on Tuesday, March 26th, James Clark, aged 91 Years," page unknown; "Death of Alex Clark, Sr.," page unknown.

32 Garrad, "Mary McKee," 4; S.B. Burton, "Indians of North America, Katie Qua Qua," *Detroit Free Press*, 20 October 1907.

33 Garrad, "Mary McKee," 4.

34 The original picture of Mary McKee is part of the Charles Garrad Private Collection. This picture was copied and republished in Barbeau, *Huron and Wyandot Mythology*, 425.

35 Sources conflict as to whether Mary refused to marry the man because of his family's objections, or whether it was his family that forced the couple to cancel the wedding. Charles Garrad interview with Cecil Wallace in Garrad, "Mary McKee," 4.

36 *Wyandot Tribal Roll 1867*, RG75, US microfilm, roll 951, frame 0234. She is also mentioned in letters from Robert McKenzie (Minister of the Interior) RG10, vol. 2004, file 7719 (31 March, 10 April, and 16 July 1877) (Ottawa: Library and Archives Canada); "Death of an Aged Indian Woman," page unknown.

37 *Wyandot Tribal Roll 1867.*

38 "Mary McKee Died," *The Seneca News*, 16 June 1922.

39 Document #364, Charles Garrad Private Collection; Peter Jones, *Life and Journals of Kah-Ke-WaQuo-Na-By* (Toronto: Anson Green, 1860), 127–8.

40 Palmer, "The McKee Treaty of 1790," 25–6. Susan Sleeper-Smith, *Indigenous Prosperity and American Conquest: Indian Women of the Ohio River Valley, 1690–1792* (Williamsburg, VA: Omohundro Institute, 2018).

41 Sallie Cotter Andrews, "History Timeline," Wyandotte Nation, https://www.wyandotte-nation.org/culture/history/timeline.

42 The origin of the name "Anderdon" is not entirely clear, but there is reason to believe that because this community comprised mostly members from the Arendaeronnon Clan, Anderdon could be a mispronunciation of the clan name. Velma Nieberding, "Notes," Charles Garrad Private Collection.

43 Garrad, "Mary McKee," 3.

44 Garrad, *Petun to Wyandot*, 525; Canada Department of Indian Affairs, *Indian Treaties and Surrenders From 1680 to 1890 in Two Volumes* (Ottawa: Brown Chamberlin Printer to the Queen's Most Excellent Majesty, 1891), 1:272.

45 Garrad, *Petun to Wyandot*, 515.

46 Chief Warrow, "Statement of Treaty and Land Surrenders of 1836," in Clarke, *Origin and Traditional History of the Wyandotts*, 123–4.

47 The cabin is now located in Willow Metropark. The original plaque that accompanies the historic site reads, "The last reservation of the Wyandot Tribe of Indians in Michigan Occupied 1818–1842." Garrad, "Mary McKee," 3; "Memorial to Chief Quo Qua," photograph, 1982, Charles Garrad Collection.

48 It is important to note that contrary to popular belief, not all We^{n}dat/Wa^{n}dat enfranchised. There remain We^{n}dat/Wa^{n}dat of Anderdon members who still have status under the Canadian Indian Act. Garrad, "Mary McKee," 5.

49 There is some debate over this because "Caty Cuqueh" is listed on the Muster Roll in 1843 as a Michigan Wyandot with two members of her household under the age of 25 (page 6); Thomas McKee is listed as a Canadian Wyandot separately (page 7) with no dependants.

50 Garrad, "Mary McKee," 4; Cotter Andrews, "Mary McKee."

51 Mary McKee, "Petition to the Minister of the Interior," 13 January 1877, RG10 vol. 2004, file 7719, Ottawa: Library and Archives Canada.

52 Garrad, "Mary McKee," 4; "Turtle Hill," *Kansas City Star*, 7 June 1959.

53 Garrad, "Mary McKee," 5.

54 Sallie Cotter Andrews folder, Index 19, Ohio State University Archives, Aubrey Buser Collection.

55 Charles Garrad interview with Cecile Wallace, in Garrad, "Mary McKee," 6.

56 "Mary McKee Grave Site," photograph (2003), Charles Garrad Private Collection.

57 Barbeau, *Huron-Wyandot Traditional Narratives*, 2.

58 Ibid., 1.

59 Ibid., xi.

60 Barbeau, *How the Huron-Wyandot Language Was Saved*, 231; Barbeau, *Huron and Wyandot Mythology*, xi.

61 Canadian Museum of History Collections, Object #III-H-71.

62 Ibid., Object #III-H-308.

63 Ibid., Object #III-H-86 a–b; III-H-73; III-H-74; III-H-183; II-H-182.

64 Barbeau, *Huron and Wyandot Mythology*; Barbeau, *How the Huron-Wyandot Language Was Saved*; Barbeau, *Huron-Wyandot Traditional Narratives.*

65 Barbeau, *Huron and Wyandot Mythology*, xi, 5, 40, 59, 287; Barbeau, *Huron-Wyandot Traditional Narratives*, 49.

66 Barbeau, *Huron and Wyandot Mythology*, 4n1.

67 Ibid., xi, 287.

68 "Copy of a letter from Alexander McKee, Esquire, D.A. to ye Board, 23 May 1790," in *Third Report of the Bureau of Archives for the Province of Ontario*, ed. Alexander Fraser (Toronto: L.K. Cameron, 1906), 10.

69 "No. 2," in *Indian Treaties and Surrenders* 2:2; Dean Jacobs, "Indian Land Surrenders," in *The Western District: Papers from the Western District Conference*, ed. K.G. Pryke and L.L. Kulisek (Windsor: Essex County Historical Society, 1983), 64.

70 "No. 2," in *Indian Treaties and Surrenders*, 2:2.

71 "Anderdon Reserve: Wyandots Petition that their Land May Be Surrendered and Sold," RG10, Indian Affairs, vol. 1911, file 247311, Red Series, R216-244-6-E, Ottawa: Library and Archives Canada; Steckley, *Beyond Their Years*, 216.

72 "Wyandot Petition," RG10, vol. 1911, file 2473; Steckley, *Beyond Their Years*, 217.

73 "Anderdon Map of Allotments," Document #3452, Charles Garrad Private Collection.

74 Garrad, "Mary McKee," 3.

75 "Captain Brant's Account of What Passed at Fort Stanwix Prior to the Treaty in October 1784," Frontier Wars Fonds, vol. 23, Draper Manuscript Collection, Wisconsin Historical Society.

76 "Copy of the Transactions between the Five Nations & the Western Indians, at their late meeting in the Indian Country," papers relating to the Western Indians and Indian Affairs at Detroit, Michilimackinac &c. 1771–1885, RG10 A3d, Reel C-1224, Ottawa: Library and Archives Canada.

77 Ibid.

78 Palmer, "The McKee Treaty of 1790."

79 "No. 46," in *Indian Treaties and Surrenders*, 1:113–15.

80 This, according to Joseph Warrow, is "a statement of facts, as I have been able to retain them in memory. Handed down to me from my ancestors, the Wyandotts," in Clarke, *Origin and Traditional History of the Wyandotts*, 123–4; Document #324, Charles Garrad Private Collection.

81 Warrow in Clarke, *Origin and Traditional History of the Wyandotts*, 123–4; Document #324, Charles Garrad Private Collection.

82 Steckley, *Beyond Their Years*, 230–1.

83 "Clarke Letter," 26 October 1884, Document #038 in Charles Garrad Private Collection.

84 Peter D. Clarke to Minister of Interior, 1 October 1877, Charles Garrad Private Collection.

85 Ibid.

86 Ibid.

87 Joseph Warrow to Mary McKee, 5 November 1895, Charles Garrad Private Collection.

88 Robert Mckenzie to unknown recipient, 6 April 1877, Charles Garrad Private Collection.

89 Deed is registered with Indian Affairs, 2 March 1887. See Document #012, Charles Garrad Private Collection; Ted Douglas, "Famed Tribe Slowly Dying Out," *Windsor Daily Star*.

90 Document #012, Charles Garrad Private Collection; Douglas, "Famed Tribe Slowly Dying Out."

91 "The Gathering of Traditions: A Centennial Celebration of Dr. Charles Marius Barbeau in Oklahoma," Wyandotte Nation, https://www.wyandotte-nation.org/wp-content/uploads/2012/07/Barbeau-Exhibit-Flyer.pdf.

92 Richard Zane Smith, personal correspondence with author, 22 June 2018. For an example of work done by Smith to revitalize the language see Richard Zane Smith, *Daughters, Sisters, Mothers and Wives: A Wa^{n}dat (Wyandot) Language Workbook* (Toronto: Ontario Native Literacy Coalition, 2019).

93 Louis Goulet, *Potier's Essex County Census* (Amherstburg: Echo Printing, 1925), 11.

94 Joseph Warrow to Mary McKee, 5 November 1895, Charles Garrad Private Collection.

95 "Daughter of Chief," *Windsor Daily Star*, 17 February 1949.

96 "Annie Splitlog, "Obituary," Charles Garrad Private Collection.

97 "Daughter of Chief," *Windsor Daily Star*, 17 February 1949.

98 Ibid.

99 Douglas, "Famed Tribe Slowly Dying Out."

100 Charles Garrad to P.W. Beaman of Canada Trust Company, New York, 9 July 1976, Charles Garrad Private Collection.

101 Jim Kasuba, "Wyandot of Anderdon Nation Acquires Land in Gibraltar," *News-Herald*, 11 September 2015.

102 Wyandot of Anderdon Nation Website, "Six Points Master Plan," http://www.wyandotofanderdon.com/wp/?page_id=385.

103 Ibid.

CHAPTER FIVE

1 *Wyandotte County and Kansas City, Kansas. Historical and Biographical. Comprising a Condensed History of the State, a Careful History of Wyandotte Country, and a Comprehensive History of the Growth of the Cities, Towns and Villages* (Chicago: Goodspeed, 1890), 170–1.

2 Carol Swihart, title unknown, *The Wyandot County Republican Newspaper*, 21 August 1890, transcribed in Thelma R. Marsh, *Daughter of Grey Eyes: The Story of Mother Solomon* (T.R. Marsh, 1984), 49–51.

3 Conley was accepted to the Kansas bar in 1910. Henry Van Brunt, "Three Sisters Defense of Cemetery Continued for Nearly Forty Years," *Kansas City Times*, 7 June 1946.

4 Kathryn Magee Labelle, "'Faire la chaudière': The Wendat Feast of Souls, 1636," in *French and Indians in the Heart of North America, 1630–1815*, ed. Robert Englebert and Guillaume Teasdale (Winnipeg: University of Manitoba Press, 2013), 4.

5 Erik R. Seeman, *The Huron-Wendat Feast of the Dead: Indian-European Encounters in Early North America* (Baltimore: Johns Hopkins University Press, 2011); Bruce G. Trigger, *The Children of Aataentsic: A History of the Huron People to 1660* (Montreal & Kingston: McGill-Queen's University Press, 1976), 88; Allan Greer, ed., *The Jesuit Relations: Natives and Missionaries in Seventeenth-Century North America* (Boston: Bedford/St Martin's, 2000), 61; Denys Delâge, *Bitter Feast: Amerindians and Europeans in Northeastern North America, 1600–64* (Vancouver: University of British Columbia Press, 1995), 73; Georges E. Sioui, *Huron-Wendat: The Heritage of the Circle* (Vancouver: University of British Columbia Press, 1999), 153.

6 Reuben Gold Thwaites, ed., *The Jesuit Relations and Allied Documents: Travels and Explorations of the Jesuit Missionaries in New France 1610–1791, The Original French, Latin, and Italian Texts, with English Translations and Notes*, 52 vols (Cleveland: Burrows, 1897) [hereafter *JR*], 17:209.

7 Examples of newspapers that published articles on the Conley sisters and the cemetery include the *Herald Newspaper* (Kansas City), *Kansas City Star, Wyandotte Gazette, Kansas City Times, Kansas City Kansan, Kansas City Post*, and *Kansas City Times.*

8 Exceptions are: William E. Connelley, *Huron Place: The Burial Ground of the Wyandot Nation in Wyandotte County, Kansas* (Kansas City: Community Development Program of the City, 1896); William E. Connelley, "The Wyandots," *Transactions of the Kansas State Historical Society* 6, no. 17 (1899); Grant W. Harrington, *Historic Spots or Mile Stones in the Progress of Wyandotte County, Kansas* (Merriam, KS: Mission Press, 1935); Kim Dayton, "'Trespassers, Beware!': Lyda Burton Conley and the Battle for Huron Place Cemetery," *Yale Journal of Law & Feminism* 8, no. 1 (1995), 1–30; Kathryn Worley, "Women Lawyers in and Around Kansas City," *The Westporter* (March 2005); Bill Gregg, "Huron Place," *The Historical Journal of Wyandotte County* 2, no. 10 (2008), 557–60; Samantha Rae Dean, "'As Long as Grass Grows and Water Flows': Lyda Conley and the Huron Indian Cemetery" (master's thesis, Fort Hays State University, 2016); Kara Evans, "Lyda Conley: Wyandot Guardian and Lawyer," *KC History*, 22 June 2018, http://www.kchistory.org/blog/lyda-Conley-wyandot-guardian-and-lawyer.

9 *Kansas City Star*, 7 July 1911; US Census, 1870, Kansas City, Kansas, population schedule, Wyandotte, 51, household 367, Lyda Conley; microfilm publication, FamilySearch.org, https://familysearch.org/ark:/61903/1:1:MCJ1-YJX; Van Brunt, "Three Sisters Defense of Cemetery."

10 US Census, 1870.

11 Jacob Burnet, *Notes on the Early Settlement of the North-Western Territory* (New York: D. Appleton, 1847), 223–6 (brackets in the original).

12 Dean, "'As Long as Grass Grows and Water Flows,'" 13n31.

13 Charles Aubrey Buser, "Tarhe," Wyandotte Nation, https://www.wyandotte-nation.org/culture/history/biographies/tarhe-grand-sachem/.

14 Dayton, "'Trespassers, Beware!'" 17.

15 "Wyandot Tribal Roll 1867 according to 13 Treaty 1867," transcribed from US Microfilm M234, roll 951, frames 0208–0249, Wyandot Nation of Kansas Archives.

16 "Letters Received by the Office of Indian Affairs," 1821–81, National Archives Publications, microformed on microcopy no. 234, roll 951, frame 221; Dayton, "'Trespassers, Beware!'" 12.

17 *Herald Newspaper* (Kansas City), 21 July 1879.

18 Dean, "'As Long as Grass Grows and Water Flows,'" 49; *Herald Newspaper* (Kansas City), 21 July 1879; Van Brunt, "Three Sisters Defense of Cemetery."

19 Dayton, "'Trespassers, Beware!'" 7.

20 Ibid.

21 Janith English, "Unpublished Chronology of the Wyandot Nation," Wyandot Nation of Kansas Archives, 2017.

22 Alan W. Farley, "Annals of Quindaro: A Kansas Ghost Town," *The Kansas Historic Quarterly* 22, no. 4 (1956), 305–20.

23 Dayton, "'Trespassers, Beware!'" 8.

24 *The Quindaro Chindowan*, 13 May 1857.

25 Ibid.

26 *Kansas City Star*, 7 July 1911.

27 Farley, "Annals of Quindaro," 305–20.

28 English, "Unpublished Chronology of the Wyandot Nation," 5.

29 John P. Bowes, "Subtraction through Division: Delawares, Wyandots, and the Struggle for Kansas Territory," in *Exiles and Pioneers: Eastern Indians in the Trans-Mississippi West* (New York: Cambridge University Press, 2007), 208–9.

30 English, "Unpublished Chronology of the Wyandot Nation," 8.

31 *Wyandot Nation of Kansas, aka Wyandotte Tribe of Indians v. United States*, United States Court of Appeals, Federal Circuit, decided 8 June 2017, https://caselaw.findlaw.com/us-federal-circuit/1863573.html.

32 Lucy Armstrong, *Wyandotte Gazette* (4 June 1890) in *History of Wyandotte County Kansas and Its People*, ed. Perl W. Morgan (Kansas City: Lewis, 1911), 81–3.

33 Armstrong, *Wyandotte Gazette*, 81–3.

34 Ibid.

35 Dean, "'As Long as Grass Grows and Water Flows,'" 49; *Kansas City Star*, 7 July 1911.

36 *Kansas City Star*, 7 July 1911.

37 Raymond was born in 1939; Robert was born in 1937. Interview with Raymond and Robert Bond by Louisa Libby (Wyandot Cultural Officer), Wyandot Nation of Kansas Oral History Project, 6 November 2014.

38 Dayton, "'Trespassers, Beware!'" 10.

39 *Kansas City Times*, 13 July 1911.

40 *The Kansas City Kansan*, 21 June 1906.

41 Fifty-ninth Congress, Sess. 1, ch. 3504, vol. 34, 348.

42 *Kansas City Post*, 17 April 1918.

43 This information was found in William Connelley's files: William E. Connelley, *Kansas City Post*, 1 August 1909, "copied by courtesy of Miss Mae Harihen, Secretary to Mayor Clark E. Tucker of Kansas City Kansas from files of William E. Connelley." Transcription is contained as part of a series of articles. Title of document is marked "The Emigrant Indian Tribes of Wyandot County, William Elsey Connelley, Address before K.C.K. High School, November 12, 1901," Wyandot Nation of Kansas Digital Archives [WNKDA].

44 The Bond brothers, however, heard that the shotgun was not loaded. Raymond and Robert Bond, interview.

45 Lyda Conley to Chief Justice and Associate Justices of the Supreme Court, 14 March 1910, in Judge Stanley Papers [JSP], WNKDA.

46 "Defend the Graves: Miss Lyda Conley Says She Will Use a Shotgun," *Leavenworth Post*, 18 July 1907, 3.

47 *Kansas City Times*, 25 October 1906.

48 William Connelley's files: Connelley, *Kansas City Post*, WNKDA.

49 Ms Conley was interviewed in 1909 while her lawsuit was pending before the US Supreme Court. The interview took place at a business college in Kansas City, Missouri, where Ms Conley was employed as an instructor. I.T. Martin, "Living in a City of the Dead," *Kansas Magazine*, June 1909, 52–3.

50 Martin, "Living in a City of the Dead," 52–3.

51 "Amendment Bill for the Injunction," 19 June 1907, DOC: 23.32.52; DOC: 23.30.29, in JSP, WNKDA.

52 Transcription, William Connelley, *Kansas City Post* (no date), WNKDA.

53 Dayton, "'Trespassers, Beware!'" 2.

54 Copy of the handwritten argument of Eliza Burton Conley, Jr, *Conley v. Ballinger*, in JSP, WNKDA.

55 Dean, "'As Long as Grass Grows and Water Flows,'" 69; Mrs Randolph Nichols, Corresponding Secretary, Associated Clubs of Kansas City, Kansas to Ida Conley (pledging Associated Clubs' support in Conley's efforts to save Huron Cemetery),

27 October 1906, Wyandotte Historical Society (original letter), in Dayton, "'Trespassers, Beware!'" 19; Van Brunt, "Three Sisters Defense of Cemetery."

56 John L. Steckley, *The Eighteenth-Century Wyandot: A Clan-Based Study* (Waterloo: Wilfrid Laurier University Press, 2013), 182.

57 McIntyre Armstrong, "Letter to the Editor," *Kansas City Star*, 8 February 1910.

58 Sixty-second Congress, Sess. 3, ch. 44, vol. 33, 668.

59 Sixty-fourth Congress, Sess. 1, ch. 468, vol. 39, 844.

60 Lyda Conley's murderer was never found. Van Brunt, "Three Sisters Defense of Cemetery."

61 Dean, "'As Long as Grass Grows and Water Flows,'" 73.

62 "Lyda Conley Defies Ditch Digging," *Kansas City Kansan*, WNKDA.

63 "Letters of Protest, 1950–1959," originally found in the Wyandotte Country Museum. Transcribed by Chief Janith English, Wyandot Nation of Kansas.

64 "Letters of Protest, 1950–1959."

65 Ibid.

66 Ibid.

67 Ibid.

68 Ibid.

69 Ibid.

70 Ibid.

71 Ibid.

72 Ibid.

73 Janith English, "Tears of My Grandmothers," unpublished manuscript, Wyandot Nation of Kansas Archives.

74 Ibid., 1.

75 Ibid., 2.

76 Ibid.

77 John W. Ragsdale, Jr, "Sacred in the City: The Huron Indian Cemetery and the Preservation Laws," *The Urban Lawyer* 48, no. 1 (2016): 67–142.

78 Ragsdale, "Sacred in the City," 119–20.

79 *JR*, 22:209.

80 It is unclear where this saying originated given the lack of written recorders, but Chief Janith English reports it is ancient Indian philosophy. A variation of this saying was also on Lyda Conley's original headstone. Janith English, "Huron Cemetery Chronology," Wyandotte Nation, https://www.wyandotte-nation.org/culture/history/general-%20history/huron-cemetery/.

CHAPTER SIX

1 Transcribed in Vine Deloria Jr, ed., *The Indian Reorganization Act: Congresses and Bills* (Norman: University of Oklahoma Press, 2002), 31.

2 For a more in-depth study of the varied strategies and outcomes of this era and in particular the various people who contested Federal Indian Policy during this time, see Joseph Genetin-Pilawa, *Crooked Paths to Allotment: The Fight Over Federal Indian Policy After the Civil War* (Chapel Hill: University of North Carolina Press, 2012).

3 Frederick E. Hoxie, *A Final Promise: The Campaign to Assimilate the Indians, 1880–1920* (Lincoln: University of Nebraska Press, 2001), 152, 161.

4 Quoted in Joseph B. Herring, *The Enduring Indians of Kansas: A Century and a Half of Acculturation* (Lawrence: University Press of Kansas, 1990), 138.

5 Colin Calloway, *Pen and Ink Witchcraft: Treaties and Treaty Making in American Indian History* (New York: Oxford University Press, 2013), 234–5.

6 Roxanne Dunbar-Ortiz, *An Indigenous Peoples' History of the United States* (Boston: Beacon Press, 2014), 159.

7 Ibid., 169.

8 Genetin-Pilawa, *Crooked Paths to Allotment*; Jon Blackman, *Oklahoma's Indian New Deal* (Norman: University of Oklahoma Press, 2013).

9 Quoted in Herring, *The Enduring Indians of Kansas*, 137.

10 Carol J. Batker, "'Her Rightful Place in the New Scheme of Things': Native American Women's Journalism in the Dawes Era," in *Reforming Fictions: Native, African, and Jewish American Women's Literature and Journalism in the Progressive Era* (Columbia University Press, 2000), 15–36.

11 Alanna K. Brown, "Mourning Dove," in Andrew Wiget, *Dictionary of Native American Literature* (1994), 145; Carol J. Batker, "'Wantin' to Wear Th' Breeches and Boss Th' Hull Shebang': Reservations and Romance in Mourning Dove's Cogewea," in *Reforming Fictions: Native, African, and Jewish American Women's Literature and Journalism in the Progressive Era* (New York: Columbia University Press, 2000), 37–52.

12 Philip J. Deloria, "Ella Deloria (*Anpetu Waste*)," in *Encyclopedia of North American Indians: Native American History, Culture, and Life from Paleo-Indians to the Present*, ed. Frederick E. Hoxie (Boston: Houghton Mifflin Harcourt, 1996), 159–61.

13 Batker, "'Her Rightful Place in the New Scheme of Things,'" 15–36.

14 Ibid., 15.

15 Jane Zane Gordon, *The Hollywood Story 7* (American Indian Unity, Inc., 1948), file number E98.R3 G68 1948, Archives and Special Collections at Amherst College, out of print.

16 Gordon, *Hollywood Story 7*, 3.

17 Batker, "'Her Rightful Place in the New Scheme of Things,'" 24.

18 Ibid., 15–36.

19 *Boston Sunday Post*, 21 July 1921.

20 Holly Zane, "Alexander H. (Zenophan) Zane," Wyandotte Nation, https://www.wyandotte-nation.org/traditions/biographical-panels/alexander-h-zenophan-zane/.

21 After Hannah died, Alexander married Lucy A. Robertson Vanslyke. They had six additional children: Noah, Henry, Isabella, Julia, Cella, and Pearl. Holly Zane, "Alexander H. (Zenophan) Zane."

22 Sallie Cotter Andrews, "Jane Zane Gordon," Wyandotte Nation, https://www.wyandotte-nation.org/culture/history/biographies/jane-zane-gordon/.

23 "Petition of the Wyandott Indians Praying Final Settlement of All Business Transactions With The Government," in *Miscellaneous Documents of the Senate of the United States for the Third Session of the Thirty-Seventh Congress* (Washington: Government Printing Office, 1863), 1–5.

24 "Petition of the Wyandott Indians," 4.

25 Holly Zane, "Alexander H. (Zenophan) Zane."

26 "Syllabus," Supreme Court of the United States, *US Reports: Wallace v. United States*, 162 US 466 (1895), no. 731, 62.

27 Copy of "Quapaw Indian Competency Commission Examination of Allottee," file 771, document 5, in Sallie Cotter Andrews Private Collection.

28 Melville Weston Fuller and Supreme Court of the United States, *US Reports: Wallace v. United States*, 162 US 466 (1895), 468. https://www.loc.gov/item/usrep162466.

29 "Wallace Testified," Melville Weston Fuller and Supreme Court of the United States, *US Reports: Wallace v. United States, 162 US* 466 (1895). https://www.loc.gov/item/usrep162466/ (page 468).

30 Jane remarried twice: first to Mr Waters and then to Mr Gordon. "Quapaw Indian Competency Commission Examination of Allottee"; Andrews, "Jane Zane Gordon."

31 "Quapaw Indian Competency Commission Examination of Allottee."

32 Rick Stansfield, "Wyandotte (tribe)," *The Encyclopedia of Oklahoma History and Culture*, https://www.okhistory.org/publications/enc/entry.php?entry=WY001.

33 Charles Marius Barbeau, *Huron and Wyandot Mythology* (Ottawa: Geological Survey of Canada, 1915), ix.

34 Andrews, "Jane Zane Gordon."

35 Stephen Warren, ed., *The Eastern Shawnee Tribe of Oklahoma: Resilience through Adversity* (Norman: University of Oklahoma Press, 2017), 92.

36 Warren, ed., *The Eastern Shawnee Tribe of Oklahoma*, 94.

37 Ibid., 95.

38 Ibid., 83.

39 Haskell is now called Haskell Indian Nations University and We^{n}dat/Wa^{n}dat continue to attend. Warren, ed., *The Eastern Shawnee Tribe of Oklahoma*, 92.

40 "School History," Haskell Indian Nations University, accessed 10 June 2019, https://www.haskell.edu/about/history/.

41 Ibid.

42 Ibid.

43 K. Tsianina Lomawaima, *They Called It Prairie Light: The Story of Chilocco Indian School* (Lincoln: University of Nebraska Press, 1994), 164.
44 Ibid., 30.
45 Warren, ed., *The Eastern Shawnee Tribe of Oklahoma*, 92.
46 Ibid.
47 Ibid., 90–1.
48 Ibid., 91.
49 Olin Downes, "Indian Girl in Boston Protests Treatment of Red Race – Says Starvation Common," *Boston Sunday Post*, 17 July 1921.
50 Ibid.
51 *Pasadena Evening Post*, 13 December 1924.
52 *The Daily Reporter* (Greenfield, IN), 18 February 1925.
53 *New York Times*, 24 April 1921.
54 *St. Louis Star*, 16 November 1920.
55 *Logansport Pharos-Tribune* (Logansport, IN), 18 November 1920.
56 *Dearborn Independent*, 26 November 1921.
57 The film *Vanishing American* (1924), for instance, starred a Richard Dix, a settler American actor, as the lead Navajo character. *Boston Sunday Post*, 17 July 1921.
58 *Dearborn Independent*, 26 November 1921.
59 Downes, "Indian Girl in Boston Protests Treatment of Red Race."
60 *Boston Sunday Post*, 17 July 1921.
61 *Dearborn Independent*, 26 November 1921.
62 Ibid.
63 *Washington Times*, 22 January 1922.
64 Ibid.
65 *Dearborn Independent*, 26 November 1921.
66 Ibid.
67 Ibid.
68 *The Tomahawk* (White Earth, MN), 15 December 1921.
69 *Dearborn Independent*, 26 November 1921.
70 *Boston Sunday Post*, 17 July 1921.
71 "Warren G. Harding," *Encyclopaedia Britannica*, https://www.britannica.com/biography/Warren-G-Harding.
72 *New York Times*, 24 April 1921; Andrews, "Jane Zane Gordon."
73 *Dearborn Independent*, 26 November 1921.
74 Ibid.
75 *New York Times*, 24 April 1921; Andrews, "Jane Zane Gordon."
76 Vine Deloria, Jr, and Clifford M. Lytle, *The Nations Within: The Past and Future of American Indian Sovereignty* (Austin: University of Texas Press, 1984), 41.
77 US Bureau of the Census, *Statistics Abstract of the United States* (1951), 14; 306.
78 Indian Arts and Crafts Board, https://www.doi.gov/iacb.

79 Despite the broad support from Indigenous activists for the IACB and its good intentions to protect Indigenous rights through art and culture, it has, at times, unintentionally enforced colonial policies. For instance, the IACB threatened to fine acclaimed Wyandot potter Richard Zane Smith in 2018 for selling "Indian Art" illegally as he was not an enrolled member of a federally recognized tribe. The accusation was the result of the complicated and problematic history of the We^{n}dat/Wa^{n}dat nations and the enduring legacy of forced removals and enfranchisement. Ironically, Smith won the battle with the support of the Wyandotte Nation's Business Committee by highlighting his clear connections to Wyandot/Wyandotte ancestors like Jane Zane Gordon (the very people who initiated the IACB in the first place).

80 William Swaim, "Wyandotte Nation Opens Doors to New Cultural Centre," Wyandotte Nation, https://www.wyandotte-nation.org/tribal-news/wyandotte-nation-opens-doors-to-new-cultural-center/.

81 Swaim, "Wyandotte Nation Opens Doors to New Cultural Centre."

82 Sallie Cotter Andrews, "Biographical Panels," Wyandotte Nation, https://www.wyandotte-nation.org/traditions/biographical-panels/.

CHAPTER SEVEN

Aspects of this chapter have been published before. See Kathryn Labelle, "'Mother of her Nation': Dr. Éléonore Sioui (1924–2006)," *Ethnohistory* 64, no. 2 (2017): 167–90.

1 Éléonore Sioui, "A Huron-Wyandot Woman's Life Story: The Realization of an Impossible Dream" (PhD thesis, Union for Experimenting Colleges and Universities, 1988), 8.

2 Duncan Campbell Scott, quoted in John Leslie, *The Historical Development of the Indian Act*, 2nd ed. (Ottawa: Department of Indian and Northern Affairs, Treaties and Historical Research Branch, 1978), 114.

3 Linda Tuhiwai Smith, *Decolonizing Methodologies: Research and Indigenous Peoples* (London: Zed Books, 1999), 112.

4 Ibid., 114. For examples of global Indigenous organizations see the World Council of Indigenous Peoples (WCIP), the International Treaty Council (IITC), and the Inuit Circumpolar Conference (ICC).

5 There is a growing body of literature since the 1990s that addresses ways that Indigenous women have created their own unique feminist movement(s) outside of settler/white feminism. For examples of this scholarship see Sarah A. Nickel and Amanda Fehr, eds., *In Good Relation: History, Gender, and Kinship in Indigenous Feminisms* (Winnipeg: University of Manitoba Press, 2020); Sarah A. Nickel, "'I Am Not a Women's Libber Although Sometimes I Sound Like One': Indigenous

Feminism and Politicized Motherhood," *The American Indian Quarterly* 41, no. 4 (2017): 299–335; Mishuana R. Goeman and Jennifer Nez Denetdale, "Native Feminisms: Legacies, Interventions, and Indigenous Sovereignties," *Wicazo Sa Review* 24, no. 2 (2009): 9–13; Andrea Smith, "Native American Feminism, Sovereignty, and Social Change," *Feminist Studies* 31, no. 1 (2005): 116–32.

6 Joyce Green, ed., *Making Space for Indigenous Feminism* (Halifax: Fernwood Publishing, 2007); Cheryl Suzack, Shari M. Huhndorf, Jeanne Perreault, and Jean Barman, eds., *Indigenous Women and Feminism: Politics, Activism, Culture* (Vancouver: University of British Columbia Press, 2011); Paula Gunn Allen, *Off the Reservation: Reflections on Boundary-Busting, Border-Crossing Loose Canons* (Boston: Beacon Press, 1998); Rayna Green, "American Indian Women: Diverse Leadership for Social Change," in *Bridges of Power: Women's Multicultural Alliances*, ed. Lisa Albrecht and Rose M. Brewer (Philadelphia: New Society Publishers, 1999); Patricia A. Monture, *Thunder in My Soul: A Mohawk Woman Speaks* (Halifax: Fernwood Publishing, 1995); Lee Maracle, *I am Woman: A Native Perspective on Sociology and Feminism* (Vancouver: Press Gang Publishers, 1996).

7 This term refers to the "discourse and movement aimed at advancing the rights and status of indigenous people worldwide." See Rhiannon Morgan, "On Political Institutions and Social Movement Dynamics: The Case of the United Nations and the Global Indigenous Movement," *International Political Science Review* 28, no. 3 (2007): 278; Ronald Niezen, *The Origins of Indigenism: Human Rights and the Politics of Identity* (Berkeley: University of California Press, 2003).

8 Georges Sioui, personal correspondence with the author, 12 June 2004.

9 The North American Indian Nation Government was established in 1947. This organization included elected representatives from Canada and the USA and sought to address grievances related to federal recognition, treaty rights, women's status, and language revitalization (among others). Original executive leadership included Chief Bernard Commanda (Nipissing Band, Ontario), Chief John Chabot (Maniwaki Band, Quebec), Jules Sioui (Lorette Band, Quebec), and Chief Silver Star (Pontiac Branch Band, Michigan). "The Second Session of the North American Indian Nation Government," Detroit, 1947, 1–12, https://kerrycoast.files.wordpress.com/2016/12/north-american-indian-government-2nd-session-1947-from-ubcic-archive.pdf.

10 Georges Sioui, "Éléonore Sioui, My Mother," conference presentation, Native American and Indigenous Studies Association, Saskatoon, SK, February 2013.

11 Georges Sioui, personal correspondence with author, 3 July 2013. According to Georges Sioui, the Forty Arpents was a small village associated with, but autonomous from, the nearby We^{n}dat/Wa^{n}dat reserve of Jeune Lorette, Quebec. In 1904, the Forty Arpents We^{n}dat/Wa^{n}dat were forced by the Canadian government to relocate to Jeune Lorette.

12 Éléonore Sioui, "A Huron-Wyandot Woman's Life Story," 7.

13 Ibid., 11–12. This would later become a conflicted space for Éléonore and although she would send her children to church, she herself refused to attend.

14 Ibid., 7.

15 Georges Sioui, "Éléonore Sioui, My Mother."

16 Ibid.

17 Georges Sioui, *Histories of Kanatha, Seen and Told, Essays and Discourses, 1991–2008* (Ottawa: University of Ottawa Press, 2008), 204.

18 They were divorced in 1970. E. Sioui Private Collection [SPC], *Supreme Court of Canada Document*, July 1970, IMG 7950.

19 Letter to Family, 25 February 1998, SPC, *Biography Folder.*

20 Éléonore Sioui, "A Huron-Wyandot Woman's Life Story," 38.

21 Ibid., 46.

22 Ibid.

23 R. David Edmunds, "Tecumseh, The Shawnee Prophet, and American History: A Reassessment," *Western Historical Quarterly* 14, no. 3 (1983), 261–76; Alfred A. Cave, "The Shawnee Prophet, Tecumseh, and Tippecanoe: A Case Study of Historical Myth Making," *Journal of the Early Republic* 22, no. 4 (2002): 637–74.

24 George Jones, *Tecumseh and the Prophet of the West: An Historical Israel-Indian Tragedy* (London: Longman, Brown, Green & Longmans, 1844), act 4, scene 1.

25 *Kanatha* Magazine 4, ed. Éléonore Sioui (Quebec, 1976), 3.

26 Ibid.

27 Morgan, "On Political Institutions and Social Movement Dynamics," 278.

28 Alain Beaulieu, "Hurons-Wendat of Wendake," *The Canadian Encyclopedia*, https://www.thecanadianencyclopedia.ca/en/article/hurons-wendat-of-wendake.

29 An arpent is an old French unit of land area equivalent to 3,420 square metres (about 1 acre), the standard measure of land in those areas settled during the French regime and in use until the 1970s.

30 "March 7, 1904 – Registration Number X14632: Surrender 511," in *Village Des Hurons, Wendake*, Legal Surveys Division, Historical Review, https://www.nrcan.gc.ca/sites/www.nrcan.gc.ca/files/earthsciences/pdf/land-surveys/VILLAGE_DES_HURONS_ANG.pdf.

31 Ibid.

32 The reserve was originally called Jeune Lorette, but was legally changed in 1985 to "Village Des Hurons, Wendake." Marguerite Vincent Tehariolina, *La Nation Huronne: Son Histoire, Sa Culture, Son Esprit* (Quebec: Septentrion, 1995), 158; *Village Des Hurons, Wendake*, Legal Surveys Division, Historical Review.

33 Alexander Fraser, *Fifth Report of the Bureau of Archives for the Province of Ontario 1908* (Toronto: L.K Cameron, 1909), 456.

34 Thomas Peace, "Maintaining Connections: Lorette during the Eighteenth Century," in *From Huronia to Wendakes: Adversity, Migrations, and Resilience, 1650–1900*,

ed. Thomas Peace and Kathryn Magee Labelle (Norman: University of Oklahoma Press, 2016), 76.

35 Ibid., 76–7.

36 Brian Gettler, "Economic Activity and Class Formation in Wendake, 1800–1950," in *From Huronia to Wendakes: Adversity, Migrations, and Resilience, 1650–1900*, ed. Thomas Peace and Kathryn Magee Labelle (Norman: University of Oklahoma Press, 2016), 144–81.

37 Antoine O. Bastien, Report on the Jeune Lorette Agency, 15 July 1899, in *Indian Affairs Annual Report, 1899*, 50.

38 Tehariolina, *La Nation Huronne*, 186.

39 L.-S.-G. Lindsay, *Notre-Dame de la Jeune-Lorette en la Nouvelle-France: Étude historique* (Montréal: La Revue Canadienne, 1900), 30–3.

40 Lindsay, *Notre-Dame de la Jeune-Lorette*, 236–7.

41 The original church was destroyed in a fire and was rebuilt in 1835.

42 Tehariolina, *La Nation Huronne*, 321–2; Bruce G. Trigger, *The Children of Aataentsic: A History of the Huron People to 1660* (Montreal & Kingston: McGill-Queen's University Press, 1976), 523–4.

43 For discussion of the family connection between Louis Vincent Sawantanan and Nicolas Vincent Tsawenhohi, see Peace, "Maintaining Connections," 74–110.

44 Jean-Pierre Sawaya, "Les amérindiens domiciliés et le Protestantisme au XVIIIe siècle: Eleazar Wheelock et le Dartmouth College," *Historical Studies in Education / Revue d'histoire de l'éducation* 22, no. 2 (2010): 1; Jonathan Lainey and Thomas Peace, "Louis Vincent Sawantanan: Premier bachelier autochtone canadien," in *Vivre la Conquête: Des parcours individuels*, ed. Gaston Deschênes and Denis Vaugeois (Quebec: Septentrion, 2013), 216–26.

45 Éléonore Sioui, "A Huron-Wyandot Woman's Life Story," 13.

46 Cynthia Wesley-Esquimaux and Magdelena Smolewski, *Historic Trauma and Aboriginal Healing* (Ottawa: Aboriginal Healing Foundation, 2004), 25.

47 Éléonore Sioui, "A Huron-Wyandot Woman's Life Story," 8–9.

48 J.R. Miller, *Shingwauk's Vision: A History of Native Residential Schools* (Toronto: University of Toronto Press, 1996), 217–50.

49 Royal Commission on Aboriginal Peoples (RCAP), 1996, 1:287.

50 Éléonore Sioui, "A Huron-Wyandot Woman's Life Story," 10.

51 Ibid., 14–15.

52 Marie Battiste, "Enabling the Autumn Seed: Toward a Decolonized Approach to Aboriginal Knowledge, Language, and Education," *Canadian Journal of Native Education* 22, no. 1 (1998): 22.

53 The United States government passed several acts to support Indigenous post-secondary education: the Indian Education Act (1972), the Self Determination Act (1975), the Education Assistance Act (1975), and the reauthorization of the Indian Education Act (1988).

54 Although the sources provide no definitive evidence concerning why Sioui chose the University of Miami, it is interesting to note that the institution offered an American Indian Scholarship and that a fifth of the scholarships were offered by the Bureau of Indian Education.

55 Union Institute, *Doctoral Program Information 1995–1996* (Cincinnati: The Union Institute, 1995) 3–5; Union for Experimenting Colleges and Universities, *University without Walls: First Report* (Yellow Springs, OH: Union for Experimenting Colleges and Universities, 1972).

56 Éléonore Sioui, "A Huron-Wyandot Woman's Life Story," 13.

57 Ibid.

58 Ibid., 12.

59 Ibid., 30.

60 Kim Anderson, *A Recognition of Being: Reconstructing Native Womanhood* (Toronto: Sumach Press, 2000), 140–1.

61 Éléonore Sioui, "A Huron-Wyandot Woman's Life Story," 51.

62 Ibid., 3.

63 Ibid., 10.

64 Ibid., 50.

65 These are poems that have been published in books that are no longer in print. See *Andatha* (Val-d'Or: Éditions Hyperborée, 1985); *Femme de l'île* (Rillieux, France: Sur le Dos de la Tortue, 1990); *Corps à coeur éperdu* (Val-d'Or: D'ici et d'ailleurs, 1992).

66 Richard Henault, "Mme. Éléonore Sioui: Une Amérindienne," *Le Soleil* (Quebec, QC), 9 November 1985.

67 Éléonore Sioui, *Andatha*.

68 Indian Affairs to Léonard Paul (Principal), 12 November 1985, SPC, IMG 7976.

69 Bill Clinton to Éléonore Sioui, 19 January 1993, SPC, IMG 7917.

70 William J. Clinton, "Inaugural Address," *The American Presidency Project*, compiled by Gerhard Peters and John T. Woolley, accessed 24 November 2014, https://www.presidency.ucsb.edu/documents/inaugural-address-51.

71 Éléonore Sioui to Frank Vieni, 28 May 1986, SPC, IMG 7942.

72 Éléonore Sioui, "A Huron-Wyandot Woman's Life Story," 15.

73 "Job description," SPC, *Education Folder*.

74 Letter of recommendation by Peter G. Ross, 27 July 1977, SPC, *Education Folder*.

75 It is unclear what the response to these requests was, but Sioui does not return to Dominica. Reference letter, 11 August 1977, SPC, *Education Folder*.

76 Éléonore Sioui, "A Huron-Wyandot Woman's Life Story," 38.

77 Ibid., 14.

78 English translation is my own. *Collectifs Grenoblois 1492–1992* conference pamphlet, November 1991, SPC, IMG 7460–7461.

79 Ibid.

80 Ibid.

81 Richard Griggs, "The Meaning of 'Nation' and 'State' in the Fourth World," (Cape Town: University of Cape Town, Center for World Indigenous Studies, 1992), paper #18.

82 Video, CPAC, *Conference of Languages, Culture and Values in Canada*, session 5, 2 June 1995.

83 Ibid.

84 Ibid.

85 Ibid.

86 Ibid.

87 Éléonore Sioui, "A Huron-Wyandot Woman's Life Story," 9.

88 Ibid., 15.

89 Letter from Georges Erasmus to Éléonore Sioui, 1 November 1988, SPC, IMG 7955.

90 Ibid.

91 University of Ottawa, "Matrilineal Societies: Dedication," workshop website, accessed 12 April 2014, http://web5.uottawa.ca/www5/iculture/conferences/matrilineal/english/DedicationBio.html.

92 English translation is my own. Jean Chrétien to Éléonore Sioui, 18 May 2001, SPC, IMG 7428.

93 University of Ottawa, "Matrilineal Societies: Redefinitions, Survival and Worldviews" workshop website, accessed 3 March 2014, http://web5.uottawa.ca/www5/iculture/conferences/matrilineal/english/programme.html.

94 Éléonore Sioui, "A Huron-Wyandot Woman's Life Story," 31.

95 Marlee Kline, "Complicating the Ideology of Motherhood: Child Welfare Law and First Nation Women," *Queen's Law Journal* 18, no. 2 (1993): 310.

96 Ibid.

97 Ibid., 312.

98 Georges Sioui, *Histories of Kanatha*, 141.

99 Éléonore Sioui, "A Huron-Wyandot Woman's Life Story," 32, 35–6.

100 Éléonore Sioui, *Andatha*; Éléonore Sioui, *Femme de l'île*; Éléonore Sioui, *Corps à coeur éperdu*.

101 Georges Sioui, "Éléonore Sioui, My Mother," 9.

102 Éléonore Sioui, "A Huron-Wyandot Woman's Life Story," 2, 39.

103 Éléonore Sioui, "Global Psychology: Leaves, Roots and Barks of the Huron Wyandot Medicine," unpublished manuscript, SPC, IMG 7534.

104 Georges Sioui, "Éléonore Sioui, My Mother," 8.

INDEX